Frommer's®

25 GREAT drives in FRANCE

9th Edition

WILEY

Wiley Publishing, Inc.

Updated by Penny Phenix

First published January 1991
Revised second edition 1995, published in this format 1997
Reprinted December 1997
Revised third edition published 2000
Revised fourth edition published 2003
Revised fifth edition published 2005
Revised sixth edition published 2007
Revised seventh edition published 2009
Revised eighth edition published 2011

Edited, designed and produced by AA Publishing.

Published by AA Publishing

Published in the United States by
John Wiley & Sons, Inc.
111 River Street, Hoboken, NJ 07030

Find us online at Frommers.com

Frommer's is a registered trademark of Arthur Frommer.
Used under license.

ISBN 978-0-470-90448-0

Color separation: AA Digital Department

Printed and bound by G. Canale & C. S.P.A., Torino, Italy

A04405
Atlas mapping in this title produced from mapping © ISTITUTO GEOGRAFICO DE AGOSTINI S.p.A., NOVARA - 2008

CONTENTS

ABOUT THIS BOOK

This book is not only a practical touring guide for the independent traveller, but is also invaluable for those who would like to know more about the country. It is divided into 6 regions, each containing between 3 and 5 tours which start and finish in major towns and cities considered to be the best centres for exploration. Each tour has details of the most interesting places to visit en route. Panels catering for special interests follow some of the main entries – for those whose interest is in history, wildlife or walking, and those who have children. There are also panels which highlight scenic stretches of road and which give details of events, crafts and customs. The simple route directions are accompanied by an easy to use tour map at the beginning of each tour, along with a chart showing how far it is from one town to the next in kilometres and miles. This can help you to decide where to take a break and stop overnight. (All distances quoted are approximate.) Before setting off it is advisable to check with the information office at the start of the tour for recommendations on where to break your journey and for additional information on what to see and do, and when best to visit.

★ This symbol on the maps represents other attractions seen along the routes, often mentioned in the panels.

Tour Information
See pages 165–77 for addresses, telephone numbers and opening times of the attractions mentioned in the tours, including telephone numbers of tourist offices.

Accommodation and restaurants
See pages 160–64 for a list of recommended hotels for each tour. Also listed are restaurants where you may like to stop for a meal. There are, of course, other possibilities to be found along the way.

Business Hours

Banks: normal banking hours are 10–1 and 3–5 weekdays and they are closed either Mondays or Saturdays, all Sundays and public holidays. Banks close at noon on the day before a national holiday, and all day on Monday if the holiday falls on a Tuesday.

Post offices: main post offices are open 8–7 on weekdays, and 8–noon on Saturdays, though some small offices have shorter hours and may close for lunch. Stamps may also be bought in tobacco shops (*tabacs*) or cafés marked with a red cigar sign. Letter boxes are yellow.

Credit Cards

International credit cards are accepted widely throughout France, but check before you use them in rural areas. French credit cards contained ID information on a chip several years before 'chip and pin' was introduced in the UK. Consequently, their card-reading machines should recognise a UK-issued card when the correct PIN is entered, and there should be no problems with cash dispensing machines.

Currency

The unit of currency is the euro (€). Bank notes come in denominations of 5, 10, 20, 50, 100, 200 and 500 euros; coins come in denominations of 1, 2, 5, 10, 20 and 50 cents, 1 and 2 euros.

Customs Regulations

There is no limit on the importation into one EU country of tax-paid goods purchased in another, provided they are for personal use.

However, all EU customs authorities have fixed indicative limits on alcohol and tobacco. Beyond these limits the importer must be able to prove that they are for personal use.

Electricity

220 volts (50 cycles AC), with the standard continental two- (or three-) pin round plug, making an adaptor essential for British and American appliances (110 volt appliances need a transformer).

Embassies

British: 35 rue du Faubourg St Honoré, 75363 Paris, tel: (1) 44 51 31 00.

Canadian: 35 avenue Montaigne, 75008 Paris, tel: (1) 44 43 29 00.

US: 2 avenue Gabriel, 75382 Paris, tel: (1) 43 12 22 22.

Emergency Telephone Numbers

Police tel: 17
Fire tel: 18
Ambulance tel: 15

Entry Regulations

No visas are required for nationals of EU and Schengen Area countries, Andorra, Australia, Bermuda, Brazil, Brunei, Canada, Chile, Costa Rica, Croatia, El Salvador, Guatemala, Honduras, Israel, Japan, Liechtenstein, Malaysia, Mexico, Monaco, New Zealand, Panama, Paraguay, San Marino, Singapore, South Korea, Vatican City, Uruguay and USA.

Visas are required for all others. Check, though, with a travel agent or the French Government Tourist Office, since visa policy is subject to review.

Health Matters

There are no special health requirements or regulations. Visitors other than EU citizens, to whom reciprocal medical services may not be available, are advised to take out medical insurance.

Motoring

For information on all aspects of motoring in France see pages 158–59.

Public Holidays

1 January – New Year's Day
Easter Sunday and Monday
1 May – Labour Day
8 May – VE Day
6th Thursday after Easter –
  Ascension Day
2nd Monday after Ascension –
  Whitsun
14 July – Bastille Day
15 August – Assumption Day
1 November – All Saints' Day
11 November – Remembrance
  Day
25 December – Christmas Day

Roche Tuilière and Roche
Sanadoire, near Le Mont-Dore
in the Auvergne

Telephones

Insert coin after lifting the receiver; the dialling tone is a continuous tone. Most booths now take phonecards (*télécartes*). Buy them for €7.50 or €15 from post offices, tobacconists and newsagents. For international calls dial 00, wait for a new tone, then dial the national code, followed by the local code, omitting the initial 0, and then the number. For the operator dial 13, for enquiries 12.

Time

France follows Greenwich Mean Time, plus one hour, with clocks put forward for a further hour from late March to late October.

Tourist Offices

Where no address is given for a separate tourist information office, enquire at the *Mairie* (mayor's office), the *Hôtel de Ville* (town hall) or perhaps the *Syndicat d'Initiative* office. In some places the tourist offices open only seasonally, and the *Mairie* or *Hôtel de Ville* will handle enquiries out of season.

Useful Words

The following words and phrases may be helpful.

English *French*
I need petrol *j'ai besoin*
  d'essence
my car has broken down *ma*
  voiture est en panne
oil *huile*
the road for *la route pour*
traffic lights *les feux*
after *après*
behind *derrière*
before *avant*
here *ici*
left *à gauche*
near *près*
opposite *en face*
right *à droite*
straight on *tout droit*
there *là*
where? *où?*
where is? *où est?*
I do not understand *je ne*
  comprends pas
do you speak English? *parlez-*
  vous Anglais?
help! *au secours!*
how much is it? *ça coute*
  combien?
I'm sorry *pardon*
thank you *merci*
please *s'il vouz plaît*

ANDY & BRITTANY

Normandy has rebuilt itself since World War II into a region of cheerful holiday resorts, attractive farmlands and archetypal rustic villages. Here and there, you will pick up eerie echoes of an earlier invasion which went from Normandy across the English Channel. The original Normans were Norsemen – Vikings who swept down from Scandinavia and, in the 10th century, created the dukedom of Normandy. William the Conqueror was Duke of Normandy, with a legal claim to the English throne, long before he invaded England in 1066. From that point on, the histories of Normandy and England intertwined.

The Normandy coastline is a succession of resorts. Look for the seafood restaurants in the fishing ports. Inland, the livestock farms supply a cuisine which is rich in butter, cheeses, cream and hefty helpings of meat. Apples and pears are major crops. The wooded farmlands of Normandy create some of the most beautiful landscapes in northern France.

Brittany becomes more Breton as you move further west. A wonderful coastline and an airy, high-level interior are linked by a wooded middle district which could easily be in Devon or Cornwall.

Waves of colonists from Britain started arriving in the 5th century. Britain and Brittany, Briton and Breton are all from the same basic word; but the close connection was lost long ago.

Bretons, particularly in the west, retain a feeling of 'apartness' from the rest of France, and you will not be long there before being aware of something Celtic in the air. Traditional costumes and religious processions, not always as well supported as they have been in the past, underline the differences in culture and background.

In both Brittany and Normandy, regional nature parks are very well organised, with wildlife reserves, museums of traditional ways of life and places where you can see products such as bread and cider being made in the old pre-industrialised way.

Caen

You cannot miss William the Conqueror's influence on Caen, which has risen again from the devastation of 1944. Its centrepiece is the château of the dukes of Normandy. Inside this massive fortress, founded by William in 1060, you will find the Musée des Beaux-Arts with its splendid collection of French and Italian paintings, and the Musée de Normandie, devoted to archaeology, history and traditional life. William also endowed the monastery of the Abbaye aux Hommes, just as his wife built the original convent of the Abbaye aux Dames. William's tomb is in the Church of St-Étienne at the Abbaye aux Hommes, which now serves as Caen's Hôtel de Ville.

The Musée d'Initiation à la Nature here concentrates on the wildlife of coast and country. The Mémorial de Caen has impressive displays and audio-visual presentations recalling World War II and the D-Day landings. New galleries are dedicated to postwar events and hopes for a peaceful future.

Dieppe

Like Caen, Dieppe has erased most of the scars of World War II. Its harbour area includes ferry, freight, fishing and pleasure ports. Morning fish stalls are set up by the roadside.

The best view of Dieppe is from the 15th-century hillside château. It houses a fine museum and art gallery with extensive maritime rooms and a glorious collection of ivories, including a full-rigged ship with billowing sails.

Rennes

Rennes is the historic and flourishing provincial capital of Brittany. The city centre is a delightful mix of grand civic architecture and medieval timber-framed buildings on pretty cobbled streets and squares. Cultural heart of the city is the Champs Libres, with the Espace des Sciences, the six-storey modern library, and the Musée Bretagne, which recounts Brittany's fascinating history. On quai Émile Zola, beside the River Vilaine, the Musée des Beaux-Arts has a rich display of paintings, drawings,

Opposite: Le Mont-St-Michel, steeped in magic and history
Above: brightly painted fishing boats in the harbour at Dieppe

engravings and sculptures, many confiscated from religious houses during the Revolution. Sisley, Rubens, Gauguin, Boudin and Picasso are all represented.

Quimper

Quimper is more Breton than Rennes, and is the home of the Musée Départemental Breton. The pleasant old quarter centres on a square dominated by the twin spire of the Cathédrale St-Corentin. Here is an architectural curiosity: the 15th-century nave is accidentally out of alignment with the 13th-century choir.

Quimper's Musée des Beaux-Arts is well provided with 17th-century Flemish paintings. In the same era, Quimper began the production of the glazed pottery for which it is still famous. Factories and ceramic artists' workshops welcome visitors and there is a museum containing some 500 pieces.

Legacy of D-Day

Normandy is a land of apples and cider, of spacious sands, of lovely inland *bocage* country with hedges and tree-lined fields, but behind the peaceful present-day scenes the region hides a land once devastated by the D-Day landings in June 1944, when the huge invasion force of Operation Overlord stormed the German defences.

3 DAYS • 456KM • 283 MILES

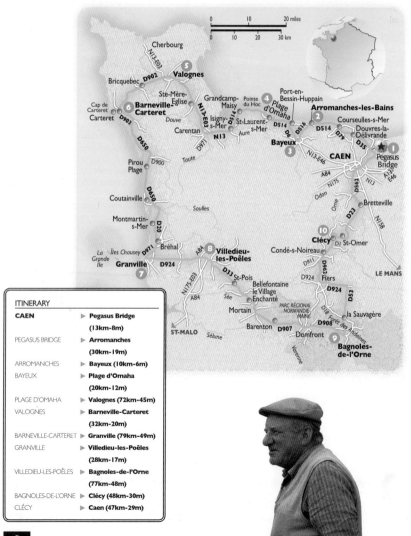

ITINERARY

_i_ *Place St-Pierre, Caen*

▶ *Leave Caen on the **D513** as for Cabourg. Go left on the **D37**, then take the **D514** as for Ouistreham to Pegasus Bridge.*

❶ Pegasus Bridge,
Normandy
In the eastern sector of the D-Day landings, the years of planning and training came down to one amazingly audacious feat. Just after midnight on the morning of 6 June 1944, three gliders with no room for a conventional approach suddenly crash-landed beside this ugly but vital little tilting bridge on the Caen–Ouistreham canal. British troops poured out and after four minutes' fierce fighting secured the bridge. They held it until reinforcements arrived, most decisively the Commandos led by Lord Lovat, who reached here exactly two-and-a-half minutes behind schedule after fighting their way inland from Sword Beach.

Three columns in the scrubland southeast of the bridge show where the gliders landed. On the west side, a museum tells the story of that dramatic engagement and on summer evenings there is a *Son et Lumière* presentation. In 1994 the original bridge was replaced by something more appropriate to modern traffic.

▶ *Take the **D35** to Douvres then follow the 'Bayeux' signs. Go right on the **D79** to Courseulles-sur-Mer, then left on the **D514** and follow signs to Arromanches-les-Bains.*

✔
❷ Arromanches, Normandy
Without massive supplies, the D-Day landings could not have developed into an advance across the whole of France. Arromanches was the scene of one of the greatest engineering feats of the war – the building, from thousands of tons of prefabricated parts shipped across the Channel, of Port Winston, the giant Mulberry (artificial) harbour. It threw a 5.7km (3½-mile) breakwater round the sea approaches to Arromanches, from which pontoon bridges reached to the shore, and was operational within 12 days.

Today, Arromanches is a busy but unremarkable little resort on a bay between all but vertical cliffs. Up on these cliffs is Arromanches 360, where visitors experience the action of D-Day amid circular projections on to nine giant screens. Down on the seafront, the well-presented Musée du Débarquement illustrates, with working models, films and photographs, the creation and operation of 'the key to the liberation of France'.

_i_ *2 rue Maréchal Joffre*

┌─────────────────────────┐

BACK TO NATURE

In the busy resort of Courseulles, part of Juno Beach on D-Day, the Maison de la Mer features aquariums with a tunnel, seahorses and conger eels, a splendid display of shells and a diorama on the local cultivation of oysters.

└─────────────────────────┘

▶ *Leave Arromanches-les-Bains for Bayeux on the **D516**.*

❸ Bayeux, Normandy
Most of the fine historic buildings here, which have been restored, survived the 1944 campaign. You can stroll through old streets and over narrow bridges, admiring the

The Café Gondrée, Pegasus Bridge

Bayeux's splendid Norman Gothic Cathedral of Notre Dame

d'Omaha Beach, with its military vehicles, weapons, uniforms, insignia and exhibits on the planning and accomplishing of the D-Day landings.

> **FOR HISTORY BUFFS**
>
> Turn right off the D514 after Omaha Beach for Pointe du Hoc, to learn about the desperate struggle of the American Rangers to scale the cliffs on D-Day. Later, the landings were re-staged here for the film *The Longest Day*.

▶ Continue on the **D514** then go right on the **N13** as for Cherbourg and continue to Valognes.

5 Valognes, Normandy
In its 17th- to 19th-century heyday, Valognes was 'the Versailles of Normandy'. Aristocratic families owned town houses here, and there was a high-flying social life. The bombardments of 1944 wrecked the centre, which has been rebuilt, and destroyed part of the Church of St Malo. A modern reinforced concrete nave and tower stand beside the 14th-century chancel.

However, several of Valogne's mansions survived. The elegant 18th-century Hôtel de Beaumont is open to visitors. The Hôtel de Thieuville houses the Musée de l'Eau de Vie et des Vieux Métiers, whose two main subjects are apple brandy and leatherwork. An

> **FOR HISTORY BUFFS**
>
> Ste-Mère-Église near Utah Beach was the first French town liberated on D-Day. A museum describes the action, with the help of a 20-minute film and interactive terminals, and explains why the figure of a paratrooper hangs from the church tower every summer.

gleaming stonework of the mills on the River Aure. On the ring road, the Musée de la Bataille de Normandie is 'guarded' by British, American and German tanks. Everything in Bayeux, however, pales beside the priceless 11th-century tapestry, displayed in the Centre Guillaume le Conquérant, with its lively scenes of the Norman Conquest of England. Weavers and lacemakers still have studios in the town. Alongside the cathedral, the Musée Baron Gérard (closed for restoration) contains paintings, lacework and ceramics. It is off a little courtyard shaded by the famous 'liberty tree', planted according to the Revolutionary calendar (France's official calendar from 1793 to 1805) on 10 Germinal of the year V – otherwise 30 March, 1797.

ⓘ Pont St-Jean

▶ Leave Bayeux on the **D6** to Port-en-Bessin-Huppain. Go left on the **D514** for Plage d'Omaha.

4 Plage d'Omaha, Normandy
Most side roads to the right of the D514 reach memorials above the Americans' principal D-Day landing beach, although signs for the Plage d'Omaha lead to a holiday camp. Look for Wn 62, a high-set German strongpoint, with American monuments as well as explanations of the D-Day action and the fearsome German defences.

The American military cemetery is close by. It has a superb visitor centre, where displays based on personal stories complement the exhibits at the Musée Mémorial

annexe has displays on the French Revolution with some unusual themes, such as the role of scientists in Revolutionary times. Close at hand the Musée Régional du Cidre et du Calvados, once a dyer's workshop, then a barracks and then a smithy, covers five centuries of cider-making with tableaux of traditional Normandy life.

[i] *Place du Château*

▶ *Leave Valognes for Barneville-Carteret on the D902.*

BACK TO NATURE

Until early this century, the huge sand dunes north of the Cap de Carteret were moved steadily inland by the wind, engulfing roads and a mill. You can see how, classified as a nature reserve, they have now been stabilised by the planting of marram grass thickets. Look for birds such as Dartford warblers and stonechats as well as numerous lizards.

▶ *Leave Barneville as for La Haye-du-Puits on the D903, then keep right on the D650. Go straight on along the D20, to Bréhal, then right on the D971 and into Granville.*

7 Granville, Normandy
Granville grew from a fortified town on a promontory rock, and, thanks to the contortions of history, it was first fortified by the English against the French! The story of the town is illustrated in the Musée du Vieux Granville, just inside the

6 Barneville-Carteret, Normandy
These two little towns, administratively linked together, form a family holiday resort with excellent sands, a spectacular rocky headland and a very sheltered tidal river harbour. This is a pleasant walking and watersports area, and summer ferries sail to the Channel Islands. Make for the lighthouse on Cap de Carteret, a wonderful viewpoint towards Jersey, Sark, Herm and, on the northern horizon, Alderney.

Take care in the sea. Every year people ignore the notices warning that, while the town beaches have a lifeguard service, the quieter one north of the Cap does not. There, it is all too easy for youngsters and less strong adult swimmers to be taken well out of their depth.

[i] *10 rue des Écoles*

RECOMMENDED WALKS

At Barneville-Carteret, start from either of the beaches flanking the Cap de Carteret along the exhilarating Sentier des Douaniers (the Excisemen's Path), which contours the lichen-clad cliffs and passes the site of an 18th-century coastal gun battery.

The beach at Barneville-Carteret, north of Cap de Carteret

preserved drawbridge gateway of the Haute Ville (High Town).

The 15th-century Notre Dame Church stands among the alleyways here; a good aquarium includes shell and mineral collections; and a scenic path follows the cliffs below the lighthouse, with views of the low-lying Chausey archipelago. Ferries sail to La Grande Île, with its château built by motor magnate Louis Renault.

On no account miss Granville's Jardin Christian Dior. Its lush lawns, pine trees and beautifully laid-out flower beds surround the pink-and-white villa, now the Musée

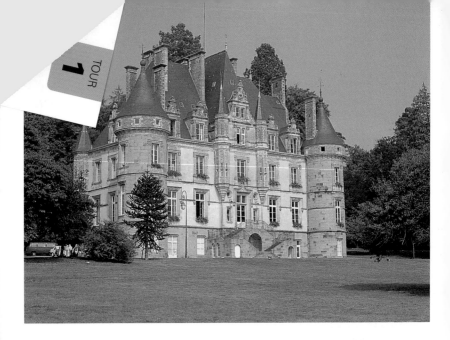

Christian Dior, once owned by the couturier. In late July, a 'Pardon of the Sea' melds religion with spectacle. Other attractions include the Musée Richard Anacréon, featuring modern art and haute couture.

[i] *4 Cours Jonville*

▶ *Leave Granville for Villedieu-les-Poêles on the D924.*

8 Villedieu-les-Poêles, Normandy

If every place-name tells a story, how to explain Villedieu-les-Poêles – 'God's Town of the Pots and Frying-pans'? The Knights of Malta (a military religious order) established here in the 16th century, called the place Villedieu, and it became a famous centre of craftsmen and metalworkers.

You can watch hand-beaten copper being worked at the Atelier du Cuivre and pewter-ware at the Maison de l'Étain. At the extremes of Villedieu's historic product range, the Fonderie de Cloches is a bell-foundry, and the Musée de la Poeslerie and Maison de la Dentellière display the lacework for which the women of the town were well known.

[i] *8 place des Costils*

▶ *Leave Villedieu-les-Poêles on the N175 as for St Hilaire. Go right on the D524, right on the D999, then left on the D33 and continue through Mortain. Turn left on the D907, go through Domfront-centre then follow 'Bagnoles-de-l'Orne' signs along the D908 and right on the D335.*

9 Bagnoles-de-l'Orne, Normandy

Retaining its old prominence as the most popular spa town in the west of France, Bagnoles, with the linked Tessé la Madeleine, lies among woodlands rising from the banks of the La Vée river. People come here for spa cures and to 'take the waters', but Bagnoles also offers excellent sporting facilities: golf, tennis, swimming, horse-riding, fishing and archery.

Wooded walks extend through the parks of the spa buildings and the château at Tessé. One fine scenic path leads to the Roc du Chien (the Dog's Rock) above the narrow river valley where the spa itself is located.

Bagnoles' casino backs on to a very pleasant lake where pedaloes can be hired. Close to the lake there are several restaurants specialising in the substantial Normandy cuisine.

The château at Bagnoles-de-l'Orne adds to the attractions of this famous spa town

---

FOR CHILDREN

On the way from Villedieu-les-Poêles to Bagnoles-de-l'Orne, turn off the D33 for Le Village Enchanté, a beautiful estate where fairy-tale tableaux are laid out in the woodland.

SPECIAL TO...

At Bagnoles-de-l'Orne is the Musée des Sapeurs-Pompiers, which shows off France's finest collection of horse-drawn and hand-pumped fire engines. Look for La Distinguée, which operated as long ago as pre-Revolutionary times. Normandy is famous for its apples and pears. The region's rich tradition in apple- and pear-growing, and the making of cider, are all explained in the Maison de la Pomme et de la Poire. Reached by turning right after Barenton on the D335, it has indoor displays as well as a walk through an orchard specially planted with many varieties of apple and pear trees.

[i] *Place du Marché*

▶ *Leave Bagnoles-de-l'Orne for
St-Michel-des-Andaines on
the D53. Go forward on the
D53 until it meets the D924.
Turn left for Flers. Go right as
for Caen along the D962,
then take the D562 to Clécy
and turn off for Clécy-centre.*

10 Clécy, Normandy
The River Orne at Clécy makes
a dramatic curve below the
densely wooded cliffs of La
Suisse Normande (Norman
Switzerland). Clécy is the main

resort in this district, whose
name should not lead you to
expect a Swiss-like landscape
of lakes and mountains; but it
is one of the most beautiful
parts of inland Normandy
nevertheless.

In the pleasant town centre
with its 18th-century houses,
look for the Musée Hardy
which displays the work of a
local artist. An exhilarating
walk climbs to the magnificent
viewpoint of the Pain du Sucre
(the Sugarloaf), high on the
cliffs overlooking the Orne.
The 16th-century Manoir de
Placy has a miniature railway
and a train museum in the
grounds.

FOR CHILDREN

In Clécy, the Musée du Chemin
de Fer Miniature shows off
more than 250 locomotives
operating on the biggest model
railway layout in Europe, with
more than 460m of track.

Bridge over the River Orne in
the resort of Clécy

[i] *Place du Tripot*

▶ *Leave Clécy on the D133c,
then go left as for St-Rémy.
Just over the brow of a hill, go
sharp right and follow Routes
des Crêtes to St-Omer. Avoid
St-Rémy itself. In St-Omer
turn right as for Pont-d'Ouilly.
Ignore the 'La Suisse
Normande' turning. Go left at
a stop sign to Bretteville and
follow the D23. In Bretteville
turn left on the D132, left at
a give way sign, then return to
Caen on the D562.*

Green &
Pleasant Normandy

West of the cross-Channel port and fishing town of Dieppe, the white cliffs and deep valleys which slice into them are hidden from the main roads, but this tour twists along the coast to some very attractive holiday resorts whose sweeping curves border the Forêt de Brotonne and the Marais Vernier.

3 DAYS • 434KM • 270 MILES

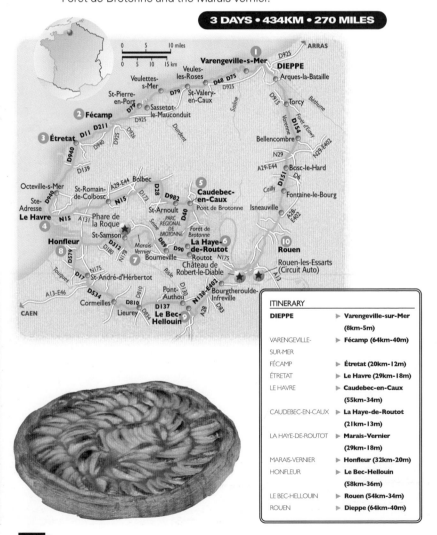

ITINERARY	
DIEPPE	▶ **Varengeville-sur-Mer** (8km-5m)
VARENGEVILLE-SUR-MER	▶ **Fécamp (64km-40m)**
FÉCAMP	▶ **Étretat (20km-12m)**
ÉTRETAT	▶ **Le Havre (29km-18m)**
LE HAVRE	▶ **Caudebec-en-Caux** (55km-34m)
CAUDEBEC-EN-CAUX	▶ **La Haye-de-Routot** (21km-13m)
LA HAYE-DE-ROUTOT	▶ **Marais-Vernier** (29km-18m)
MARAIS-VERNIER	▶ **Honfleur (32km-20m)**
HONFLEUR	▶ **Le Bec-Hellouin** (58km-36m)
LE BEC-HELLOUIN	▶ **Rouen (54km-34m)**
ROUEN	▶ **Dieppe (64km-40m)**

The painter Georges Braque (1882–1963) is buried in the churchyard at Varengeville-sur-Mer

i Pont Ango, Dieppe

FOR HISTORY BUFFS

On Dieppe seafront, look for the memorial to the disastrous raid of August 1942, by a force of mostly Canadian and Scottish troops.
The bitter lessons learned from its failure were put into practice on D-Day. Appropriately, Canadians liberated Dieppe in 1944.

► Leave Dieppe on the **D75** to Varengeville-sur-Mer.

❶ Varengeville-sur-Mer, Normandy

You might be deep in the heart of an English county here, with villas and cottages in discreetly private grounds, wooded and grass-banked lanes, and half-timbered farms fitted like jigsaw pieces in between. There is a wonderful English-style garden at the Parc Floral des Moutiers, the garden of the house called Bois des Moutiers created by architect Sir Edwin Lutyens and landscape gardener Gertrude Jekyll. Up on the farmland plateau, the Manoir d'Ango is a Renaissance manor house with a beautiful dovecote.

At the foot of the Petit Ailly gorge you can wander along the stony shore under the towering cliffs. The artist Georges Braque, a founder of Cubism, is buried beside Varengeville's parish church, for which he designed one of the stained-glass windows.

RECOMMENDED WALKS

At Varengeville, three very attractive colour-coded walks follow pleasant country lanes and footpaths behind the great chalk cliffs of the coast. They all meet up close to the Parc Floral des Moutiers.

► Continue on the **D75**, then go into St-Aubin and follow signs to St-Valery-en-Caux, leaving it on the **D925**. Turn right to Veulettes-sur-Mer on the **D79** then follow signs to Fécamp.

❷ Fécamp, Normandy

A fishing, freight and pleasure port at a dip in the cliffs, Fécamp has a shingle-bank beach and some remarkable places to visit. The Palais Bénédictine is the home of the liqueur of the same name, a distillation first carried out by monks of the Benedictine order, of 27 aromatic plants and spices whose precise recipe is a very closely guarded secret. There is a museum in the palace – a glorious 19th-century architectural confection of Gothic and Renaissance styles – which traces the history of Benedictine and also displays items of reli-

gious art, furnishings and, in the Gothic hall, a magnificent oak and chestnut ceiling built by Fécamp shipwrights. The early Gothic abbey church, has one of the longest naves in France.

As well as the Palais Bénédictine, the town also has the Musée des Terre-Neuves et de la Pêche. While its displays go back to the Vikings, who colonised this coast, it concentrates on the years when the local fishing fleet used to spend months among the great cod banks of Newfoundland.

i Quai Sadi Carnot

► Leave Fécamp on the **D940** as for Etretat, then go right on the **D211** through Yport and follow the **D11** to Étretat.

has the largest collection of Impressionist paintings outside of Paris, including works by Monet, Renoir, Pissarro and Boudin, as well as Fauvist and Cubist collections. There is a Natural History Museum in the 18th-century Tribunal, with exhibits ranging from dinosaur eggs to a living beehive.

> [i] *186 boulevard Clémenceau*

FOR HISTORY BUFFS

In June 1940, while most of the British troops in France were being evacuated from Dunkirque, the 51st Highland Division was ordered to pull back to Le Havre. In this sacrificial manoeuvre, which helped to divert 10 German divisions, the Highlanders fought until their ammunition was exhausted, and thousands had to surrender at St-Valéry-en-Caux. A granite memorial on a hillside at St-Valéry commemorates the event, and the town is twinned with Inverness, the Highland capital.

3 Étretat, Normandy

Étretat lies behind a beach at the foot of a wooded valley. To north and south rise tall white cliffs with weathered natural arches and a great isolated needle rock off shore. Paths climb to the cliffs called Falaise d'Amont north of town and the Falaise d'Aval to the south. Amont probably has the finer view, as well as a seafarers' chapel with fish carved in the stonework, and a museum to the aviators Nungesser and Coli, whose plane was last seen over Étretat before disappearing during the first attempt in 1927 to fly the Atlantic from east to west.

> [i] *9 place Maurice-Guillard*

> ► *Leave Étretat on the **D940** to Le Havre.*

4 Le Havre, Normandy

Much of Le Havre was reduced to rubble during World War II, and its reconstruction by architect Auguste Perret, gave it a

Guy de Maupassant compared the Falaise d'Aval to 'a carved elephant dipping its trunk in the sea'

pleasing uniformity and earned it a place on the UNESCO World Heritage List. One of Perret's flats is open to the public, showing his innovative design for post-war living.

The town is a major freight and ferry port – the second busiest in France, occupying the harbour and miles of riverside along the Seine. You can take a harbour cruise to get a close-up view of some of the vessels. The Musée Malraux

FOR CHILDREN

Visit the Forêt de Montgeon, 279 hectares (690 acres) of mixed woodland laid out as a leisure park with waymarked walks, a camping site, sports circuits and games, including canoeing on the lake.

> ► *Leave Le Havre on the **N15** as for Rouen. Turn right for Trouville on the **D40**, then go straight on along the **D29** and **D28**. Follow the **D28** left as for Anquetierville, but bear right to avoid the village. Turn left at the T-junction on to the **D982** for Caudebec-en-Caux.*

5 Caudebec-en-Caux, Normandy

Just downstream from the Pont de Brotonne suspension bridge which soars over the Seine, Caudebec is ideally situated to show off the commercial life of the river, to and from the container port at Rouen. The Musée de la Marine de Seine covers the history of river boats and river traffic.

Look for the remarkable Church of Notre Dame in 15th- and 16th-century Flamboyant Gothic style. It has a lovely fretted roof and a west frontage like lacework in stone, with 300 now heavily weathered figures of saints, prophets, musicians and gentlefolk of the town.

A stunning memorial beside the main road commemorates the Caudebec-built Latham seaplane which was lost in 1928 during a rescue mission in the Arctic. Roald Amundsen, discoverer of the South Pole, was one of the crew.

> [i] *Place du Général de Gaulle*

▶ *Leave Caudebec-en-Caux on the **D982** then turn right to cross the Pont de Brotonne. Go right on the **D65**, left on the **D40**, then bear left to La Haye-de-Routot.*

6 La Haye-de-Routot, Normandy

This fascinating village lies in farmland on the edge of the Fôret de Brotonne. La Haye's Four à Pain is a restored 19th-century brick-built bakehouse, run as a working museum. The Musée du Sabot is a workshop museum devoted to clogs (*sabots*). In early summer, look for the 15m (50-foot) pyramid of wood which, on the morning of 16 July, is set alight to create the Feu de St Clair, an old pagan ritual taken over by the

Christian church. Opposite the Four à Pain, a half-timbered cottage features a wall-niche model of the Feu de St Clair.

From the Café des Ifs (Yew-tree Café), marked walking routes radiate through the village and the forest.

▶ *Leave La Haye for Routot. Go left, then right, at stop signs, then continue through Bourneville as for Quillebeuf-sur-Seine. Go left on the **D95** to Ste-Opportune and straight on at crossroads following the 'Réserve Naturelle des Mannevilles' sign. Turn right at the T-junction. Turn left at the 3.5t sign, then left at the T-junction. Follow Honfleur signs uphill to the view indicator.*

7 Marais-Vernier, Normandy

Bounded by an amphitheatre of wooded hills, this area was once marshland flooded by the Seine (*marais* means marsh). After vague earlier reclamation efforts, it was at the beginning of the 17th century that Dutch workers dug channels to drain the southern part of the marsh. They are still recalled in the name of the Digue des Hollandais (the Dutchmen's Dyke) alongside the D103.

North of that road, the work was tackled only in 1947. Now the Marais-Vernier is mostly lush grazing land for Camargue horses and Highland cattle. Some pockets of boggy ground can still be found, and there are central scrubby woodlands. In spring, pink and white blossom embellishes the surrounding farmland. La Grande Mare is the lake into which most of the drainage water flows on its way eventually to the Seine.

BACK TO NATURE

Where the main route turns sharp right after Ste-Opportune, bear left and after about 0.8km (½-mile) watch for the 'Réserve Naturelle des Mannevilles' car park. A steeply stepped viewing tower overlooks the nature reserve around the Grande Mare. You will often see mallards, coots, grebes, teal, pochard and tufted duck on the lake itself or in the reed beds and drainage channels round it. Grey herons and Cetti's warblers are present, but more secretive.

Fifteenth-century Notre-Dame Church at Caudebec-en-Caux

▶ *After the view indicator, go right on the D100 to St-Samson then left past the church on the D39. Bear right to the give-way sign then left* at the T-junction on the *N178. Go first right and follow the signs to Honfleur.*

8 Honfleur, Normandy

To all its other attractions, Honfleur adds the lovely old slate-roofed houses overlooking the harbour of the Vieux Bassin and, near by, some splendid survivals like the Grenier à Sel (salt stores) in Rue de la Ville.

Erik Satie, the composer, was born in this fishing town. So was the artist Eugène Boudin, still admired for his skyscapes and his ability to 'paint the wind'. His work is featured in the museum which bears his name.

The Musée d'Ethnographie has 12 rooms in which traditional Norman homes have been re-created and offers visits to the old town prison. The Musée de la Marine is lavishly stocked with ship models and other memorabilia of the sea.

Honfleur commemorates Samuel de Champlain. It was from here, on eight great voyages between 1603 and 1620, that he explored Canada, claimed it for France and founded the city of Québec.

ℹ *Quai Lepaulmier*

▶ *Leave Honfleur by the rue de la République as for Pont-l'Evêque, then go left as for Tancarville on the D17. Turn right on to the N175 then left on the D534 to Cormeilles. Leave Cormeilles on the D810, continue into Lieurey and follow the D137 to Pont-Authou. Go right on the D130 then left on the D39 to Le Bec-Hellouin.*

9 Le Bec-Hellouin, Normandy

This is a lovely hillside village, massed with flowers, including rosebeds by the timbered houses on the square. Many old buildings survive here, from the tiny red-tiled wash-house by a fast-flowing stream to the stalwart ruins of what was once a powerful abbey dating back to 1040. It has a great reputation as a centre of theological learning, and three of its 'sons' went on to become archbishops of Canterbury – Lanfranc in 1070, Anselm in 1093 and Theobald in 1138.

Closely linked with the abbey is the Ste-Françoise

The calm of Honfleur harbour belies the town's turbulent past

monastery near by. Workshops can be visited and the products are sold in the abbey shop.

16th centuries – contributed to its appearance, but from a distance the most remarkable feature is the tall steeple added in the 19th century. Built entirely of fretted cast iron, it arrows towards the sky.

After Rouen was lost to the English in the Hundred Years' War, it was here than Joan was brought as a prisoner and subjected to a shameful trial. Its aftermath was even more despicable when, her life having been previously spared, she was burned at the stake in the old

▶ *Continue on the **D39** then go left on the **N138**. At the stop sign, go straight ahead on the **D3** as for Rouen, through Moulineaux. Turn right at traffic lights as for Elbeuf, and right over the level crossing. Go sharp left on the **N138** and follow the signs to Rouen.*

10 Rouen, Normandy
The revitalisation of the quaysides, smart new shopping facilities and an ambitious modern public transport scheme have transformed much of Rouen, but the glory of the historic capital of Normandy remains its magnificent Gothic Cathedral of Notre-Dame. It stands in the midst of a splendid carefully restored 'old town'.

Architects and artists of many different eras – mainly 13th to

marketplace. She was canonised in 1920. A surviving tower of the castle she was imprisoned in can be visited, and the Musée de Cire Jeanne d'Arc portrays her story. Other museums include the Musée Flaubert, with displays on the history of medicine in the former home of novelist Gustave Flaubert, the Musée Maritime Fluvial et Portuaire, relating the city's seafaring heritage, and the Musée des Beaux-Arts with a good collection of 17th- to 20th-century French paintings.

ℹ️ *25 place de la Cathédrale*

▶ *Leave Rouen on the **A28** then go left on the **D928**, right on the **D151** to Bellencombre and left on the **D154** to Dieppe.*

Richard the Lionheart's tomb in Rouen Cathedral

The Emerald
Country

Starting from Rennes, the capital of Brittany, this tour is drawn briefly into Normandy to visit Mont-St-Michel on its fortified tidal island. Along the Brittany coastline there are headlands offering magnificent views, then it's inland to historic towns such as Vitré, Fougères and Dinan, and St-Malo, on the coast.

3 DAYS • 392KM • 243 MILES

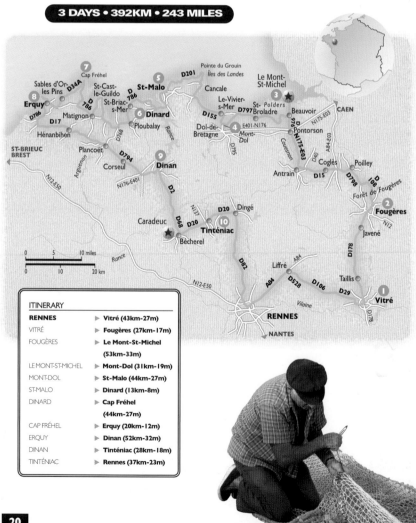

ITINERARY	
RENNES	▶ **Vitré (43km-27m)**
VITRÉ	▶ **Fougères (27km-17m)**
FOUGÈRES	▶ **Le Mont-St-Michel**
	(53km-33m)
LE MONT-ST-MICHEL	▶ **Mont-Dol (31km-19m)**
MONT-DOL	▶ **St-Malo (44km-27m)**
ST-MALO	▶ **Dinard (13km-8m)**
DINARD	▶ **Cap Fréhel**
	(44km-27m)
CAP FRÉHEL	▶ **Erquy (20km-12m)**
ERQUY	▶ **Dinan (52km-32m)**
DINAN	▶ **Tinténiac (28km-18m)**
TINTÉNIAC	▶ **Rennes (37km-23m)**

▶ Leave Rennes as for Fougères on the **A84**. Go right on the **D528** to Liffré and in the town centre turn right for Vitré via La Bouëxière. Enter Vitré on the **D857**.

FOR HISTORY BUFFS

The Manoir de l' Automobile on the A84 after Rennes, tells the story of the French motor industry through such fine exhibits as a 1904 Renault with a basketwork canister for the passengers' canes and parasols. Veteran posters and accessories are also on display.

---

1 Vitré, Brittany
In the days when Brittany was separate from France, Vitré was a frontier fortress. Its triangular-plan castle, high above the River Vilaine, houses the town museum in three of its towers. A fourth provides an all-encompassing viewpoint. Many medieval and Renaissance buildings are still in use. The Centre Social, for instance, occupies a splendid 16th-century mansion with elaborate windows, doors and rooflines. Beautifully restored, the rue de la Beaudrairie was the leatherworkers' quarter.

Walks lead down into the pleasant valley of the Vilaine. The manor house and outbuildings of the 'Bocage Vitréen' house the Musée de la Faucillonnaie, devoted to rural life and crafts, while Le Château des Rochers-Sévigné manor house reflects a grander style of living, with one wing devoted to former resident Madame de Sévigné.

i Place Général-de-Gaulle

▶ Leave Vitré for 'Fougères par Taillis' on the **D179**.

2 Fougères, Brittany
The most important feature of this second medieval fortress town is the huge and superb castle on a peninsula site all but encircled by the Nançon river. But delay going to the castle itself until you have looked at it from the attractive Jardin Public in the high town. Its situation and layout are seen to best effect from the garden (despite the background scar of a modern quarry). Below the castle, the low town retains many fine buildings, such as the Flamboyant Gothic Church of St-Sulpice and the 17th-century houses round the Place du Marchaix. In the high town, one 16th-century house is now the Musée Emmanuel de la Villéon, devoted to the locally born artist who was one of the last Impressionists.

i 2 rue Nationale

RECOMMENDED WALKS

Ask at the tourist office at Rennes or Fougères for the leaflet showing the footpaths in the Forêt de Fougères. One, which crosses the route at the Carrefour du Père Tacot, wanders through the beechwoods, passes a line of druids' stones and follows the shore of Chédenet Lake.

Traditional-style half-timbered houses in Rennes

natural phenomena of the bay with audiovisuals and exhibits, and includes a splendid view from its observatory.

ⓘ *Corps de Garde des Bourgeois*

▶ *Return to Beauvoir. Turn right for Les Polders, over the bridge and immediately left. Turn left at the first stop sign and right at the second stop sign. Go right on the **D797** through St-Broladre, left on the **D80** then right on the **V5** to the village of Mont-Dol. Watch for a right turn before the Hôtel du Tertre up a steep and narrow road to Sommet du Mont-Dol.*

> ### FOR CHILDREN
>
> On the way back from Le Mont-St-Michel, call in at Alligator Bay in Beauvoir to see 200 aligators and crocodiles, iguanas, lizards, snakes and giant tortoises.

▶ *Leave Fougères as for St-Hilaire on the **D177**. Immediately after leaving Fougères bear right along a 'route forestière'. Go left at Carrefour du Père Tacot then straight on across the main road. At Carrefour des Serfilières bear left, taking the fourth exit. Turn right at the stop sign (this is the **D108**) to Parigné. Leave Parigné on the **D108** as for Mellé. At the crossroads go straight on, avoiding the right turn to Mellé. Go right at the stop sign along the **D798**. Turn left on the **D15** through Coglès, left briefly on the **D296** then right on the **D15** again. In Antrain, turn right at the stop sign to Pontorson and continue via Beauvoir to Le Mont-St-Michel.*

Fougères Castle – a fine example of medieval military architecture

magnificent abbey whose highest steeple spears the sky. Reached by a causeway, Mont-St-Michel lies among the mazy channels of a vast bay. The lowest towers and medieval sea-wall protect a village of lanes and stairways, where the Musée Historique tells the story of the abbey and island community in a series of tableaux, and the Archéoscope elaborates it with sound and lighting. More prosaically, the Musée de la Mer places the island in its marine and tidal context.

Crowning the summit, the abbey dedicated to the Archangel Michael is a triumph of Romanesque and Gothic design. Finest of all the architecture are the 13th-century buildings which include the refectory and cloisters.

On the mainland, the Maison de la Baie du Mont-St-Michel illustrates the history and

❸ Le Mont-St-Michel,
Normandy
From whatever angle, a first sight of this isolated tidal rock is stunning. It rises from rampart walls and a clustered village to a

❹ Mont-Dol, Brittany
From this hilltop with its marvellous 360-degree view, note the great area of rich, reclaimed marshland of the 'polders' that you crossed after Beauvoir. Beyond them, across the bay, lies Mont-St-Michel.

A good display map shows the features of Mont-Dol itself – which include the scenes of the legendary struggle between St Michael and the Devil. There is also a chapel, an old seaward signalling tower, two 19th-century windmills and walks among the pines, gorse and rock outcrops.

▶ *Return from the summit. Go right to pass the Hôtel du Tertre. Leave Mont-Dol village on the **D123**. Turn right on the **D155** and follow the signs towards Cancale on the **D76**. Go right on the **VC15** signed 'Cancale le Port'. Leave Cancale following 'St-Malo par la Côte' and 'Pointe du Grouin' signs along the*

*D201. Go straight on along the **C6** to Pointe du Grouin then return to the **D201** for St-Malo.*

SPECIAL TO...

Cancale, to the east of St-Malo, is famous all over France for the high-quality oysters cultivated extensively in the bay. They taste nowhere better than in the town's own seafood restaurants. Visit the Ferme Marine to learn more.

RECOMMENDED WALKS

One of the most glorious coastal walks in Brittany is the GR34 north of Cancale on the way between Mont-Dol and St-Malo. It takes a clifftop route with high-level views to offshore islands and faraway Mont-St-Michel, on the way to the magnificent bay at Port Briac.

BACK TO NATURE

On the breezy headland of Pointe du Grouin, telescopes are aimed at the rugged nature reserve of the Île des Landes. It houses Brittany's biggest colony of cormorants.

⑧ St-Malo, Brittany

An extensive area of sheltered harbours continues the long maritime tradition of a town which was the historic base for privateers, explorers and the 16th-century Newfoundland fishing fleets. The heart of St-Malo is the granite-built district known as Intra Muros, inside the coastal rampart walls. It is almost entirely a reconstruction from the rubble of World War II. Look here for the historical Musée d'Histoire in the 15th-century castle whose great keep and towers command impressive views of the harbour and the Fort National on its rocky outcrop, open for visits when the French flag is flying. There are two well-stocked aquariums as well as a museum of dolls and old-time toys.

Ferries sail to destinations along the coast, and there is a hydrofoil service to Jersey. But the Tour Solidor recalls much grander voyages: it houses displays on the Cape Horners.

i Esplanade St-Vincent

▶ *Leave St-Malo as for Dinard. Go right on the **D114** and right on the **D266** into Dinard.*

SPECIAL TO...

After St-Malo, on the main road across the estuary of the Rance is an innovative hydro-electric generating station which uses tidal power in both directions – at the ebb and at the flow. The main road across the estuary runs along the dam, and you can take a guided tour of this splendid pollution-free scheme.

St-Malo was named after a Welsh monk called Maclow

6 Dinard, Brittany

To a beautiful seafront of bays, promontories, sandy beaches and offshore rocky islets, Dinard adds hotels, restaurants, a casino, a golf club, an equestrian centre and other sporting facilities to maintain its reputation as the premier resort of Brittany's Emerald Coast. The weather is mild and some of the vegetation is Mediterranean along the footpaths which meander along the coast.

Fine villas stand in lovely wooded grounds, many of them dating from the turn of the century when British high society favoured Dinard – Edward VII and George V are remembered in street names today.

Dinard attracts many musical, film and artistic events. Every summer evening at dusk there is a *son et lumière* presentation on the seafront Promenade du Clair de Lune.

i 　2 boulevard Féart

▶ *Leave Dinard on the **D786** through St-Briac-sur-Mer and continue as for St-Brieuc. After Port-à-la-Duc turn right to Cap Fréhel on the **D16**.*

7 Cap Fréhel, Brittany

In the 1920s a company tried to sell off building plots on this dramatic cliff-ringed headland. Fortunately, the misbegotten scheme failed – much of the ground is too marshy. From the approach road, you may think that the cape ends at the two lighthouses – one built in the 1950s and the other completed in 1847, immense care having been paid to the design and the masonry work – and the 18th-century fortification known as the Tour Vauban. In fact, Fréhel extends much further out to sea.

A stroll around the cape, whose majestic rock stacks are a nature reserve, opens up views into precipitous wave-lashed inlets as well as southeastwards to the spectacularly located Fort la Latte, a medieval fortress situated on a headland some 4km (2.5 miles) away.

i 　Place de Chambly

BACK TO NATURE

Cap Fréhel and its offshore rock stacks are busy with gulls, fulmars, cormorants and guillemots, for whom this is France's premier nesting area. In summer the approach to the cape is purple with heather and gold with the flowers of gorse and bird's-foot trefoil.

FOR CHILDREN

Sables-d'Or-les-Pins, after Cap Fréhel, caters well for children, with sandy beaches, pony rides, 'bouncy castles' and beach clubs with organised activities. There are facilities for watersports, and behind the beach are plenty of places to eat.

▶ *Return from Cap Fréhel and turn right on the **D34a** as for St-Brieuc. Rejoin the **D786** for Erquy.*

8 Erquy, Brittany

Built round a west-facing bay well sheltered from the northerly wind, Erquy is a pleasant and unpretentious little resort with no trace of obtrusive modern building. The bay is busy with courses in canoeing and windsurfing, and there is a local shellfish fleet.

Take the road to the Cap d'Erquy and you will climb to an exhilarating headland where the heath and low-lying scrub are criss-crossed by wandering footpaths. There are cliff edges to be carefully explored, views to the broken water over dangerous offshore reefs, and a splendid if unexpected east-

The medieval town of Dinan on the River Rance, where boats depart for St-Malo and Dinard

facing beach. There are also ditches and other signs of prehistoric fortifications, some as old as 4,500 years.

ⓘ *3 rue du 19 Mars 1962*

▶ *Leave Erquy on the **D786** as for St-Brieuc, then left on the **D17** for Dinan via Plancoët. Enter Dinan via the **N176**.*

❾ Dinan, Brittany
Since its appearance in the Bayeux Tapestry, in the 11th century, Dinan has had a clear line of history, each era marked by its own architectural styles in ramparts, towers, gateways and attractive houses. Streets in the old town bear the names of medieval trade guilds. The castle is a fortress of mellow stonework whose unusual 14th-century oval keep houses the local museum. You can admire Dinan from the upper viewing gallery of the 15th-century belfry, the Tour de l'Horloge

(Clock Tower). Another good viewpoint, although disappointing as an actual garden, is the Jardin Anglais (English Garden). It overlooks the valley of the Rance, in which enticing footpaths lead under the stately viaduct over which you approached the town, towards the downstream quays.

In the Church of St Saveur is buried the heart of Bertrand du Guesclin, who fought in single combat in the Place du Champ Clos in 1359 to free his brother from his English captors.

ⓘ *9 rue du Château*

▶ *Leave Dinan from Lanvallay and turn right through Évran on the **D2**, which becomes the **D68** as for Bécherel. In La Barre turn left for Tinténiac on the **D20**.*

❿ Tinténiac, Brittany
On the D2, turn left to visit the enormous Château de la

Bourbansais, which reputedly has 1 ha (2.5 acres) of roof; the grounds are home to a well-established zoo.

The church in Tinténiac, with its cupolas and sturdy but ornate stonework, looks slightly puzzling. In fact it is a complete turn-of-the-century rebuilding of an old ecclesiastical site, and well worth a visit.

Tinténiac lies on the Canal d'Ille et Rance. At the quai de la Donac, a redundant grain store is now the Musée de l'Outil et des Métiers (Museum of Tools and Trades), displaying tools and machinery from half-forgotten rural trades.

FOR HISTORY BUFFS

Before Tinténiac, turn right in La Barre, through Bécherel to the Parc de Caradeuc and its château. The 18th-century lawyer Caradeuc de la Chalotais was devoted to the independence of the Breton parliament. Louis XV imprisoned him without trial. A message he smuggled out of jail, written with a toothpick in ink made from soot, vinegar and sugar, caused a sensation.

▶ *Continue on the **D20** to Dingé. Watch for a right turn on the **D82** before the Confiserie/Épicerie shop. Return to Rennes.*

SCENIC ROUTES

Approaching Vitré, the D22 runs through a pleasant rural landscape, which continues along the D179 to Fougères, with long eastern views. Even at times of hectic traffic, the approach to stately Mont-St-Michel has a magic all its own.

The coastal stretch of the D155 looks over salt marshes and oyster beds to the rocky islets off Cancale. A succession of cliffs and sandy bays follows the D34a after Cap Fréhel.

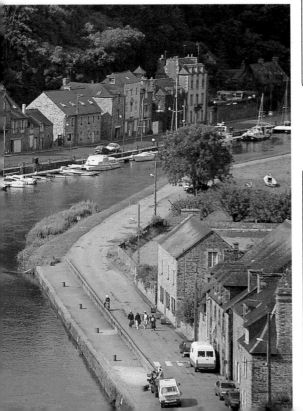

The Celtic
Connection

Quimper is the capital of old Cornouaille. This is Celtic country, as you will see from the place-names. The Breton language is still spoken by more than half a million people, giving western Brittany the position in France which Wales occupies in the UK.

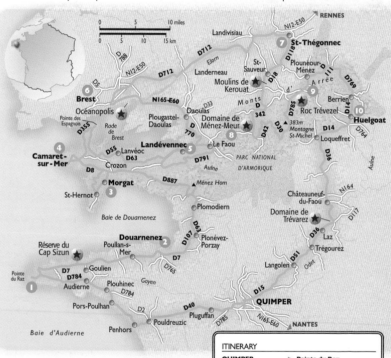

4 DAYS • 496KM • 309 MILES

ITINERARY	
QUIMPER	▸ **Pointe du Raz (60km-37m)**
POINTE DU RAZ	▸ **Douarnenez (41km-26m)**
DOUARNENEZ	▸ **Morgat (53km-33m)**
MORGAT	▸ **Camaret-sur-Mer (24km-15m)**
CAMARET-SUR-MER	▸ **Landévennec (48km-30m)**
LANDÉVENNEC	▸ **Brest (63km-39m)**
BREST	▸ **St-Thégonnec (51km-32m)**
ST-THÉGONNEC	▸ **Ménez-Meur (28km-17m)**
MÉNEZ-MEUR	▸ **Monts d'Arrée (32km-20m)**
MONTS D'ARRÉE	▸ **Huelgoat (29km-18m)**
HUELGOAT	▸ **Quimper (67km-42m)**

i *Place de la Résistance, Quimper*

▶ *Leave Quimper on the **D785** as for Pont l'Abbé, then through Pluguffan and follow the **D40** through Pouldreuzic to Penhors. Bear right as for Plozévet, then left, and follow signs to Pors-Poulhan. Climb from the harbour, then turn sharp left following 'Allée Couverte' sign. Turn left at two stop signs. In Audierne, look for 'Pointe du Raz' signs and take the **D784** to Pointe du Raz.*

❶ Pointe du Raz, Brittany
One of Brittany's classic headlands plays host to a commercial square of souvenir shops and cafés. A wasteland of bare, trodden earth and rock leads beyond the coastguard station to the actual point, and then the atmosphere changes. No careless exploitation can damage the magnificent seaward views. Pointe du Raz looks over a savage strait where jagged rocks, the last topped with a lighthouse, march towards the weird outline of the Île-de-Sein – reminiscent of a Pacific atoll moved to the

windswept Atlantic edge. Guides escort parties of visitors round the cliff paths, and with or without them it is easy to appreciate why the statue near the point is to *Notre-Dame des Naufragés* – Our Lady of the Shipwrecked. Knowing that Sein was once the mainland coast makes the legend of the drowned city of Ys, out in the Bay of Douarnenez, something to ponder.

> **FOR HISTORY BUFFS**
>
> The Alée Couverte, at Pors-Poulhan, is a restored ancient burial chamber. Great rock slabs form the walls and others are laid across them as the roof.

▶ *Return from Pointe du Raz and turn left for 'Douarnenez par le CD7' on the **V8** and **D7**. On the approach to Douarnenez, follow 'Autres Directions' and 'Toutes Directions' signs at roundabouts, then turn left on the **D765** and left to Centre-Ville.*

Pointe du Raz, Cap Sizun – a sanctuary for seabirds

> **BACK TO NATURE**
>
> Turn left off the D7 for the Réserve Ornithologique on the seabird cliffs of Cap Sizun. This was the first bird reserve in France with a definite educational programme. The movements and associations of whole gull colonies are followed by computer.

❷ Douarnenez, Brittany
Douarnenez is the fifth busiest fishing port in France. The narrow river inlet of Port-Rhu slices deep into Douarnenez, but the main harbour of Rosmeur is on the east side of the peninsula which it helps to form. There are early morning fish auctions here, and cruise boats visit the cliffs, inlets and grottoes of the bay. Beaches are scattered in some unexpected locations, and a good coastal walk leads from Rosmeur along the Sentier des Plomarc'hs. Le Port-Musée is located here. A tidal wall has been built to dam

a basin 2km (1 mile) long at Port Rhu. Visitors can explore 250 full-sized boats (summer only) and admire the skills of craftsmen engaged in restoration work. This floating museum is unique in France.

i 2 rue Docteur Mével

▶ *Leave Douarnenez as for Brest on the D7, then turn left*

South of Morgat, just before the village of St-Hernot, the interesting Maison des Minéraux houses a fascinating array of crystals, fossils and semi-precious stones, such as agates and amethysts, from all over Brittany, in their natural state as well as cut and polished. Make sure you see the fluorescent cabinet where many of them gleam in exotic colours.

museum in the Tour Vauban recalls events such as the British and Dutch landing of 1694, which was furiously and famously repulsed.

The prehistoric standing stones of Lagatjar retain their strict straight-line alignment and, to the south, the Pointe

Camaret-sur-Mer's beach is strewn with shipwrecks

on the D107 to Plonévez-Porzay. Watch for the left turn on to the D63, then take the D47 through Plomodiern and left to Ste-Marie. Turn left on the D887, right to the Ménez-Hom summit and return to the D887. Follow 'Morgat' signs through Crozon, watching for an unexpected left turn. In Morgat, follow 'Maison des Minéraux' signs towards St-Hernot.

❸ Morgat, Brittany
This resort on the sheltered side of Douarnenez Bay is well equipped for watersports and enjoys good, extensive beaches with coastal promenades. There are daily summer cruises to the marine caverns of La Chambre du Diable (the Devil's Chamber), La Cheminée des Cormorans (the Cormorants' Chimney) and the loveliest, l'Autel (Altar Grotto).

▶ *After the Maison des Minéraux, bear right as for Kerdreux then almost immediately right at crossroads. Go straight on at the stop sign, follow 'Crozon' signs, then turn right at a T-junction (D308) into Crozon. At the roundabout, take the third exit along the D8 to Camaret-sur-Mer.*

❹ Camaret-sur-Mer, Brittany
Set on a stunning peninsula within the Armorique regional park, Camaret is a resort surrounded by beaches facing in different directions. A substantial crayfish fleet is based here, and lobster is also fished locally, so the seafood restaurants, naturally, are well and freshly stocked.

Vauban, the great 17th-century military architect, fortified Camaret. The local history

de Penhir is a majestic viewpoint with dramatic rock formations – a natural amphitheatre of 70m (230-foot) high cliffs.

i 15 quai Kléber

> ### BACK TO NATURE
>
> Well out of reach of any road approach, the dramatic rock stacks of the Tas des Pois – the Pile of Peas – can be visited on the *Sirène IV*, which sails from Camaret. Their cliffs teem with gulls, fulmars, cormorants, guillemots and storm petrels.

▶ *Leave Camaret-sur-Mer on the D355 to Pointe des Espagnols and through Roscanvel. At a roundabout take the D55 to Lanvéoc, then the D63 as for Brest. At the brow of a hill at Maison*

*Blanche, watch for a left turn at crossroads. Turn right at the crossroads at a stop sign. At the give-way sign, turn left on the **D60** to Landévennec.*

5 Landévennec, Brittany
Occupying an attractive peninsula where the estuaries of the Aulne and the Faou combine, Landévennec is a village in which a glance down almost any lane offers a view of the water. Brittany's oldest abbey was founded here in 485 by the Welsh missionary St Guénolé. It crumbled away after the Revolution. The ruins of the final Romanesque buildings are approached by a palm-tree avenue. Exhibitions explain the history of the abbey itself, and also how Brittany rose from the wreckage of the Roman Empire, colonised in Guénolé's time by Celts driven from Britain by the Anglo-Saxon invasions.

▶ *Return along the **D60** to the **D791** and turn left. In Le Faou go left as for Hanvec, over a bridge and left – at first along the riverside – through Lanvoy. Turn left at a T-junction and through Daoulas on the **D770**. Follow signs for Brest on the **N165**.*

ℹ *Mairie, Landévennec*

6 Brest, Brittany
For almost 2,000 years, the sea has been Brest's delight and its despair. From Roman times its great roadstead – perhaps the most beautiful in Europe, with its bays, peninsulas and feeder rivers – has been a naval base. Such places are vulnerable in time of conflict. Brest came out of World War II shattered by bombing raids. Even the street plan was redrawn at the time of rebuilding. This remains the home of many capital ships. Only French citizens may visit the base itself, but foreigners are more than welcome at the Musée-Château National de la Marine, repository of Brest's tumultuous history, housed in the medieval castle, which is open to all. Excellent parks include the Vallon du Stang-Alar, with its lawns, lakes, tree-shaded walks and Conservatoire Botanique, preserving hundreds of endangered plant species.

Océanopolis is a fascinating complex of aquariums (the largest in Europe, including a stunning polar habitat, a tropical environment that contains sharks and a 13m (42-foot) living coral reef, and Brittany's rich marine life.

SPECIAL TO...

Breton is a Celtic language, related to Cornish and Welsh, which has survived consistent attempts to crush it by French governments of the past. The late 20th century saw a growing movement to preserve and promote its use, and secondary schools now offer Breton courses to thousands of pupils.

Only the ruins of the Abbey of St Guénolé testify to Landévennec's monastic beginnings

ℹ *Place de la Liberté*

FOR CHILDREN

Children are always delighted by a boat trip, and across the bay at Rade de Brest, gleaming white pleasure cruisers are waiting to whisk you around the harbour, with views of the warships, merchant ships and pleasure craft on the waters. The duration of the trips vary between half an hour for the straight crossing and three hours for the restaurant cruise.

▶ *Leave Brest for Landerneau on the **D712**. Follow the 'Centre Ville' sign at a roundabout in Landerneau. Continue to Landivisiau, still on the **D712**, then as for Morlaix on to the **N12**. Take the exit for St-Thégonnec.*

7 St-Thégonnec, Brittany

In the past, Breton villages would vie for glory with their neighbours, particularly in the splendour of their churches. Consequently, at St-Thégonnec, the 16th- to 18th-century masonry work of the church is far more elaborate than is justified by the status of the little place. The churchyard gateway and the funeral chapel are similarly ornate, and the calvary of 1610, its clustered figures telling the story of the Passion, was one of the last in the exuberant Breton style. Inside the church, look for the intricately carved pulpit of 1683.

RECOMMENDED WALKS

The Pont Hir walk at St-Thégonnec follows a waymarked route across rural landscapes to an eerie tunnel taking the River Coatoulsac'h through a railway embankment. Another feature of the walk is a wood where quiet walkers may sight roe deer.

SPECIAL TO...

At the stop sign after Croas-Cabellec, turn left for the Écomusée Moulins-de-Kerouat, with its two antique watermills. Lessons are sometimes given on how to bake your own country-style bread.

There is also the miller's home with its traditional furniture and an exhibition relating the history of the village through the lives of five generations of millers.

▶ Leave St-Thégonnec as for Sizun on the **D118**, then the **D18**. After St-Sauveur, carry straight on at the crossroads at Croas-Cabellec, following '5 Sizun' sign. After a double-bend sign, take the first left, then go straight on at the stop sign as for Goas ar Vern. Follow the 'Barrage du Drennec' sign, then continue to St-Cadou. Turn right on the

The numerous statuettes on St-Thégonnec's elegant 1610 calvary depict the Passion

D30, left on the **D130** as for St-Eloy, and watch for a left turn to Ménez-Meur.

8 Ménez-Meur, Brittany

The wooded surroundings of this estate conceal a series of open grazing areas where you can admire red, Sika and fallow deer, wild boars, several breeds of horses, and other domesticated specialities such as the long-haired Highland cattle and Swaledale sheep.

Ménez-Meur is approached along a beautiful avenue, where interlocking trees arch over from mossy walls. There are three waymarked trails within the estate, which have animal, forest and general countryside themes, and the estate is famous for its displays, fairs and festivals celebrating the sturdy Breton horse.

▶ Continue to St-Rivoal on the **D30**, then turn left on the **D785**.

9 Monts d'Arrée, Brittany

The D785 runs along the upper reaches of the Monts d'Arrée, where the Parc Naturel

Régional d'Armorique opens out in a world of moorland summits. Montagne St-Michel is one of the highest points, at 383m (1,256 feet). From it, a superb all-round view gives a slightly perplexing impression of a completely circular horizon. Roc Trévezel, further along the road, is a granite tor which offers another fine viewpoint.

RECOMMENDED WALKS

Off the D785 is an access point to the footpaths shown in the *Yeun Elez* leaflet published by the Parc d'Armorique. One of the paths climbs the open moorland to Mont-St-Michel de Brasparts and circles back by the lovely countryside around St-Rivoal.

▶ *Continue on the **D785** to Plounéour-Ménez. Turn right on the **D111**, right on the **D769** and follow signs to Huelgoat, turning right on the **D14** in Berrien.*

🔟 Huelgoat, Brittany

Built beside a peaceful lake, this is an inland resort with two contrasting characters. The town is bright and open, with lakeside walks, pedalo hire and fishing. In the centre, the peaceful Arboretum du Pöerop has a collection of trees and shrubs from several continents. Close by is the Jardin de l'Argoat, set around a 16th-century fountain and pond. Go to the bridge over the lake's outflow and you look immediately into a more dramatic world. From a chaos of jumbled rocks, footpaths wander through the most beautiful forest in Brittany. Beech, oak and conifers clothe a landscape of leafy glades, tumbling streams and mysterious Celtic stones, where the legends of King Arthur, Merlin and the Druids survive.

ℹ️ *18 place Aristide Briand*

Great moss-covered boulders litter the streams and tumbled hills in Huelgoat Forest, a delightful place for strolling

FOR HISTORY BUFFS

On the return route to Quimper, the Maison des Pilhaouerien in Loqueffret recalls the 'rag and bone' families who, until the 1950s, toured the district with their donkey carts.

After Châteauneuf-du-Faou, the rose castle in the beautiful park of Trévarez was one of the last built in France. During World War II it was a rest centre for the German Navy, until gutted in an RAF bombing raid. History, art and floral exhibitions are held here.

▶ *Leave Huelgoat for Loqueffret on the **D14**. Turn sharp left on the **D36** through Châteauneuf-du-Faou. Follow 'Domaine de Trévarez' signs, then continue on the **D36** to Trégourez. Turn right on the **D51** and return to Quimper.*

SCENIC ROUTES

The Ménez-Hom road, the D83, climbs to one of the finest viewpoints in Brittany. After Camaret, the D355 rounds a peninsula with a beautiful outlook over the roadstead of Brest. Later, look for the view from the suspension bridge that takes the D791 over the River Aulne. Around St-Rivoal, the D342 is a lane set in wooded combes.

THE LOIRE & CENTRAL FRANCE

As it sweeps from the mountain country of the Massif Central, by the Loire Valley and the Cognac vineyards, to the coastline and islands around La Rochelle, this area illustrates the great variety of landscape in France.

Not far from the industrial city of Clermont-Ferrand you drive through a country of ancient volcanoes, with high cattle pastures closed till the clearance of winter snows. In the valleys of the Loire and its principal tributaries you will encounter many of France's most magnificent castles. The 'conspicuous consumption' they represented was one of the elements which brought about the French Revolution. Fortunately, the major castles such as Chenonceau and Blois survive.

At high levels you will find windy, upland pastures and conifer plantings, and there is a chance of snow flurries even in late spring. Lower down lies a pastoral area of arable farms, but the finest ground, especially near Tours and along the valley of the River Charente, is reserved for vineyards. This is the country of Pays Nantais, Vouvray, Rosé d'Anjou, Cognac and Côtes d'Auvergne wines.

The two islands of Ré and Oléron are microcosmic worlds of their own. Rimmed by beautiful beaches and holiday resorts, with fine climates tempered by the Atlantic breezes, they have a strong off-season life. Farms, vines and oyster beds all play their part, and the little towns enjoy intriguing histories. Ré, for instance, was the last place on metropolitan French soil seen by criminals shipped to Devil's Island.

As in most of France, the road network is extensive. In some places, for instance approaching Angoulême on the La Rochelle tour in the attractive valley of the Charente, you should keep a close watch on the route instructions.

In 1988, ferries to the major islands were replaced. The drive to Ré is notable for the splendidly proportioned toll bridge from the mainland. This is how an island should be approached, on a dramatic, high-level curve.

Clermont-Ferrand

Clermont-Ferrand, a great industrial centre in the heart of France, is the world headquarters of the Michelin tyre company; it's also where they bottle mineral water. The city is dominated by its splendid Gothic cathedral, but not far from it there stands another church of equal if not greater architectural merit, the 12th-century Notre-Dame-du-Port. The Musée Lecoq contains some fine natural history exhibits, and there are two other museums in town, as well as exhibitions in the new information centre.

Limoges

Limoges is the city of porcelain. Its Musée National Adrien-Dubouché shows porcelain in all its colour, elegance and stages of preparation. Enamelware is one of the specialities of the Musée Municipal de l'Évêché. As in Clermont-Ferrand, there are attractive individual houses, churches and public buildings in Limoges, as well as botanical gardens and craft displays in the Cité des Métiers et des Arts overlooking the River Vézère.

La Rochelle

La Rochelle carefully guards its waterfront. Le Gabut is an engaging modern harbourside development whose colour-washed wooden buildings, with stairs and gangways, have a maritime air. The older houses have an agreeably regular appearance, forced on the builders by strict town-planning laws.

Museums here include one of mechanical toys, another of model ships, planes and railways, and a third devoted to a century and a half of yacht racing. The maritime collection occupies a sturdy harbour-entrance tower, and there is a fine weathership museum and a major modern aquarium.

Nantes

Very much a river city, Nantes includes two channels of the Loire, three of its tributaries and, for good measure, a canal. The city centre has undergone a major face-lift and has an efficient modern tram network. Look for the moated castle of the dukes of Brittany, the cathedral, begun in 1434, the old quarters and the half-dozen parks, including a peaceful Japanese garden. A pᵣ um complements the ᵣ museum devoted to the ᵢ and works of the sciencᵉ fiction pioneer Jules Verne.

Tours

The capital of Touraine is spacious and unhurried, with elegant public buildings and a beautiful cathedral. There are promenades on rivers – the Loire and the Cher. The Château-Royal houses Historial de Touraine, where waxworks tableaux illustrate local history. The Musée des Beaux-Arts is in an archbishops' old palace. Archaeology, and Renaissance and medieval art are found in the Musée Archéologique in the superb 16th-century mansion called the Hôtel Gouin. Other museums and studios cover the wines of Touraine, dolls, gemstones and enamelwork, military transport, the story of journeymen-craftsmen and the handloom weaving of silk.

Opposite: Fontenay-le-Comte, an old market town on the Vendée
Below: Tours has managed to preserve (with much restoration) its historic heart

d of Quiet
Volcanoes

Clermont-Ferrand has the advantage of backing immediately on to hill country, and these are no ordinary hills. They are the relics of huge volcanic convulsions thousands of years ago. Now green and wooded, they provide space in the valleys for holiday resorts, including spas whose thermal waters were famous in Roman times. The area's 20 mineral springs supply the world with bottled water.

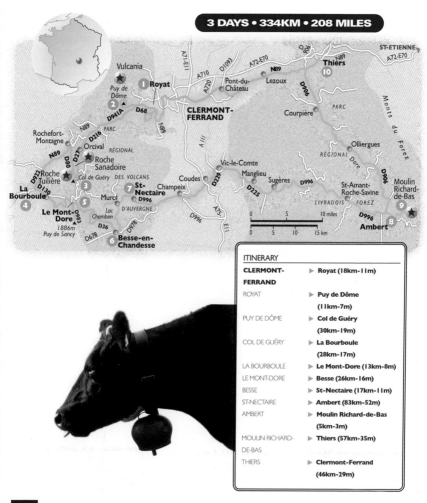

3 DAYS • 334KM • 208 MILES

ITINERARY	
CLERMONT-FERRAND	▶ **Royat (18km-11m)**
ROYAT	▶ **Puy de Dôme (11km-7m)**
PUY DE DÔME	▶ **Col de Guéry (30km-19m)**
COL DE GUÉRY	▶ **La Bourboule (28km-17m)**
LA BOURBOULE	▶ **Le Mont-Dore (13km-8m)**
LE MONT-DORE	▶ **Besse (26km-16m)**
BESSE	▶ **St-Nectaire (17km-11m)**
ST-NECTAIRE	▶ **Ambert (83km-52m)**
AMBERT	▶ **Moulin Richard-de-Bas (5km-3m)**
MOULIN RICHARD-DE-BAS	▶ **Thiers (57km-35m)**
THIERS	▶ **Clermont-Ferrand (46km-29m)**

[i] *Place de la Victoire, Clermont-Ferrand*

▶ *Leave Clermont-Ferrand on the N89 as for Tulle. Go right on the D767 then right on the D941c to Royat.*

❶ Royat, Auvergne
Royat is a perfect example of a French spa which has moved with the times. Since Roman times, people have drunk the mineral waters and relaxed in thermal baths here, but its development as a fashionable spa dates from the 19th century. Today, Roman remains and fine old churches mix with attractive modern buildings.

Its central area is crammed into a narrow river valley where there is still room for parks and open spaces as well as for the Établissement Thermal and the inevitable casino. Among the alleyways of the upper town, look for the Maison du Passé (House of the Past), the museum of old Royat, and for the Taillerie, where crystals and gemstones are cut and polished.

[i] *1 avenue Auguste Rouzaud*

Imposing Puy de Dôme, the highest peak (1,465m/4,806 feet) in an extinct volcanic chain

---

SPECIAL TO…

At St-Ducs-les-Roches, off the Clermont-Ferrand to Limoges road, is Vulcania, the European Volcano Centre. The imaginative building is partially underground, and its exhibition galleries simulate the rocky depths, complete with fissures showing glowing red imitation lava. On to screens of rock, dramatic images of volcanic action are projected. Outside the centre has some of the most spectacular views in the whole of Europe.

▶ *Leave Royat on the D68. Go left on the D941a and immediately right on the D68. Go straight on to join the toll road to the summit of Puy de Dôme. Check for 'ouvert' sign.*

❷ Puy de Dôme, Auvergne
An electric rack railway to the summit of the Puy de Dôme is due to open in 2012, with a pendulum system that will replenish its energy during every ascent. During construction work vehicular access to the summit will not be possible, leaving a 45-minute climb on the chemin des Muletiers as the only option. For anyone with the stamina, it is well worth the effort. The Puy de Dôme is a glorious viewpoint, a spectacular hang-gliders' launch area, the site of a Roman temple, dedicated to Mercury and an exhilarating walkers' hill.

The story of access to the Puy de Dôme is a fascinating one. The first car reached the summit in 1913, but in those days the usual way up was by a steam train. The toll road opened only in 1926. On the

summit look for the statue of Eugène Renaux. In 1911 his biplane landed safely on the plateau at the end of a prize-winning flight from Paris. The elegant lava and wood buildings covered with copper roofs house a reception and information centre.

SPECIAL TO…

Just before the junction with the D941a, the Village Auvergnat is a shopping centre where many of the specialities of the region are on sale, including honey, jams, liqueurs, the well-known local cheese and Côtes d'Auvergne wines.

...uring
...ring
...eopled
by l... ...nights,
troubadours ...sants, who
involve children (and adults) in
the day-to-day life of a
medieval castle.

BACK TO NATURE

At 1,465m (4,806 feet) the Puy
de Dôme is the highest of 80
extinct volcanoes in the
district. It dominates a characteristic volcanic landscape.
Some hills retain their hollow
crater shapes; others are the
old volcanic cores. Flowers and
butterflies are abundant, and
look for red kites and honey
buzzards in the skies above.

▶ *Return to the **D941a** and
turn right. Go straight ahead
on the **D216** then on the
D27 and on the **D983**. Stop
at a major car park immediately before the junction with
the **D80**.*

8 Col de Guéry, Auvergne

This is one of the most dramatic
viewpoints in the Auvergne,
looking down the precipitous
valley between La Roche
Tuilière and La Roche
Sanadoire.

These two huge rock towers
rise from a wooded crater and
are the remains of a volcanic
eruption which occurred something like two million years ago.
Like the Puy de Dôme, they
are included in the biggest
regional nature park in France,
the Parc des Volcans
d'Auvergne (Regional Nature
Park of Auvergne Volcanoes).

Tuilière, as you will see close
up later from the D80, was the
vent of the volcano, whose lava
spewed out from the earth's
molten core and cooled into the
tall, brittle columns exposed
today. Sanadoire was part of the
cone. But the landscape was
shaped by more than just
volcanic activity: the valley
between the rock towers was
ground out by a retreating Ice-
Age glacier.

▶ *Turn right on the **D80** to
Rochefort-Montagne, then
turn left and follow the **N89**
and **D922** to La Bourboule.*

4 La Bourboule, Auvergne

Two thermal establishments
continue the spa traditions of
this little valley town where
tree-lined streets follow the
banks of the upper Dordogne.
The mineral waters here
contain arsenic – in medicinal,
not murderous proportions. La
Bourboule is very well supplied
with sports facilities, and its
Musée de Géologie Botanique
organises a variety of themed
geological outings of discovery
into the surrounding area.

The Parc Fenestre is a pleasant wooded area with pathways,
a lake and a narrow-gauge railway. It also houses the town
station for the cable-car system
to the Plateau de Charlannes. At
1,250m (4,100 feet), Charlannes
is a place of wide-ranging views,
and a ski resort in winter. For a
more intimate view of La
Bourboule itself, walk up to the
granite boulder called Le
Rocher des Fées (the Fairies'
Rock) which rises some 50m
(165 feet) over the town to the
northwest.

ℹ️ *15 place de la République*

The pretty spa of La Bourboule
is also a thriving winter resort

RECOMMENDED WALKS

Many people visit Orcival, to the north of La Bourboule, for its beautiful pilgrimage church. This village in the deep wooded valley of the Sioulet is also an excellent walking centre. Waymarked paths climb through forests, to the crater-lake of Servière, and to the dizzily balanced Roche Branlante (the Rocking Stone).

but a forest clearing reached by a funicular railway (built in 1898 and now a historic monument) and then a final climb on foot. The superlative high-spot of Le Mont-Dore is up the D983 as it climbs a steeply wooded valley to the ski runs and chairlifts on the alpine meadows below the Puy de Sancy. Be ready for a drop in temperature. Take a cable-car and then walk to the summit at 1,886m (6,188 feet), to admire the colossal views from the highest point in the Auvergne.

SPECIAL TO...

The annual Le Mont-Dore Car Race in August sees rally cars hurtling down the Puy de Sancy on a 5km (3-mile) course with a 300m (984ft) descent. A cycle race tackles the massif at the end of August.

⑥ Besse-en-Chandesse, Auvergne
This is an engaging little town which has preserved, in narrow

▶ Leave La Bourboule on the *D130 to Le Mont-Dore.*

⑤ Le Mont-Dore, Auvergne
Upstream from La Bourboule, here is another spa resort. Le Mont-Dore is well known for activities as diverse as fishing, mountaineering and amateur classical music. Instrumentalists and singers from all over France gather here to practise, rehearse and perform in concert. The Promenade des Artistes is a pleasant walk on the woodland ridge overlooking the town. There are higher attractions here, too: the Salon du Capuchin for instance, is not some elegant town-centre hall,

ⓘ *Avenue de la Libération*

FOR CHILDREN

At Le Mont-Dore, the Parc Animalier du Cezalier is more than just a zoo, with an exhilarating summer toboggan ride, a carousel, water cascades and an Apache fort adding to the fun.

▶ Return on the *D983 from the Puy de Sancy, then right on the road signed 'Besse par Col-Croix St-Robert'. Check 'ouvert' sign. Follow the D36 to Besse-en-Chandesse.*

The pleasant little village of Orcival nestles among the hills on the banks of the Sioulet

streets and tiny squares, many old houses from the 15th and 16th centuries. Some have connecting doors which allow the townspeople – walking through their neighbours' homes – to reach the church in winter while avoiding the chill open air. The Auvergne has snowy winters, and Besse has created a satellite ski resort called Super-Besse. One fascinating place to visit in the old town is a ski museum, the first in France. Here, Pierre-André Chauvet has assembled a

remarkable collection of skiing memorabilia. There are skis and bindings, ancient and modern, of many different styles, from France, Switzerland, Norway, Sweden and the Austro-Hungarian empire. Illustrations cover curiosities such as historic Russian army snowploughs, and early events of the pioneering ski club of Besse, founded in 1902.

i *Place du Docteur-Pipet*

▶ *Leave Besse on the **D5** to Murol then go right on the **D996** to St-Nectaire.*

7 St-Nectaire, Auvergne
One of the most exuberant of the typical Romanesque churches of the Auvergne is the one in this village split into upper and lower parts in the winding and wooded valley of the Courançon. Over a hundred ornamented pillars surround the nave and the choir.

The Maison du St-Nectaire has a video presentation as well as the chance to sample the local cheese – St-Nectaire gave its name to a round, nut-flavoured cheese made in many parts of the Auvergne – as well as the wines and bayberry liqueur special to the district.

St-Nectaire is another spa. There are modern thermal baths, but at the Cornadore grotto you can see the naturally warm water welling up. Try the mineral waters at a little pavilion in the parkland at Les Thermes.

i *Les Grands Thermes*

▶ *Continue on the **D996** to Champeix. Follow signs to Coudes and Vic-le-Comte, then continue on the **D225** and **D996** (sometimes signed **N496**) to Ambert.*

FOR HISTORY BUFFS

A Scottish-Auvergne connection exists in the 16th-century Sainte-Chapelle at Vic-le-Comte, built for Jean (or John) Stuart, a descendant of the Scottish royal family and regent of Scotland during James V's minority. He was Duke of Albany and Comte d'Auvergne.
The chapel features an unexpectedly light interior and a splendid balustraded gallery with statues of the Apostles. There are also remains of the castle of the Comtes d'Auvergne.

The Puy de Sancy, at 1,886m (6,188 feet), is the highest peak in the Massif Central

8 Ambert, Auvergne
Two notable buildings here are the granite church of St John and the curious town hall. Begun in 1471 in Flamboyant Gothic style, and decorated by a master mason obviously enjoying himself, St-Jean Church has later additions such as a frisky little Renaissance belfry. Look for the carved coat of arms of Ambert's old trade guilds – saddlers, shoemakers and the rest – and for the optical illusion which makes the interior seem longer than it really is.

The Hôtel de Ville (town hall) is entirely circular and arcaded all the way round. It was built in 1820 as the grain market. In the industrial area, a splendid museum of steam and traction engines, road rollers, tractors and mobile distillation plants is known, thanks to the French passion for acronyms, as AGRIVAP.

In the centre of town a museum is devoted to the 'divine cheese', Maison de la Fourme d'Ambert et des Fromages d'Auvergne.

i *4 place de l'Hôtel de Ville*

▶ *Leave Ambert on the **D57** for Moulin Richard-de-Bas.*

9 Moulin Richard-de-Bas, Auvergne

Traditional papermaking is one of the most fascinating industrial processes. This restored 14th-century mill is in the valley of the River Laga, which still turns its waterwheel. It tells the story of papermaking, from ancient Egyptian papyrus via the strict rules of the craft laid down by the Chinese in about AD105, to the Arabs' discovery of its secrets from Chinese soldiers captured in the defence of Samarkand in 751, and on beyond the invention of mechanical printing.

All the traditional processes of crushing linen into the basic pulp, the smoothing, drying and pressing are displayed. There are early manuscripts on show, a gorgeous 18th-century atlas, a mid-19th-century printing press, parchments, vellums and thousands of watermarks.

Richard-de-Bas also produces papers of the highest quality. One speciality, made when the petals of cornflowers and marigolds from the mill's own gardens are mixed with the pulp, is flowered paper, where each sheet is individually patterned.

▶ *Return to Ambert and take the **D906** then the **N89** to Thiers.*

RECOMMENDED WALKS

Much of this tour is in the Livradois-Forez regional nature park.
There are dozens of official footpaths here, one starting from the Salle Polyvalente in Olliergues on the D906 between Ambert and Thiers. Taking about three hours, it explores the farmlands, woods, old village churches and rural lanes above the valley of the Dore.

10 Thiers, Auvergne

France's 'capital of cutlery' is an attractive town with its red roofs rising on a hillside from a bend on the River Durolle. Many fine medieval and later half-timbered houses survive along the steep streets of the old quarter.

The museum and workshop of La Musée de la Coutellerie displays an astonishing variety of knives, scissors, table settings and hallmarks. There are workshops all over the town where modern craftsmen and designers keep up the ancient tradition. Down on the Durolle, several little waterfalls used to provide power for the cutlery factories. Look for the Creux d'Enfer, much less forbidding than its name – the 'Drop to Hell' – suggests.

i *Château du Pirou*

▶ *Return from Thiers on the **N89** and continue to Clermont-Ferrand.*

SCENIC ROUTES

The D27 is a high road through typical Auvergne countryside of cattle farms, woodlands, attractive villages and little valleys. Then the tour enters the magnificent volcanic landscapes around the Roche Sanadoire. The Col de la Croix St-Robert road, brightened by splashes of hillside broom, looks to deep valleys and wooded summits. Beyond St-Nectaire, the D996 goes through a narrow glen with thickly wooded sides and exposed rock faces.
After Vic-le-Comte, it wanders past farms and broadleaved woodlands, conifer plantations and little river valleys, then swoops down to Ambert on the plain.

A papermaker at work in Moulin Richard-de-Bas

Heartland
of France

Porcelain from Limoges and tapestries from Aubusson are two of the main features of this tour, where historic towns are matched by fine recreational facilities, especially on and around two beautiful wooded reservoirs. Limoges, the starting point, has been an industrial centre for centuries and is still expanding.

3/4 DAYS • 411KM • 255 MILES

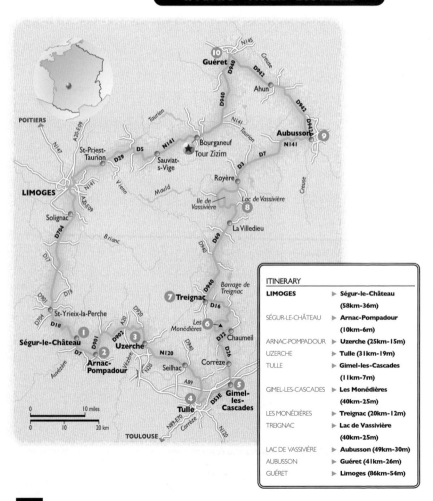

ITINERARY

LIMOGES	▶ **Ségur-le-Château (58km–36m)**
SÉGUR-LE-CHÂTEAU	▶ **Arnac-Pompadour (10km–6m)**
ARNAC-POMPADOUR	▶ **Uzerche (25km–15m)**
UZERCHE	▶ **Tulle (31km–19m)**
TULLE	▶ **Gimel-les-Cascades (11km–7m)**
GIMEL-LES-CASCADES	▶ **Les Monédières (40km–25m)**
LES MONÉDIÈRES	▶ **Treignac (20km–12m)**
TREIGNAC	▶ **Lac de Vassivière (40km–25m)**
LAC DE VASSIVIÈRE	▶ **Aubusson (49km–30m)**
AUBUSSON	▶ **Guéret (41km–26m)**
GUÉRET	▶ **Limoges (86km–54m)**

[i] *Boulevard de Fleurus, Limoges*

▶ *Leave Limoges on the D704 to St-Yrieix-la-Perche. Take the D18, which later becomes the D6, to Ségur-le-Château.*

❶ Ségur-le-Château,
Limousin

Visitors to Ségur-le-Château may be mystified by the number of rivers here. In fact, there is only one – the Auvézère – which double loops through a narrow, winding valley. The tiny medieval town has long since lost its influential position, but the once-aristocratic mansions survive. Riverside mills remain in place, and the ruined 12th-century castle (closed) broods absent-mindedly on its hilltop overlooking the town.

[i] *28 avenue du Château*

Medieval Ségur-le-Château

RECOMMENDED WALKS

Clearly waymarked from the D6 through Ségur-le-Château, four numbered pathways explore a beautiful countryside of modest hills and woodlands. The 'rivers and streams' walk wanders along the banks of the Auvézère, and there are fine views down to the river from the low ridges which follow its winding course.

SPECIAL TO...

Ségur-le-Château is noted for the craft of working with chestnut wood. By the riverside here look for the little hut with a display illustrating the work of the *feuillardiers* – the woodcutters – who supplied the chestnut stakes for the plants in the Périgord vineyards. Dozens of craftsmen in the district still work with chestnut wood.

▶ *Continue on the D6, then the D7 to Arnac-Pompadour.*

FOR HISTORY BUFFS

Turn right at the entrance to St-Yrieix on the way from Limoges to Ségur-le-Château, for the unobtrusive but well-stocked Musée National de la Porcelaine Adrien Dubouché at the Les Palloux china factory. Limoges, Meissen, Delft, Chinese and Japanese figures, vases and dinner services are all on display. It was the kaolin deposits of St-Yrieix which launched the porcelain industry at Limoges.

On the return route to Limoges is the restored La Tour Zizim in Bourganeuf, the home (or, in some versions of the story, the prison) of an exiled 15th-century Ottoman prince who equipped it with Turkish baths and even a harem.

---

❷ Arnac-Pompadour,
Limousin

In the 18th century this was the estate of the Marquise de Pompadour. Since 1872 it has been the home of the French National Stud Farm, devoted principally to the breeding of Anglo-Arab horses. The stallions are stabled in the Puy Marmont; La Jumenterie de la Rivière is the home of the mares and their foals. Flat and cross-country races, show-jumping and carriage-driving events are held regularly.

[i] *Entrée du Haras, place du Château*

▶ *Leave Arnac-Pompadour on the D901 to Lubersac, then follow the D902 and turn right on the D920 to Uzerche.*

3 Uzerche, Limousin

Historic gateways and fine old houses with towers, turrets, carved lintels, ornamented windows and heraldic designs are all preserved here. Uzerche stands on a peninsula ridge bounded on three sides by the River Vézère, and there are attractive views from the high-set esplanade de la Lunade. Behind the esplanade, the Romanesque Church of St-Pierre features an eerily impressive crypt built around 1030.

[i] *Place de la Libération*

▶ *Leave Uzerche heading south on the* ***D3****, then take the* ***N120*** *to Tulle.*

4 Tulle, Limousin

This is a place of odd contrasts. The pleasant approach road swinging down wooded valleys arrives at a town whose modern parts are dull; but it has a fascinating old quarter crossed by lanes and stairways, and there is a bustle around its riverside quays. Tulle gave its name to a fine-woven silk, but one of its main industries now is armaments. There is some fine modern stained glass in the 12th-century cathedral, and the Musée du Cloître, built round the arcades and gardens of a dignified old Benedictine monastery, illustrates local history in a quiet and peaceful setting. Paintings, sculptures, porcelain and archaeological finds share a building with historic firearms.

You will need a strong stomach to look over some of the illustrations in the Musée de la Résistance et de la Déportation, which recalls the grim days of World War II when many local men were deported, never to be heard of again.

[i] *2 place Emile Zola*

▶ *Leave Tulle as for Clermont-Ferrand. After a hairpin climb out of the built-up area, go straight on under a bridge, following the* ***D9*** *then the* ***D53e*** *to Gimel-les-Cascades.*

5 Gimel-les-Cascades, Limousin

On the approach to Gimel, try to catch a passing glimpse of the dashing waterfalls of the Montane which gave the village its name. From Gimel itself there is a dramatic outlook down a steeply wooded ravine. Footpaths wander past the spray-soaked triple falls. Although nowadays it is off the main road, a hint of Gimel's previous religious importance is given by the great treasure of its parish church – a 12th-century gold and bejewelled reliquary of St Stephen. The saint's stoning to death is one of the scenes picked out in fine enamel and precious stones.

▶ *Leave Gimel-les-Cascades following the 'Tulle 13' sign. Turn right following the 'Étang de Ruffaud' signs, then follow 'Gare de Corrèze' and 'vers RN 89' signs. Cross the* ***N89*** *and continue on the* ***D26*** *through Corrèze. Go right on the* ***D32*** *to Chaumeil, left on the* ***D121****, right on the* ***D128*** *as for Lestards, then take a side road right to Les Monédières.*

Uzerche, the 'Pearl of Limousin', stands on a spur above the Vézère

6 Les Monédières, Limousin
At about 911m (2,990 feet) above sea-level, the summit here is a magnificent all-round viewpoint. Many of the faraway hills are *puys* – the remains of extinct volcanoes. The hilltop is a favourite launching-place for hang-gliders.

BACK TO NATURE

On the Monédières hills, conifer plantations rise above the lower deciduous woodland. The original forest was deliberately set on fire, once by Julius Caesar and again during the 16th-century religious wars. *Myrtilles*, or bilberries, grow in profusion and are sold locally. Wild boar are occasionally seen in autumn and fungi grow in profusion.

▶ Return to the **D128** and turn right following 'Chaumeil' sign. Go left on the **D32** to Lestards then left on the **D16** to Treignac.

Lac de Vassivière offers many facilities for sports

7 Treignac, Limousin
Roofs are slaty-grey colour here, a sign that this is a different part of the country from the warmer villages visited before Les Monédières. There is a fine view of the town from a view-point tower in the centre. Closer investigation reveals medieval and Renaissance buildings descending to the Vézère river, which is crossed by a 15th-century bridge. A museum exhibits historic furnishings, craft and farm tools, weaving equipment and local ironwork. The restored parish church displays locally-worked stained glass and there is a simple little chapel, reached by a walk past the Stations of the Cross, which offers a good view westwards through a woodland clearing.

ℹ️ Place de la République

▶ Leave Treignac on the **D940** as for Eymoutiers. Turn right on the **D132e** which becomes the **D69**, signed 'Lac

RECOMMENDED WALKS

Treignac offers high- and low-level paths, some to hilltop viewpoints. Best of these is the walk past the local hospital, by wooded lanes and an open hillside, to the poised granite boulder called La Pierre des Druides (the Druids' Stone).

BACK TO NATURE

In the winding gorge of the Vézère just below Treignac, the Rocher des Folles is a series of granite pillars on the edge of a weathered cliff.

de Vassivière'. Go right on the **D992** to La Villedieu, where you should watch for a left turn on the **D34**. Go straight on avoiding a '19t' sign, left at a 'stop' sign as for Beaumont, then follow signs 'Île de Vassivière'.

visitors. Their designs range from reproduction style Louis XIV to something suitable for TGV trains.

ℹ️ *Rue Vieille*

▶ *Leave Aubusson on the **D942a** and turn left on to the **D942** to Guéret.*

🔟 Guéret, Limousin
You may be tempted to skip through Guéret, but its museum deserves a visit. Occupying an 18th-century mansion surrounded by pleasant formal gardens, the Musée de la Sénatorerie has valuable collections of tapestries; ceramics from France, the Netherlands and Ming dynasty china; and some wonderful religious art, especially 12th-century enamelwork. The Courtille leisure park close by has a lake with beaches, water sports and picnic spots.

ℹ️ *1 rue Eugène France*

▶ *Leave Guéret on the **D940** then follow 'Limoges' signs through Pontarion and remain on the **D940**. Go through Bourganeuf and continue before turning right on the **D5** as for Ambazac then watch for a junction where you should bear left uphill on the **D29** at the 'Limoges 27' sign. Return to Limoges.*

8 Lac de Vassivière,
Limousin
The route here stops before a bridge across to the main island in an extensive and well-wooded reservoir. The lake offers sports and leisure activities along its 45km (28-mile) shoreline, and visitors can walk

Aubusson's museum proudly displays the town's heritage

to the island, where there are woodland paths, outdoor sculpture displays and a castle.

▶ *Retrace your route and turn right on the **D222** as for Peyrat-le-Château. Turn right at the stop sign to Royère. Go left on the **D3**, watch for a right turn signed 'Aubusson 24' and continue to Aubusson.*

9 Aubusson, Limousin
At heart Aubusson is a dignified old town with many discreetly restored buildings. Most of all, though, it is the capital of French tapestry, introduced here in the 14th century by Flemish weavers.

The Musée Départemental de la Tapisserie displays hundreds of tapestries, from classical works of the 17th century to dazzling modern abstracts. Several tapestry workshops and studios are open to

---

FOR CHILDREN

There are sandy beaches at the wooded Barrage de Treignac reservoir, formed by a dam on the Vézère. It is ideal for fishing, swimming and sunbathing parties. Swimming from the main beach, beside the D940, is supervised in summer.

Further on, the Lac de Vassivière offers tuition in sailing, windsurfing and horse and pony rides. This beautiful reservoir is a noted recreational area, and there are easy walks, suitable for children, in the forest which surrounds it.

SCENIC ROUTES

From St-Yrieix to Ségur-le-Château the D18 and D6 run through pleasant undulating country of low hills and little valleys, and woodlands interspersed with grazing land.

The N120 sweeps down wooded valleys to Tulle, the D9 to Gimel is a fine winding road with views to the tumbling waterfalls, and after Gimel there are attractive roadside fishing lakes. West of Chameil, alpine-like country rises to conifer-clad summits.

Of Rivers
& Islands

The coat of arms of La Rochelle feature a full-rigged ship with cannons at the ports. That mixture of war and sea dominates the history of the coast and islands here. Inland, this is the country of the Cognac vineyards, and in the gentle Marais Poitevin you will be tempted to explore the canals of what was once the Gulf of Poitou.

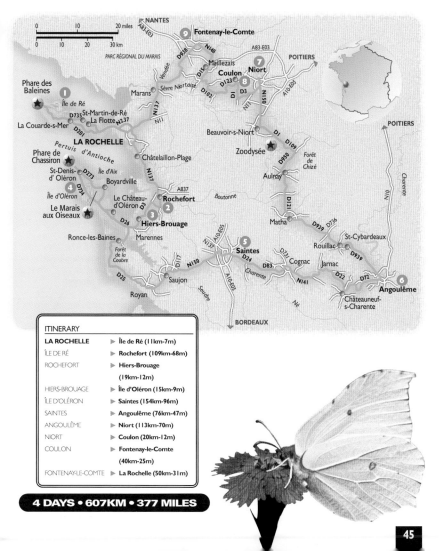

ITINERARY

LA ROCHELLE	▶ **Île de Ré (11km-7m)**
ÎLE DE RÉ	▶ **Rochefort (109km-68m)**
ROCHEFORT	▶ **Hiers-Brouage**
	(19km-12m)
HIERS-BROUAGE	▶ **Île d'Oléron (15km-9m)**
ÎLE D'OLÉRON	▶ **Saintes (154km-96m)**
SAINTES	▶ **Angoulême (76km-47m)**
ANGOULÊME	▶ **Niort (113km-70m)**
NIORT	▶ **Coulon (20km-12m)**
COULON	▶ **Fontenay-le-Comte**
	(40km-25m)
FONTENAY-LE-COMTE	▶ **La Rochelle (50km-31m)**

4 DAYS • 607KM • 377 MILES

☐ *Le Gabut, La Rochelle*

▶ *Leave La Rochelle over the toll bridge to Île de Ré. Take the 'Itineraire Nord', visiting La Flotte and St-Martin-de-Ré on the way to Phare des Baleines. Return by the D201 via Le Bois-Plage, then right on the D735 back over the toll bridge.*

1 Île de Ré, Poitou-Charente
Linked to the mainland by a modern toll bridge, the island is 28km (17 miles) long and 3–5km (2–3 miles) wide, ringed with holiday beaches. The old fishing and trading port of La Flotte once shipped salt and brandy to America. St-Martin-de-Ré, the principal town, has unexpected rampart walls, a town centre virtually on an island, and the Musée Ernest-Cognacq, which is named after a native of St. Martin. There is also a citadel where visitors can admire the outer defences and the old quay. The inner part is a state prison.

At the northern point of the island you can visit the Phare des Baleines, a lighthouse named after the whales that used to be seen offshore.

☐ *2 quai Nicolas Baudin, St-Martin-de-Ré*

FOR CHILDREN

The Île de Ré has more for children than its glorious beaches. Activities include watersports, canoeing through the marais and pony riding.

St-Martin-de-Ré, the principal town of Île de Ré

BACK TO NATURE

The Réserve de Lilleau des Niges, towards the tip of the Île de Ré, is a stopover for migratory birds and in winter there are thousands of geese, ducks, oystercatchers, redshanks and other bird species. There are footpaths, cyclepaths and guided tours.

▶ *Follow the D735 as for La Rochelle, on to the dual-carriageway N237 then N137. Continue to Rochefort.*

2 Rochefort, Poitou-Charente
You may wonder, entering it through unremarkable suburbs, if Rochefort is worth a visit, but this is a special town. In 1666 thousands of workers, under the orders of Louis XIV's chief minister Jean Baptiste Colbert, built a huge arsenal and naval shipyard here. There are guided tours of the beautiful mansard-roofed Corderie Royale, with its huge hall where the ropes were twisted. Museums in Rochefort cover art, medicine, trades and history, and its background as a military port. The exotically furnished Maison de Pierre Loti, house of Pierre Loti (1850–1923), a marine officer and novelist of the sea, stands in a quiet side street.

☐ *Avenue Sadi Carnot*

▶ *Take the D733 as for Royan, then go right on the D238e to Soubise and left on the D3 signed 'Hiers-Brouage'.*

3 Hiers-Brouage, Poitou-Charente
Away from main roads, this fine little fortified town is now also away from the sea and today it stands half deserted among the salt marshes. The retreat of the waters ruined its position as a busy trading port. From the ramparts, the French tricolour and the maple leaf of Canada fly side by side. Samuel de

Champlain, founder of Quebec, was born here in 1567. There is a comprehensive exhibition in the church on the founding of what was at first 'New France'.

i *2 rue de Québec*

▶ *Continue on the **D3**, turn right at the traffic lights over the toll bridge on to Île d'Oléron. Bear right on the **D734** through Le Château-d'Oléron. Go right in Dolus on to the **D126** through Les Allards and Boyardville, then via Foulerot, Port du Douhet, La Brée and St-Denis to the Phare de Chassiron. Return to St-Denis, then take the **D734** to Dolus and follow 'Le Viaduc' signs back over the toll bridge.*

FOR HISTORY BUFFS

Reached by ferry from Boyardville on the Île-d'Oléron, the Napoleonic museum on the little island of Aix, Maison de l'Empereur, recalls how Napoleon spent his last night on French soil before surrendering to the British ship *Bellerophon*.

4 Île d'Oléron, Poitou-Charente

Larger than Ré (30km/18 miles long and 6km/3½ miles wide), this is another holiday island of villages, picturesque harbours, vineyards, woodlands and fine sandy beaches.

Look for the grassy site of the 12th-century fortress which gave the island's main town of Le Château-d'Oléron its name, the river resort of Boyardville with its pinewood dunes and beach, and the lighthouse tower of the Phare de Chassiron, where the waves are seen breaking over offshore reefs and shallows.

RECOMMENDED WALKS

Go north through Boyardville on the Île d'Oléron to the Forêt des Saumonards, where you can follow any number of pinewood paths behind the sand dunes. In the channel between Oléron and Aix, look for the isolated rock prison of Fort Boyard, for a time in the 19th century a French equivalent of Alcatraz.

The fortified town of Brouage was once an important port

i *Place Henri Barbusse, Bourcefranc*

BACK TO NATURE

On the Île d'Oléron, turn left in Les Allards for the nature reserve of woodland, pools and canals at the Marais aux Oiseaux, featuring wildfowl, waders, storks and birds of prey.

FOR CHILDREN

If the ocean should lose its charm, children will enjoy the Iléo Parc Aquatique at Dolus d'Oleron, with its indoor and outdoor pools, including a wave pool and waterslides.

▶ *Follow the **D26** off the island then turn right at the 'La Tremblade' sign. Go right opposite Camping les Pins, and right at the T-junction over another toll bridge. Go right on the **D25** to Royan, then take the **N150** to Saintes.*

L'Arc de Germanicus, Saintes' Roman triumphal arch

▶ Leave Angoulême on the **D939** to Matha. Turn right to Aulnay, following the **D121**. After Aulnay, go right on the **D950** left on the **D109** and join the **D1** through Chizé. Turn right on the **N150** to Niort.

RECOMMENDED WALKS

Turn right off the D939 on the way between Angoulême and Niort, at St-Cybardeaux, for the informal paths which penetrate a hilltop woodland and reveal the unexpected sight of a Gallo-Roman theatre with tiers of stone-blocked seats facing what was once the stage.

5 Saintes, Poitou-Charente
Back from the resorts and islands of the coast, this is a handsome district capital. There is a good town museum, and others concentrating on fine arts, folklore and archaeology. Roman remains include an amphitheatre and a triumphal arch. Saintes lies astride the River Charente, and cruise-boats sail from its garden-backed quays.

ℹ️ Place Basson Pierre

SPECIAL TO...

At Cognac and Jarnac are such world-famous cognac houses as Hennessy, Martell, Rémy Martin and Courvoisier and Hine. Contact the tourist office for visitor information.

▶ Leave Saintes on the **D24**, which becomes the **D83**. Go right on the **N141** and right on the **D83** to Cognac. Take the **N141** through Jarnac, then turn right on the **D22**. After Vibrac watch for a left turn – away from Châteauneuf-sur-Charente – to St-Simeux. Go right through Sireuil, left on the **D53**, right on the **D84**, left on the **D41** and right on the **D72** to Angoulême.

6 Angoulême, Poitou-Charente
This is a busy industrial town, but its old upper town is worth a visit. Of special note are its imposing hilltop location, the views from the wooded paths round its ramparts, and the glorious façade of its cathedral (much restored in the 19th century). There are museums, exuberant Renaissance buildings, and rare active survivors of the papermills which once made Angoulême's fortune.

ℹ️ 7 bis rue du Chat, Place des Halles

7 Niort, Poitou-Charente
Niort, on the River Sèvre, is a working town with various industries. The riverside has walks and footbridges, gardens and vestiges of old mill streams. Past and present town halls are richly ornamented, and there is much fine Renaissance design. Customers bustle around the glass-and-wrought-ironwork market hall. The multi-towered castle or donjon may have been built by the 12th-century English Kings Henry II and Richard the Lionheart.

ℹ️ Place de la Brèche

▶ Leave Niort on the **N11** towards Rochefort. Turn right on the **D3**, then right on the **D1** to Coulon.

8 Coulon, Poitou-Charente
In the heart of one of the most appealing landscapes in France – the farms, market gardens, woodlands and waterway maze of the Marais Poitevin – Coulon is an attractive village where punts are available for hire, and escorted cruises also start, on some of the 40,000km (25,000 miles) of water channels. Not all, of course, are navigable, but they are an enchanting haven. Some picnic sites, accessible by

water, are remote from any road. In Coulon, the Maison des Marais Poiterin is a visitor centre that tells the story of the marshes, and the boutique sells local products and books on marsh wildlife.

ℹ️ *Place de la Coutume*

▶ *Leave Coulon on the D123 as for Le Vanneau, then go right on the D102, which becomes the D104 through Damvix. Go straight on at the give way sign, then right on the D15 through Maillezais. Go left on the N148 to Fontenay-le-Comte.*

🅽 **Fontenay-le-Comte,**
Loire Valley West

There are no fishing-smacks now, sailing under the Pont des Sardines (Sardine Bridge) at Fontenay, but the riverside is a pleasant recreational area with footpaths and little gardens. Fontenay preserves its historic buildings – even the tourist office was once a toll-house for the port. The Église Notre-Dame is an impressive Gothic church with a beautiful walnut pulpit and, high on an outer wall, a gilded Madonna. Beside it there is a regional museum. The Château de Terre-Neuve is a splendid 16th-century castle whose richly ornamented fire-places feature alchemists' symbols and griffins. During the Renaissance, the town became the home of poets and writers, including Rabelais, who was educated in a convent here.

ℹ️ *8 rue du Grimouard*

▶ *Leave Fontenay on the D938ter for La Rochelle.*

The charming canalside village of Coulon is typical of the marsh villages of the Marais Poitevin

The Western
Loire Valley

Starting in Nantes, this tour soon leaves all Breton influences behind as it heads for the valleys of the Loire and the Sarthe. You will find some of France's finest *son et lumière* presentations here, one of the world's most famous motor-racing circuits, and the Pays Nantais and Anjou are packed with vineyards.

5 DAYS • 512KM • 319 MILES

ITINERARY

NANTES	▶ **Clisson (27km-17m)**
CLISSON	▶ **Cholet (36km-22.5m)**
CHOLET	▶ **Doué-la-Fontaine (58km-36m)**
DOUÉ-LA-FONTAINE	▶ **St-Hilaire (29km-18m)**
ST-HILAIRE	▶ **Saumur (4km-2.5m)**
SAUMUR	▶ **Baugé (44km-27m)**
BAUGÉ	▶ **Le Lude (24km-15m)**
LE LUDE	▶ **Le Mans Circuit (75km-47m)**
LE MANS CIRCUIT	▶ **Le Mans (10km-6m)**
LE MANS	▶ **Angers (106km-66m)**
ANGERS	▶ **Nantes (99km-62m)**

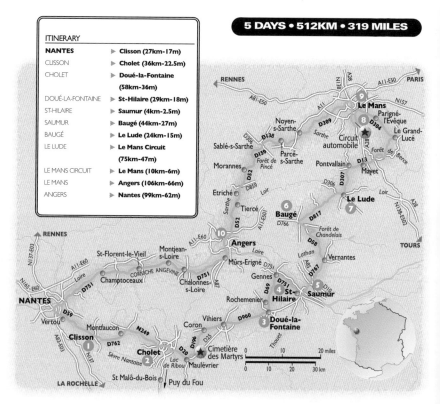

[i] *3 cours Olivier de Clisson, Nantes*

▶ *Leave Nantes for Clisson on the D59 through St-Fiacre. In Gorges go left of the D113 then take the D59 again into Clisson.*

❶ Clisson, Loire Valley West
The Vendée Wars and the savage reprisals of the Revolutionary government army all but obliterated this little town. Then it was completely rebuilt, but not as it had been before. Present-day Clisson is mostly a tribute to Palladian Italy, with colonnades, loggias and bell-towers of a style seen nowhere else in western France.

Look for the stabilised but unfurnished ruin of the 13th- to 15th-century castle, the 15th-century market hall, the two medieval bridges contrasting with the soaring 19th-century road viaduct, and Italianate creations such as the Temple d'Amitié and the Church of Notre-Dame.

There are beautiful walks in the valleys of the Sèvre Nantaise and the Moine. Local wines may be tasted. But

Clisson itself is the great attraction, especially its Italianate skyline and leafy riverside view.

[i] *Place du Minage*

▶ *Leave Clisson on the N149. Turn left as for Beaupréau on the D762 then go along the N249 and follow signs to Cholet.*

❷ Cholet, Loire Valley West
Only 20 buildings were left standing in the brutal aftermath of the Vendée Wars of 1793–96. A section of the Musée d'Art et de l'Histoire explains how the Vendée rising against the Revolutionary government's policies of mass conscription and the overthrow of all previous loyalties, was at first successful, then viciously crushed. Other exhibitions are at the Musée Paysan with its old-style dairy and country house interiors in the leisure park by the Ribou lake.

This is a famous textile town with a Musée du Textile. Its trademark is the red-and-white handkerchief – the *mouchoir de Cholet* – whose design is rooted in another incident of the

Clisson's impressive ruined 13th- to 15th-century castle sits atop a rocky outcrop

Vendée Wars. The town also has a shoe museum and at nearby Maulévrier there is a fine Oriental Garden which mirrors the Buddhist stages of human existence.

[i] *14 avenue Maudet*

▶ *Leave Cholet on the D20 as for Poitiers. In Maulévrier turn left and right as for Vihiers, then left on the D196 through Chanteloup to Coron. Go right on the D960 to Doué-la-Fontaine.*

SPECIAL TO...

Puy du Fou is a historical theme park with costumed actors and superb re-creations, including a medieval city, Renaissance castle and a full-size reproduction of Rome's Coliseum. The *Cinéscénie* spectacular, staged on certain nights, uses over 80 actors, special effects and fireworks.

FOR HISTORY BUFFS

In a forest clearing beside the D196 after Maulévrier (on the way from Cholet to Doué-la-Fontaine), the chapel at the Cimetière des Martyrs commemorates victims of the Revolutionary fury in the Vendée Wars. Virtually alone in France, the Vendée region saw little to celebrate at the bicentennary of the Revolution in 1989.

3 Doué-la-Fontaine, Loire Valley West

If you arrived in the middle of Doué without paying attention to its outskirts, you might shrug it off as an ordinary little town. It is far from that. The Bioparc, adapted from the cliffs, caverns and ditches of a disused limestone quarry, houses lions, tigers, lemurs, birds of prey, deer, emus, rarities such as snow panthers, and 15 separate monkey enclosures. Its Naturoscope has displays relating to the problems of threatened species and the destruction of their habitats.

The Musée des Commerces Anciens features seven old-style shops and a rose-water distillery, in partly restored 18th-century stables.

Nobody is certain about the origins of Doué's arena, which is Roman in style but of a much later date. However, there is no doubt about the Moulin Cartier. Built in 1910, it was the last windmill raised in the region of Anjou (closed to visitors).

BACK TO NATURE

Doué-la-Fontaine is France's great rose-growing centre. The Chemins de la Rose display dozens of different varieties, coloured crimson, scarlet and yellow – *Caroline de Monaco*, *Sarabande* and *Moulin Rouge* among them. Every July, an exhibition of 100,000 roses is held in the arena.

i *30 place des Fontaines*

▶ *Leave Doué on the **D69** to Gennes. Go right as for Saumur on the **D751** through La Mimerolle and into St-Hilaire.*

FOR HISTORY BUFFS

After Doué-la-Fontaine, turn left off the D69 for Rochemenier and its strange troglodyte village. You can visit furnished underground dwelling houses – with their cowsheds, barns, wine-cellars and even a chapel – still inhabited until early this century.

4 St-Hilaire, Loire Valley West

Just before this village – a suburb of Saumur – the Musée du Champignon, in a cave system cut into the roadside cliffs, is more than simply an exhibition about mushrooms and how they are grown. The underground galleries were dug in medieval times, part of a network of more than 480km (300 miles) throughout the district, which produces 75 per cent of France's cultivated mushrooms.

Turn right in St-Hilaire for the École National d'Équitation. This is France's national riding academy, excellently housed and staffed. In the practice arena, in front of high wall mirrors, you may see members of the acadamy's Cadre Noire put their horses through the intricate, disciplined and stylish movements for which they are famous all over Europe. They also perform summer season shows.

▶ *Continue on the **D751** into Saumur.*

5 Saumur, Loire Valley West

Straddling the Loire, this very appealing town is passionate about horses and the cavalry, wines, museums and exuberant outdoor displays. The Château de Saumur, overlooking the river, houses two separate

collections. The Musée des Arts Décoratifs concentrates on the decorative arts – ceramics, enamelware, carvings in wood and alabaster. Another, Musée du Cheval, celebrates centuries of horsemanship.

The cavalry has two separate exhibitions, one recalling its mounted days, the other taking the story to more recent times with a comprehensive display of tanks and armoured cars.

Second only to Champagne, Saumur is famous for its sparkling wines. Several firms welcome visitors to their cellars. Notre-Dame de Nantilly, dating from the 12th century, houses a valuable collection of medieval and Renaissance tapestries.

And the old quarter of Saumur with its restored 17th-century houses adds to the attractions of a justifiably self-confident town.

ⓘ *Place de la Bilange*

▶ *Leave Saumur on the **N147** as for Le Mans. At the round-about take the second exit to*

*Vernantes on the **D767**. In Vernantes, turn sharp left at the traffic lights as for Baugé, then right on the **D58** as for Baugé through Mouliherne. In Le Guédéniau go right on the **D186** as for Lasse. Turn left following 'Les Caves de Chanzelles' sign. At the round-about in the forest take the fifth exit for Baugé. Rejoin the **D58** and continue to Baugé.*

❻ **Baugé,** Loire Valley West
Plenty of space has been left around Baugé's 15th-century castle, originally a hunting lodge of Good King René, Duke of Anjou. Holding displays of

The château at Saumur has been dubbed 'the castle of love'

weapons, coins and ceramics, it stands beside public gardens dipping to an attractive riverside. The Convent of La Girouardière houses a venerated relic – a jewelled cross believed to contain a piece of the True Cross brought to France by a crusader knight. Its unusual design was adopted as the Cross of Lorraine. Look also for Baugé's charming 17th-century Hospice-St-Joseph (not open to the public).

Sometimes an unfamiliar language may be seen or spoken here, describing Baugé, for instance, as 'bela kaj malmova urbeto': the Château de Grésillon, on your exit route from 'this fine old town', is an international Esperanto centre (not open to the public).

ⓘ *Au Château*

▶ *Leave Baugé on the **D817**, which becomes the **D305**, then go right on the **D306** to Le Lude.*

❼ **Le Lude,** Loire Valley West
Pride of this little town is the richly furnished château, rebuilt in Renaissance style after an English garrison was driven out – with heavy damage to the fabric – in 1427. Its situation is most attractive, above balustraded gardens rising from the River Loir, whose waters eventually feed the larger Loire. Cultural life in Le Lude includes a number of special events and festivals featuring horticulture, theatre, music and children's activities.

ⓘ *Place Nicolay*

▶ *Leave Le Lude on the D307 to Pontvallain. Go right on the D13 through Mayet and across the N138 to Le Grand-Lucé. Turn left at the give way sign and left on the D304 as for Le Mans. Go under the bridge, then left following the 'Angers' sign, under another bridge and follow the 'Tours' signs along the N138. Go right at the roundabout on the D140 as for Arnage, then right on the D139 to the grandstands of the racing circuit.*

🖥 Le Mans Circuit, Loire Valley West
Prosaically, they may be the N138, D140 and D139, but these roads are also part of the great motor-racing circuit where

test sessions from the main grandstands, which are informally open to the public on non-competition days.

The revamped and renamed motor museum, the Musée 24 Heures, has 120 vehicles on show, including 24-hour race winners and other historic racing cars. It also recalls that this was where Wilbur Wright, over from the United States, made the first powered flight in Europe in 1908.

▶ *Continue on the D139 into Le Mans.*

🟤 Le Mans, Loire Valley West
Le Mans lies at the heart of a warren of cobbled medieval streets, lined with half-timbered buildings and Renaissance mansions.

One of the loveliest of these houses the Musée de la Reine

the Le Mans 24-Hour Race is held every June. The N138 is the Mulsanne Straight, along which Jaguars, Porsches and Mercedes howl at speeds of over 320kph (200mph).

There is a smaller but linked Bugatti Circuit. The two tracks play host to five major car and motor-cycle events, plus a 24-hour truck race! You can watch

Fascinating exhibits in Le Mans' Musée 24 Heures

Bérengère, a celebration of Sarthe history. Queen Bérengère was Richard the Lionheart's widow, and she built the Cistercian abbey outside the town.

Art lovers should make for the Musée de Tessé, which has

a superb collection of paintings, particularly French and Italian, as well as sculpture and objets d'art. In early July, a lively street festival takes over the town.

ℹ️ *Rue de l'Étoile*

▶ *Leave Le Mans on the **D309** as for Sablé. In Parcé cross the river then go first right at the crossroads, left to Solesmes then continue to Sablé-sur-Sarthe. Go straight across the **D306** for Centre-Ville. At the roundabout take the last exit, then a side road right for Pincé. This is the **D159**. Bear right on the **C15** for 'Pincé par la Forêt'. Rejoin the **D159** then follow the **D18** and **D52** through Morannes. Continue through Etriché and Tiercé. Go straight on along the **N160** then right on the **N23** to Angers.*

🔟 **Angers,** Loire Valley West
Here in the heart of Anjou lies a university town of parks, gardens and colourful floral decorations, with a grand Plantagenet castle rising in towers of banded stonework. The Cathédrale Saint Maurice, is best approached by the Montée St-Maurice, a stairway climbing from the River Maine.

The longest tapestry in France, *La Tenture de l'Apocalypse*, completed in the late 14th century to show the Apocalypse, is on display in the castle. Angers is a tapestry town. Many others, ancient and modern, are on show in the castle itself and in individual museums and galleries.

Fine Renaissance buildings survive, both around the cathedral and elsewhere. River cruises follow the Maine, and for the adventurous there are hot-air balloon flights to waft you high above the castles, vineyards and villages of Anjou. Alternatively, visit the stunningly converted 13th-century abbey, now home to the monumental sculptures of David d'Angers (1788–1856).

ℹ️ *7 place Kennedy*

▶ *Leave Angers through Les-Ponts-de-Cé on the **N160**. In Mûrs-Érigné, turn right to go through Chalonnes-sur-Loire and Champtoceaux on the **D751** and return on the **N249** to Nantes.*

Detail of Cathédrale St-Maurice's tympanum above the 12th-century west front door in Angers

---

FOR CHILDREN

Europe's first theme park with a botanical focus opened in Angers in 2010. Terra Botanica, covering 11ha (27 acres), offers a fun way to explore the nature, development and future of the world's plantlife. There's also an exciting 4D theatre experience, but don't expect rollercoasters.

SCENIC ROUTES

From Nantes to Clisson the route runs through the attractive Muscadet vineyards. Around the D13, the Forêt de Bercé is one of the most beautiful areas in the district. The D751 after Angers runs along the lovely Corniche Angevine above the Loire. The Layon vineyards are impressive, but the route is at its best near the 'panorama' viewpoint at La Haie Longue ('the long hedge'). A roadside memorial commemorates the pioneer aviator René Gasnier, whose first flights were from the level fields across the river.

SPECIAL TO...

Angers is the home of Cointreau, which has been produced here since 1849. Guided one-hour tours of the distillery (La Distillerie Cointreau) show off the processes, production methods and famous advertising posters of this much-exported liqueur, but the recipe remains a secret.

Through
Château Country

Some of the most elegant castles in Europe are within easy reach of Tours, in and around the valley of the Loire. Vineyards abound in Touraine, 'the garden of France'. Although this route starts and finishes beside the Loire, it also goes into the lonely area of pools, farms and woodlands known as the Sologne.

3/4 DAYS • 428KM • 267 MILES

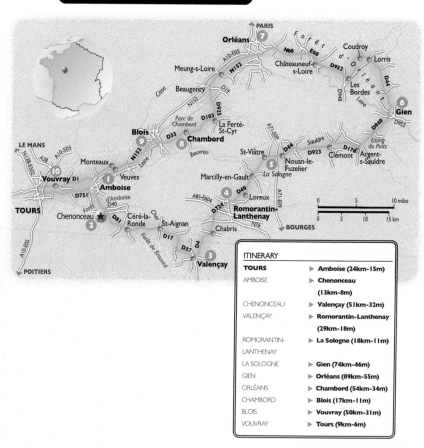

ITINERARY	
TOURS	▶ **Amboise (24km-15m)**
AMBOISE	▶ **Chenonceau**
	(13km-8m)
CHENONCEAU	▶ **Valençay (51km-32m)**
VALENÇAY	▶ **Romorantin-Lanthenay**
	(29km-18m)
ROMORANTIN-LANTHENAY	▶ **La Sologne (18km-11m)**
LA SOLOGNE	▶ **Gien (74km-46m)**
GIEN	▶ **Orléans (89km-55m)**
ORLÉANS	▶ **Chambord (54km-34m)**
CHAMBORD	▶ **Blois (17km-11m)**
BLOIS	▶ **Vouvray (50km-31m)**
VOUVRAY	▶ **Tours (9km-6m)**

i 78 rue Bernard-Palissy

▶ Leave Tours on the **D751** to Amboise.

❶ Amboise, Loire Valley Central

You will enter Amboise along a classic plane-tree avenue, with the Loire out of sight beyond the riverside embankment. The Château Royal's massive walls tower over the town centre streets. This impressive building is only a fifth of the size it was during its 16th-century heyday. Much was destroyed after the Revolution. A *son et lumière* presentation brings to life François I's glittering court of those days. Panoramic views can be enjoyed from the garden terraces planted with aromatic Mediterranean species.

On the climb out of Amboise, pause at the exotic 18th-century pagoda of Chanteloup (all that remains of a château there). The topmost gallery of this 44m (144-foot) hillside tower is a splendid viewpoint over the Loire.

i 233 quai Général de Gaulle

SPECIAL TO...

In Amboise, be sure to visit the brick and stone house called Le Clos Lucé, home till his death, in 1519, of Leonardo da Vinci. The great artist and engineer was installed here by his patron François I, King of France, who was to buy the *Mona Lisa* and *Virgin on the Rocks* after Leonardo's death. Here Leonardo worked on astonishing engineering drawings. Forty of these, featuring machines resembling an aeroplane, a helicopter and an army tank, have been turned into an amazing display of three-dimensional models such as Leonardo himself never saw in his lifetime.

▶ After the pagoda turn left then right as for Chenonceaux on the **D81**. Go left on the

D40, then right to Château de Chenonceau.

❷ Chenonceau, Loire Valley Central

Lacking the final 'x' of the similarly named little town near by, with its ivied houses and old coaching inns, this 16th-century riverside castle was one of the most striking architectural exercises of its day. The bridge which linked it to the south bank of the Cher was adapted as a gallery of two storeys and attic-level rooms, with the River Cher flowing through the arches underneath. Extending for almost 61m (200 feet) across the river, this is still the most noteworthy feature of a richly furnished castle. Chenonceau stands surrounded by water channels. The woodland grounds include formal riverside

gard
muse
ties i
There
lumière

▶ Continue on the **D40**. In Chisseaux, go straight on the **D80** to Francueil, take the **D81** to Céré-la-Ronde, then the **C5** and **D90** to St-Aignan. Go left on the **D675**, right on the **D17**, right for Valençay on the **D33**, left on the **D37** in Villentrois and right on the **D956** into Valençay.

❸ Valençay, Loire Valley Central

The great 16th-century castle here was owned by several famous financiers. A half-

Basilique St-Martin's Tour Charlemagne, in Tours

interest in the vast 19,000-hectare (47,000-acre) estate was briefly held by the Scotsman John Law, who introduced the system of credit. In 1719–20 he dominated the French banking system, until his enterprises collapsed in insolvencies and rancour.

Later, Valençay became the residence of Talleyrand, Napoleon's foreign minister, whose diplomats and dignitaries were extravagantly entertained. From 1808 to 1813 Ferdinand VII of Spain was held in virtual house arrest here, which is why the town's Hôtel d'Espagne is so named. A *son et lumière* show brings these varied characters back to life.

The castle is still lavishly furnished. Fallow deer graze in a sunken park, and you will hear peacocks' screams echoing through the grounds. Do not be put off by the ramshackle

FOR CHILDREN

On the way to Valençay turn right on the D657 in St-Aignan to the Zoo Parc de Beauval. Originally a bird garden, Beauval has expanded to house a splendid collection of big cats, primates, elephants and aquatic species in huge tanks.

appearance of the separate motor museum, whose exhibits include a spidery Bedelia cycle-car of 1914, a lovely little 1930 Amilcar sports model and an Alpine-Renault of 1971.

[i] *2 avenue de la Résistance*

▶ *Leave Valençay on the D4 through Chabris, then continue straight ahead on the D128. Cross the N76 and follow the signs to Romorantin-Lanthenay.*

4 Romorantin-Lanthenay, Loire Valley Central

In this 'capital' of the Sologne district, the River Sauldre splits into several channels. From the main-road bridge there is a most beautiful view downstream to the ivy-covered walls and colourful flower boxes of the restored watermills.

The town centre includes several attractive buildings, notably the ancient timbered Carroir Doré which houses an archaeological museum. The Musée de Sologne, which can be found in an old mill, is devoted to local rural life and traditions, with domestic, hunting and historical art displays of the Sologne.

Matra, the aerospace company, has a factory here. The town's L'Espace Matra

Valançay château is a fine example of classic Renaissance architecture

Automobile houses historic Matra competition cars, such as a Le Mans 24-Hour Race winner and Jackie Stewart's Formula 1 Matra-Ford V8.

[i] *Place de la Paix*

▶ *Leave Romorantin-Lanthenay for Loreux on the D49 and continue to Marcilly-en-Gault. Turn left at the T-junction there and first right for St-Viâtre, still on the D49.*

5 La Sologne, Loire Valley Central

At St-Viâtre you are well into the Sologne, a huge tract of more than half a million hectares (nearly 2,000 square miles). It is an all but level countryside of heath and woodland, widely separated arable and livestock farms, red-tiled brick houses and hundreds of lonely pools. In this slightly mysterious landscape, whose people are regarded in other parts of France as clannish and self-contained, only the trees create any kind of horizon.

The Sologne is also a land of hunters, wild-fowlers and fishermen. Until the second half of the 19th century much of it was unhealthily covered by even greater areas of stagnant water. Extensive drainage schemes and tree-planting created the landscape you see today.

▶ Leave St-Viâtre on the *D49*, then avoid the left turn for Lamotte-Beuvron and go straight ahead on the *D93* to Nouan-le-Fuzelier. Go left as for Orléans, then right as for Chaon on the *D122* and left on the *D44*. Go right on the *D923* as for Aubigny to Clémont. Turn left at the cross-roads on the *D7*, then follow signs to Étang du Puits. Continue to the *D948*, turn right for Argent-sur-Sauldre then left on the *D940* to Gien.

cation to St Joan is appropriate. It was here in 1429 that she first made contact with the Dauphin's army and began her mission to liberate France.

[i] *Centre Anne de Beaujeu, Place Jean-Jaurès*

▶ Leave Gien for Lorris on the *D44*. Continue as for Bellegarde. Immediately after the 'La Chaussée' sign take the first left. Go right on the *V3* into Coudroy. Turn left at the stop sign, through Vieilles-Maisons-sur-Joudry and left on the *D88*. Bend right then left, and watch for a right turn at the crossroads along a gravel forest road, passing the '3t' sign. Bear left at a junction

of forest roads, left after a 50m warning sign for give way ahead, and turn right along the tarred road (this is the D961). Turn right on the D952 and follow the N60 and the N152 to Orléans.

FOR CHILDREN

The kids will have plenty of opportunity to work off some energy at the Étang du Puits, before you reach Gien. This wooded recreational lake offers sandy beaches, rowing boat and pedalo hire, pony rides and a little children's playground. Sailing dinghies and windsurfers skim the water.

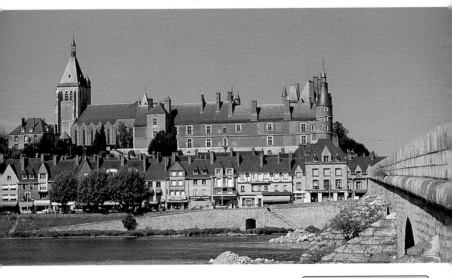

FOR HISTORY BUFFS

In Lorris, after leaving Gien, turn left on the D961 to find the Musée de la Résistance et de la Déportation. Set in well-tended gardens, it tells the story of the Resistance movement in World War II through displays of documents, photographs, maps and weapons, and newspapers of the clandestine press.

6 Gien, Loire Valley Central
From a leafy promenade by the Loire, the hillside in this town, famous for its faïenceware, rises to a little plateau shared by the 15th-century castle and the modern church, both of brick rather than stone. The castle houses the Musée de la Chasse, with displays on every aspect of hunting.

Replacing a building wrecked in World War II, the church shows inside and out, what decorative effects can be achieved in brickwork. Its dedi-

Gien has been meticulously restored since World War II

RECOMMENDED WALKS

Pause for a few minutes at Coudroy, after leaving Gien. Here, there is a short footpath which follows the bank of the Orléans Canal. Only fishermen now come to this 300-year-old waterway, long since closed to navigation.

Orléans' splendid neo-Gothic Cathédrale Sainte-Croix

i 2 place de l'Etape

▶ *Leave Orléans on the N152 as for Blois, avoiding the autoroute. Continue through Meung-sur-Loire to Beaugency. Go left on the D925 as for Limoges, crossing the river bridge. Continue straight over the D951 and on to La Ferté-St-Cyr. Go right on the D103 to Crouy, left on the D33 and continue through the Parc de Chambord to Chambord.*

SPECIAL TO...

At Beaugency, between Orléans and Chambord, follow signs to the Musée Dunois. In a 15th-century castle, the arts and traditions of the district round Orléans are preserved. Each of its rooms has a special theme, such as furniture, toys or costumes.

FOR CHILDREN

Natural history museums rarely fail to delight children, and the lively Centre Sciences in Orléans is no exception. It has four floors of exhibits, including aquariums, creepy-crawlies, mammals, birds and tropical glasshouses. Exhibits also explore astronomical, geological and environmental themes, and there are masses of interactive stations.

---

7 Orléans, Loire Valley Central

Every spring, Orléans organises a festival celebrating Joan of Arc's intervention, which raised the English siege of the city in 1429. The Maison Jeanne d'Arc, where she stayed, and Centre Jeanne d'Arc tell the story. The latter is also a repository of authentic documents of the period, kept on microfilm and microfiche.

The Musée des Beaux-Arts houses a valuable collection of French and Italian paintings. Now used for civic receptions, the luxuriously furnished 16th-century Hôtel Groslot is open to visitors. The Musée Historique et Archéologique (local history and archaeology) is housed in the Renaissance surroundings of the Hôtel Cabu.

Cathédrale Sainte-Croix dominates the townscape above the Loire. Look inside for its stained-glass windows telling the story of Joan of Arc, its beautifully carved choir stalls and its 32 18th-century medallions illustrating the life of Christ.

BACK TO NATURE

In Orléans, the magnificent Parc Floral de la Source takes its name from a curious natural feature. Officially, the River Loiret rises here. In fact, its waters are diverted from the Loire almost 30km (19 miles) upstream. They disappear underground for all that distance before welling up again in the park.

---

8 Chambord, Loire Valley Central

The Renaissance château of Chambord is the biggest of all the castles of the Loire. Begun as the favourite hunting lodge of François I, it has no fewer than 440 rooms, and stands in the midst of a 5,443-hectare (13,450-acre) estate circled by a 32km (20-mile) wall.

Most of the forested estate is a hunting reserve, but parts of it are open to visitors. Chambord is beautifully furnished, with fine paintings and tapestries. It houses an exhibition on hunting, and another on its own history. A viewing terrace stands high among the intricate rooftop decorations.

BACK TO NATURE

Turn left off the D33 in the Parc de Chambord for a high-level 'hide', from which you can watch a herd of red deer in a grazing enclosure in the forest.

▶ Continue on the D33. After Nanteuil go under the bridge through St-Gervais-la-Forêt and right on the D956 to Blois.

9 Blois, Loire Valley Central
A gorgeous open-air staircase built for François I (and possibly designed by Leonardo da Vinci) is only one of the architectural delights of the hilltop castle here. The same king commissioned the decorated façade which overlooks the lovely little garden in the Place Victor-Hugo.

Archaeological and fine arts museums are housed in the castle and there is a gallery devoted to Robert Houdin, the great 19th-century conjuror from whom the escapologist Houdini took his stage name. In the town, a street, a stairway and a statue commemorate Denis Papin, an early steam-engine pioneer. There is also an excellent museum on the natural history of the area, situated in the ancient cloisters of Les Jacobins.

Attractive old buildings include the half-timbered Maison des Acrobates, with its carvings of jugglers and tumblers. Bicycles can be hired from the railway station and several shops in town.

ⓘ 23 place du Château

RECOMMENDED WALKS

Ask at one of the tourist offices about walks around the Val de Cisse. Monteaux, between Blois and Vouvray, is a good centre for them. Using minor roads and field tracks, you can wander through farms, woods and vineyards on a fresh, airy plateau above the valley of the Loire.

▶ Leave Blois on the N152 for Tours. In Veuves, turn right on the D65 to Monteaux. Bear left for Cangey along the D58 which becomes the D1. Continue through Limeray. Keep left in Pocé-sur-Cisse as for Amboise then go right following the 'Vouvray' sign. Turn left on the D46 and continue to Vouvray.

10 Vouvray, Loire Valley Central
There hardly seem to be enough vineyards around Vouvray to justify its reputation as a white wine village, but most are on the upland plateau hidden by limestone cliffs.

A detour to the Château de Jallanges gives rewarding views over the vineyards, and the Château de Valmer is another vineyard castle, with beautiful formal and culinary gardens to visit. You can buy wine at the château or several *caves*, some of them dug into the limestone.

ⓘ 12 rue Rabelais

▶ Leave Vouvray on the N152 and return to Tours.

Royal Blois: a former capital of France and famous for its château

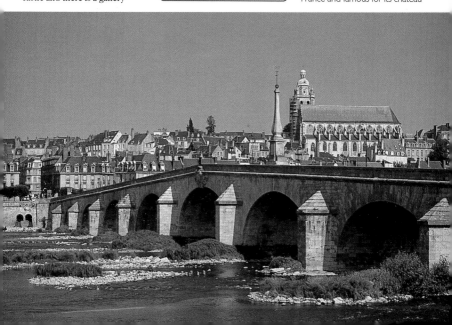

Here is another region which shows the remarkable variety of France. On the coast there are uninterrupted expanses of surf-washed beaches. Behind them stretch vast areas planted with pines. The Pyrenean foothills offer bracing spa resorts where walks by mountain streams and wildflower meadows are the order of the day. In the valleys of the Dordogne and the Vézère you will find the greatest cluster of prehistoric sites in Europe, many of them troglodytic dwellings quarried thousands of years ago.

Lourdes attracts millions of pilgrims and visitors every year. Smaller numbers make the journey to the glorious hilltop church in St-Bertrand-de-Comminges. You can visit weird underground caverns, one group bizarrely reached, not by going deep into the bowels of the earth, but by heading uphill in a cable car, and you can find out about traditional rural crafts and ways of life in display areas large and small.

Oysters are a major crop where the Bordeaux route reaches the coast. Inland, connoisseurs of wine and brandy can lose themselves among the vineyards of Armagnac, Bergerac, Barsac, Graves and Sauternes.

West and south of Bordeaux there are few natural obstacles to divert the roads from long, flat straights through the forests. Winding river valleys are the norm for Périgueux. The Pau tour, as it climbs into the Pyrenees, is for pass-stormers.

Some of France's most glorious towns and villages are here. Rocamadour is one of the most stunningly located places in Europe, but there are also Domme and Sarlat and Labastide-d'Armagnac to cherish.

Wildlife parks include bird reserves, zoos for endangered species and an atmospheric place devoted to the ancient worship of the bear. You can find out in museums and exhibitions about tobacco, seaplanes, prehistoric art, clockwork figures and hussars.

Bordeaux

Bordeaux is the capital of Aquitaine and of wine, the heart of a region of world-renowned vineyards. It was one of the first cities in France to pedestrianise its shopping streets, and a pioneer in computerised traffic management. Among its elegant public buildings, which earned the city a UNESCO World Heritage listing, look for the river façade of the 18th-century Place de la Bourse and the sumptuous Grand-Théâtre of the same era. There are bustling covered markets, craft shops and studios of every kind. Museums and galleries take in fine and decorative arts, the history of the region, vintage printing presses, natural history collections with magnificent crystal displays, military history and the Resistance movement. Cruise boats explore the Garonne and Dordogne rivers and their joint estuary, the Gironde. A helicopter jaunt over your own selection of vineyards is an exciting option.

Périgueux

Périgueux is a handsome town whose beautiful old quarter, where the merchants and craftsmen used to live, includes fine Renaissance and medieval buildings. The perhaps over-restored cathedral, Saint-Front, is a fascinating sight, all domes and cupolas, giving Périgueux an almost Ottoman-Empire skyline. The Musée de Vesunna has expanded well beyond its original brief to exhibit the results of excavated Roman sites. The Musée Militaire shows uniforms and weapons from several centuries, and tells the story of the district's war-ravaged past. There are pleasant gardens, and squares with pollarded trees. You can stroll along the rue des Gladiateurs to the site of the Roman arena. This is a cool place in summer, planted with shrubs and trees, its fragmentary Roman archways within sight and sound of an attractive modern mosaic-tiled fountain.

Opposite: vineyard in Bordeaux
Above: the opulent, fertile valley of the Dordogne at Périgueux

Pau

In the 19th century, the British invaded Pau, but not with any martial intent. Three Scots laid out a golf course for the British colony. At the turn of the century and through the 1920s, Pau was one of the great British resorts of Europe. There was American influence, too. Orville and Wilbur Wright set up the world's first aviation school here. The town has lovely parks and gardens. Find the boulevard des Pyrénées and you will see not only a fine promenade, but also a glorious southern mountain horizon. A rebuilt funicular railway climbs from a lower avenue.

Some of the finest state rooms in France are in the majestic, much restored, château, which houses a rich collection of tapestries. On one weekend in June, Pau echoes to the scream of high-pitched engines. There is a famous racing circuit here, including public roads and driveways to the leafy Parc Beaumont.

Coast, Dunes
& Forests

South of Bordeaux, the flatness of the Landes region is disguised by two notable features. Along the coast there are long fine-sand beaches backed by substantial dunes, while inland lies a huge forest area with carefully watered croplands in extensive clearings.

4 DAYS • 486KM • 301 MILES

ITINERARY		
BORDEAUX	▶	**Gujan-Mestras (47km-29m)**
GUJAN-MESTRAS	▶	**Arcachon (13km-8m)**
ARCACHON	▶	**Biscarrosse (42km-26m)**
BISCARROSSE	▶	**Mimizan (38km-24m)**
MIMIZAN	▶	**Sabres (47km-29m)**
SABRES	▶	**Mont-de-Marsan (81km-50m)**
MONT-DE-MARSAN	▶	**Labastide-d'Armagnac (29km-18m)**
LABASTIDE-D'ARMAGNAC	▶	**Barbotan-les-Thermes (16km-10m)**
BARBOTAN-LES-THERMES	▶	**Nérac (42km-26m)**
NÉRAC	▶	**Sauternes (82km-51m)**
SAUTERNES	▶	**Bordeaux (49km-30m)**

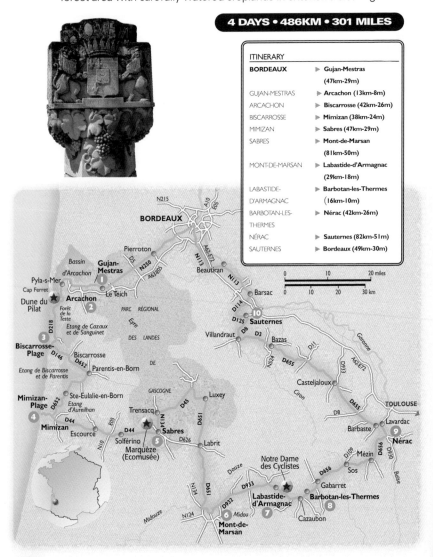

ⓘ 12 cours du 30 Juillet,
Bordeaux

▶ *Leave Bordeaux on the*
N250. Go straight ahead on
the D650 through Le Teich to
Gujan-Mestras.

BACK TO NATURE

Turn right in Le Teich, on the
way to Gujan-Mestras, at the
'Parc Ornithologique' sign. The
bird reserve here in the scrubland delta by the Bassin
d'Arcachon is especially strong
in wildfowl, but you should also
look for whiskered terns, black-
winged stilts, herons, storks
and little egrets. They have
binoculars for hire.

---

❶ Gujan-Mestras, Aquitaine
The two parts of this strung-out
cluster of villages on the southern side of the great Bassin
d'Arcachon could hardly be
more oddly matched. Take any
of the streets with 'port' signs,
to the right of the main road,
and you enter the almost timeless world of the oyster farmer.
The ports are seven rectangular
inlets of the bay, lined by identi-
cal wooden workshop cabins.

Outside lies the paraphernalia
of oyster cultivation – boat
tackle, mounds of emptied
shells – and the Maison de
l'Huître, which tells everything
there is to know about oysters.
Elsewhere, Gujan-Mestras is
a modern holiday resort. Turn
left for the 'Parc Aquatique'
(water park) called Aqualand, a
great alternative to the beach.
Its pools, wave machine, slides
and water chutes share the large
leisure area at La Hume with
the Coccinelle animal park (see
panel below).

ⓘ 19 avenue de Lattre de
Tassigny

FOR CHILDREN

Street signs in Gujan-Mestras
are decorated with ladybirds –
coccinelles – the emblem of the
town. La Coccinelle animal park
at La Hume continues the
theme. Here, in addition to
being able to touch and stroke
(and sometimes feed) the
domestic and farm animals, there's
a mine-train rollercoaster, giant
toboggan slides, a water park,
trampolines, and other activities,
plus magic shows.

Arcachon has become a very
popular beach resort

▶ *Continue on the D650 to*
Arcachon.

❷ Arcachon, Aquitaine
Although the oysters of the
Bassin d'Arcachon have been
celebrated since the 16th
century, the town itself is a
resort created in the railway age.
Arcachon has a well-equipped
yacht haven and fishing port. A
high-set figure of Christ blesses
the harbour. Walk to the end of
the breakwater and you will see
not only the far-out oyster beds
but also a stone anchor sailors'
memorial. The Musée
Aquarium specialises in the
creatures of the bay and the
open sea. You can sail to the
oyster beds, to the Île aux
Oiseaux (Birds' Island) in the
bay, and across the mouth of the
bay to the peninsula resort of
Cap Ferret. Back from the
waterfront the town has lively
shopping and café areas, and it
is generously supplied with
woods and parkland. Arcachon's
status as the most stylish resort
on the Côte d'Argent ('silver
coast') is well deserved.

ⓘ Esplanade Georges Pompidou

BACK TO NATURE

South of Arcachon, the Dune du Pilat is the greatest sand dune in Europe, more than 106m (350 feet) high and extending for nearly 3km (2 miles). You will not be able to see its imperceptible wind-driven inland movement, but take the long stairway to the summit for a beautiful view of pine forests and the sea. Heathland in the area supports Dartford warblers, red-backed shrikes and wrynecks, as well as plenty of insect life.

RECOMMENDED WALKS

After the Dune du Pilat south of Arcachon, the D218 runs through the pinewoods, scrub and sandhills of the Forêt de la Teste. Park here, and you will find many informal footpaths off to the right, leading to beaches lapped by rolling Atlantic breakers.

▶ *Leave Arcachon on the **D218** to Pyla-sur-Mer and past the Dune du Pilat to Biscarrosse.*

3 Biscarrosse, Aquitaine ·
A pinewood resort with bungalows, hotels and a few colour-washed apartment blocks, Biscarrosse-Plage has a not-yet-finished air. But there is a splendid beach here, backed by dunes, with white-topped breakers creaming in. The older part of the settlement, Biscarrosse-Bourg or Biscarrosse-Ville, is separated from the beach resort by a full 9.6km (6 miles) of open road. This is a handsome place. Its church stands among bright and well-watered gardens dotted with birch trees.

On the southwestern edge of town is an attractive lake rimmed by low wooded hills. This is a good sailing and angling centre, and it was briefly, between the wars, the French base of a flying-boat service from New York. The Musée Municipal de l'Hydraviation, on the road to the lake, recalls those flying-boat days, and there is also the Musée des Traditions et de l'Histoire.

ⓘ *55 place G Dufau*

▶ *Leave Biscarrosse on the **D652** through Parentis-en-Born to St-Eulalie, then take the **D87** to Mimizan.*

FOR HISTORY BUFFS

Parentis-en-Born, on the way from Biscarrosse to Mimizan, is a place with a rustic appearance and a pleasant lakeside. Incongruously, since 1954, oil has been pumped from the lake bed and from offshore deposits, making Parentis-en-Born France's foremost oil discovery site.

4 Mimizan, Aquitaine
This is another split-personality town, approached along the shore of the Étang d'Aureilhan, where Winston Churchill was often a guest of the Duke of Westminster on an estate here. He left several paintings of local scenes. Mimizan divides at the Papeteries de Gascogne, a huge papermill which wafts an unmistakable smell along the prevailing wind. The holiday resort is very modern, with fine beaches ideal for surfing. You can explore the forest to the south, on foot or along the cycle tracks.

The inland part of Mimizan is built round a largely derelict

Mimizan's fine sandy beach lies to the west of the town

11th-century Benedictine abbey. The Musée du Prieuré faces it. In summer the riverside bull-ring promotes *courses landaises*, acrobatic affairs, similar to the Provençal form of bullfighting in which the bulls are unharmed. Stilt-walking is another speciality.

[i] *38 avenue Maurice Martin*

▶ *Leave Mimizan on the D44 to Sabres.*

FOR HISTORY BUFFS

On the D44 before Sabres, the village of Solférino recalls a battlefield in Italy. The estate here, owned by Napoleon III, was given the name after his successful part in the battle against Austria in 1859. The estate became the largest artificial forest in Europe.

5 Sabres, Aquitaine
A pleasant if unremarkable village, with half-timbered houses and old church, Sabres still has a station on the railway built in 1890 to link it with Mimizan. The line is now used to take visitors to the remote Écomusée at Marquèze, 5km (3 miles) to the northwest.

This splendid place is part of the Parc Régional des Landes de Gascogne. A number of historic buildings – the homes of land owners, bosses and workers – have been moved into the forest clearing here to represent a farming community of the 1830s, and there's a huge pavilion for the summertime temporary exhibitions. Displays make it clear how the great forests used to support little local industries such as iron and glass works, and brick and tile kilns before the second half of the 19th century, when the government decided to manage the pine forests on a virtually industrial scale. The museum shows how the timber resources have been exploited and what kinds of activity were discarded

▶ *Leave Sabres on the N134 as for Bordeaux. In Trensacq turn right on the D45. Turn right on the D651 through Luxey, then continue to Mont-de-Marsan.*

FOR CHILDREN

Aventure Parc, near Biscarosse on the Bordeaux road, has activities in a woodland setting. Rope swings and ladders, 'Tarzan jumps' and fitness courses (for adults too) are some of the ways to diffuse excess energy.

SPECIAL TO...

On the way to Mont-de-Marsan, turn left in Luxey following the 'Écomusée' sign, and park beside the church. The nearby museum deals with the uses of resin from the vast pine forests of the Landes.

The Ecomusée de Marquèze is an open-air museum documenting the life of the Landes region

6 Mont-de-Marsan,
Aquitaine
You will not be long in Mont-de-Marsan before realising that this is a place of some consequence. Its elegant 19th-century public buildings, immaculately kept, stand among modern equivalents, which are imaginative in design, but do not clash. In fact, Mont-de-Marsan is an important government centre.

It stands where the rivers Midou and Douze merge into the waggishly named Midouze. The Parc Jean Rameau is an attractive woodland area, with many flowering shrubs, overlooking the Douze.

Musée Despiau Wlérick, the only museum in France devoted exclusively to 20th-century sculpture, is named after two local sculptors. Its terrace offers a superb view over the town and river. There are also a large number of sculptures around the town. The Church of Ste Madeleine is worth visiting for its marble-work and elegant ornamented ceiling.

Like Mimizan, Mont-de-Marsan is a centre for *courses landaises*, but the great sporting enthusiasm is for horse-racing. The impressive race-course plays host to a dozen meetings every year.

ℹ️ *6 place du Général Leclerc*

cursory mention, but go to the flowery Place Royale and you will find an architectural gem.

Away from the square, a 17th-century chapel houses an exhibition of the *bastides*, the historic fortified villages.

Beyond Labastide, turn right on the C1 for Château Garreau, with a distillery producing the local brandy, armagnac. The Ecomusee de l'Armagnac is the most fascinating of the three museums, with staff recreating the working life of the domain.

ℹ️ *Place Royal*

SPECIAL TO...

About 2.4km (1½ miles) beyond Labastide-d'Armagnac, look for the isolated 11th-century church called Notre-Dame des Cyclistes. Since 1959 this historic building has been a cyclists' sanctuary, with old machines and the jerseys of famous race-winners on display.

Cool, shady arches in the Place Royale, Labastide-d'Armagnac

▶ *Leave Mont-de-Marsan on the **D932** as for Roquefort. Bear right on the **D933** to St-Justin, then right on the **D626** to Labastide-d'Armagnac.*

7 Labastide-d'Armagnac,
Aquitaine
Almost miraculously, the arcaded square here, Place Royale, has survived with little alteration since 1291. Three sides are still taken up by arches and cool, covered walkways. The fourth features the 15th-century church. Some guidebooks give Labastide a

RECOMMENDED WALKS

Ask at the tourist office in Labastide-d'Armagnac for the map of the waymarked walks southwest of the little town. They climb gently into a lush landscape of woodlands, farms and Armagnac vineyards.

▶ *Continue on the **D626** to Cazaubon and turn left on the **D656** to Barbotan-les-Thermes.*

8 Barbotan-les-Thermes,
Aquitaine
Unlike the spa towns of some other countries, those in France have not mouldered away. Barbotan, whose thermal baths were probably known to the Romans, has been completely refurbished. Brightly decorated hotels, shops, restaurants and cafés line the busy and effectively pedestrianised main street. Sparkling new buildings house the baths which attract an increasing number of *curistes* (cure-seekers) – more than 20,000 of them every year.

There are attractive gardens, pleasant walks and an opportunity to admire relics of the past, such as the 12th-century church whose clocktower is built above one of the medieval gateways.

Just outside town is Lac de l'Uby. This leisure area offers sailing, tennis and mini-golf facilities as well as a sandy beach, pony rides, pedalo hire and a children's play park.

ℹ️ *Place Armagnac*

▶ *Continue on the D656 through Gabarret to Nérac.*

9 Nérac, Aquitaine
Only one wing remains, high above the River Baïse, of Nérac's lovely Renaissance château. Climb the stairs to the elegant, open, first-floor gallery, and you will find a museum of archaeology and history. Close by, the Church of St Nicholas has a severe frontage but some good 18th-century stained glass. There are grand views across the river to Petit Nérac, a hillside quarter of fine old buildings with dark red roofs. Its church spire soars in glorious silhouette against the sky.

River boats run cruises on the Baïse. Upstream, the promenade de la Garenne offers you a stroll through a pleasant woodland park with fountains and an open-air theatre.

ℹ️ *7 avenue Mondenard*

▶ *Leave Nérac on the D930 to Lavardac, then go left to Casteljaloux and follow signs to Bazas. Continue to Villandraut. Turn right on the D8 through Noaillan and Brouquet, then left on the D125 to Sauternes.*

10 Sauternes, Aquitaine
Arriving at Sauternes, the centre of one of the most famous white wine districts, you will come to the place de l'Église, which would be the heart of the village if there were a village for it to be the heart of. Only a handful of

buildings surround the square, one of them where the local wine producers offer their wares. There is also a map locating the eight vineyards nearby that regularly welcome visitors.

Not included in this display is the aristocratic 16th- and 17th-century Château Yquem. Its Château Yquem wine, with the superlative classification of *Premier Grand Cru Classé*, was the first to be produced from grapes affected with the 'noble rot' provoked by the misty mornings and warm afternoons of autumn.

ℹ️ *11 rue Principale*

▶ *Continue on the D125 as for Budos, then go right on the D114. Follow this road over the autoroute to the N113. Turn left there through Barsac and return to Bordeaux, avoiding the autoroute.*

The Church of St Nicholas in the town of Nérac

SCENIC ROUTES

Heading south for Biscarrosse-Plage, the D218 runs through the attractive pine and sandhill country of the Forêt de la Teste.
Later, the D146 continues in similar country over a low winding pass among the pinewood dunes.
Around Luxey, the D651 leads across a lovely quiet countryside of forests and farms, with characteristic timber-framed houses and attractive villages drowsing in the summer sun.
Immediately after Sauternes, the D125 opens up a delicious little landscape of undulating vineyards in the valley of the River Ciron.

Journey into Prehistory

Although there are remains of old Roman buildings in the heart of
Périgueux, this tour, featuring two of France's loveliest rivers, the
Dordogne and the Vézère, takes you much further back into the
history of man. Here, limestone provides the huge cliffs, the amazing caves and underground rivers, and the golden building stone of
beautiful towns like Sarlat and Domme.

4 DAYS • 383KM • 238 MILES

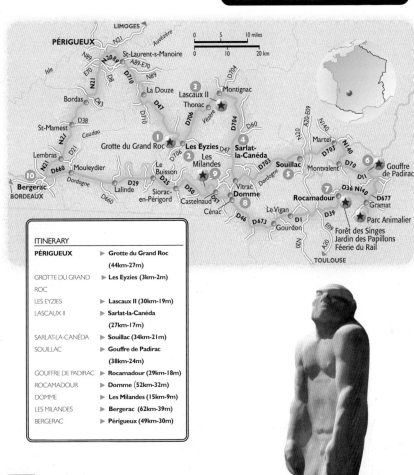

ITINERARY		
PÉRIGUEUX	▶	**Grotte du Grand Roc** (44km-27m)
GROTTE DU GRAND ROC	▶	**Les Eyzies** (3km-2m)
LES EYZIES	▶	**Lascaux II** (30km-19m)
LASCAUX II	▶	**Sarlat-la-Canéda** (27km-17m)
SARLAT-LA-CANÉDA	▶	**Souillac** (34km-21m)
SOUILLAC	▶	**Gouffre de Padirac** (38km-24m)
GOUFFRE DE PADIRAC	▶	**Rocamadour** (29km-18m)
ROCAMADOUR	▶	**Domme** (52km-32m)
DOMME	▶	**Les Milandes** (15km-9m)
LES MILANDES	▶	**Bergerac** (62km-39m)
BERGERAC	▶	**Périgueux** (49km-30m)

ⓘ 26 place Francheville, Périgueux

▶ Leave Périgueux on the
N2089 as for Brive. Go right
on the D710, left on the D45
then left on the D47 to
Grotte du Grand Roc.

SCENIC ROUTES

The approach to the Grotte du
Grand Roc on the D47
introduces the stunning
limestone cliffs that
characterise this tour.

---

❶ Grotte du Grand Roc,
Aquitaine
The great natural limestone
wall here, facing the Vézère,
with its overhangs forming the
pitched roof lines of some
bizarrely located houses, is
honeycombed with ancient
dwellings and caverns. In the
Grotte du Grand Roc you will
find an underground wonder-
land whose cave floors and
hanging gardens of fretted limestone look like a spiky coral reef
(wire grills protect some of the
formations).
    In the same magnificent cliff,
the prehistoric rock shelters of

Laugerie Haute and Laugerie
Basse, which yielded countless
objects left behind by their Ice-
Age inhabitants, are open.
    Less forbidding than its
name, the Gorge d'Enfer
(Gorge of Hell) is set in a little
wooded side valley whose caves
display 25,000-year-old wall
carvings. There is also a fishing
lake and a picnic site.

▶ Continue on the D47 into
Les Eyzies.

❷ Les Eyzies, Aquitaine
If the Vézère is the 'valley of
mankind', the village of Les
Eyzies, spectacularly located
between a northern limestone
cliff and the river, is at the heart
of the greatest concentration of
prehistoric sites. The Musée
National de la Préhistoire, built
into the cliff face, is devoted in
particular to the palaeolithic era,
starting perhaps 2½–3 million
years ago with the first traces of
primitive man.
    Near by, the Abri Pataud is a
cliff shelter dating back to more
than 20,000 years ago, and Abri
de Cap Blanc has prehistoric
sculptures of bison and horses.
There is also a museum and
research centre on site.

The G
Cazelle fea
figures dep
cave dwellers
to 1966.

ⓘ 19 avenue de la Préhistoire

▶ Leave Les Eyzies on the
D706 to Montignac. Turn right
on the D704, then right again
for Lascaux II.

BACK TO NATURE

Along the D703 from
Les Eyzies at Le Bugue is
the Aquarium du Périgord
Noir, with 3 million litres
(660,000 gallons) of water in
huge tanks containing freshwa-
ter species of Europe.

---

❸ Lascaux II, Aquitaine
The caves at Lascaux were
discovered in 1940 by some
boys, out on a rabbiting expedi-
tion. They are decorated with
the most celebrated prehistoric
paintings in the world – lively
representations of bulls, deer

Périgueux has a rich historical
mixture of architectural styles

Replicas of Lascaux's original cave paintings on show at Lascaux II

and horses created nearly 18,000 years ago by Cro-Magnon man.

The caves have had to be closed to the public to prevent deterioration of the original paintings, but painstakingly exact replicas are on display at the neighbouring site called Lascaux II. A visit here cures visitors of any notion that our ancestors of 800 generations ago were nothing more than primitive louts.

FOR HISTORY BUFFS

Off the D706, after Les Eyzies, several sites illustrate the everyday life of our very remote ancestors. La Roque-St-Christophe is an amazing troglodytic fortress town, lived in from prehistoric days to the 18th century, with five great terraces overlooking the River Vézère. At Thonac, Le Thot – Éspace Cro-Magnon explains the environment and art of prehistoric times. In the parkland, present-day animals such as red and fallow deer, bison, tarpan and Przewalski's horses can be compared with life-size replicas of mammoths and aurochs (an extinct type of ox).

Older than Lascaux, the nearby cave site of Régourdou is open to visitors. The brown bears in its park match displays in its museum about the prehistoric cult of the bear.

i *Place Bertran-de-Born, Montignac*

▶ *Return to the **D704** and turn right to Sarlat-la-Canéda.*

❹ **Sarlat-la-Canéda,** Aquitaine

The golden stone of Sarlat and the effortless grace of its Gothic and Renaissance buildings make this one of the loveliest towns in the Dordogne region. Even the tourist information office is housed in a 15th-century mansion near the handsome cathedral of the 16th and 17th centuries. Shaded alleys and courtyards in the old town are busy with a craftsmen's market and shops, many selling *foie gras*. On a wooded hillside above the square, pleasant public gardens can be found.

i *3 rue Tourny*

▶ *Leave Sarlat-la-Canéda on the **D46** for Vitrac. In Vitrac-Port watch for a left turn on to the **D703** to Carsac and Souillac. Turn left on to the **N20** in Souillac.*

❺ **Souillac,** Midi-Pyrénées

The glory of this busy centre in the Dordogne valley is the restored 12th-century Romanesque church called Abbatiale Sainte Marie, whose red-and-white tiled roofs culminate in a series of cupolas, as in the cathedral at Périgueux. The carvings in the church are particularly fine. Behind the church you may hear the incongruous music of a 1920s jazz band. This is just one of the lifelike exhibits in the Musée de l'Automate. Tableaux of moving life-size figures also include a glamorous lady snake-charmer, a clown and a splendid 19th-century Passion Play.

i *Boulevard Louis-Jean Malvy*

FOR CHILDREN

The prehistoric dwellings of Les Eyzies are as fascinating to children as they are to adults, but Préhisto-Parc wraps it all up for them in theme park style. It features outdoor tableaux of Neanderthal and Cro-Magnon (a type of 'modern' man), hunting expeditions and household scenes of 15,000 years ago.

▶ *Leave Souillac on the **D703** to Martel. Turn right on the **N140**, left on the **D70**, then right on the **D11** to Miers and left on the **D91**. Go left on the **D60**, right at the Y-junction at the stone cross, then finally right at the T-junction to Gouffre de Padirac.*

SCENIC ROUTES

After Montvalent, on the way from Souillac to Padirac, there is a landscape change as the D70 and D11 run through the parcels of sheep-grazed land on the limestone plateau known as the *causse*.

6 Gouffre de Padirac,
Midi-Pyrénées

Open since the late 19th century when it was discovered, the Padirac chasm is one of the greatest underground sights in Europe. Lifts and stairways descend to the otherworldly cavern of a subterranean river where, by boat and pathway, you can visit glorious floodlit limestone chambers like the Great Dome Gallery, walls of stalagmites and a petrified waterfall. Cafés and restaurants, a picnic area and a small zoo are clustered above ground.

▶ *Continue on the **D90** to Padirac, turn left and follow signs to Gramat. Leave Gramat on the **N140** northwards, then turn left on the **D36**. Turn left on the **D32** into Rocamadour.*

7 Rocamadour,
Midi-Pyrénées

Words and pictures rarely do justice to the reality of Rocamadour, the magnificent fortified pilgrimage town whose historic houses, sanctuary churches, bishops' palace, museums and skyline castle cascade down a terraced limestone cliff. It became a place of pilgrimage in the 12th century, visited by the great and the good of Christendom. Lifts and staircases, including the long and tiring pilgrims' Holy Way, thread through the town. Once you have turned on to the D32, pause to admire the stunning situation of the place, from the viewpoint beside the Hotel Belvédère. In Rocamadour, the finest view is from the castle ramparts.

RECOMMENDED WALKS

At busy times, you may appreciate leaving the narrow streets of Rocamadour for a walk, steep in places, based on old sheep tracks in the Alzou Valley. It starts from the bridge on the D32 below the town and heads upriver.

The D32 avoids the town centre often crammed with visitors. There are parking places in the valley.

i *L'Hospitalet*

FOR CHILDREN

Insectopia, at Gouffre de Padirac, has a collection of live insects and a big-screen cinema showing fun clips of insects in films, with and without special effects. For children who are not into bugs, La Féerie du Rail (The Enchanted Railway) is a huge model layout with 60 trains hauling coaches and freight wagons.

The ancient town of Rocamadour, situated above the Gorge of Alzou

▶ *Continue on the D32 to Couzou, go right on the D39 through St-Projet, right on the D1 then join the D673 to Gourdon. Turn left as for Sarlat then left as for Salviac, leaving Gourdon on the D673. Go right on the D6, which becomes the D46 to Cénac. Go right on the D49 to Domme.*

8 Domme, Aquitaine
This lovely, mellow hilltop town, founded with defensive ramparts and gateways around 1280, provides one of the finest viewpoints in France. The River Dordogne curves below the town, giving way to fields, farmhouses and lines of poplars on the riverside plain.

Limestone cliffs, woods and hill villages march to the horizon. In Domme itself there are beautiful townscape views round every corner. A good museum illustrates local domestic life in the past. Shops sell local honey, jams, truffles and *foie gras*. In the central square, an old covered market hall is now the entrance to a marvellous series of underground caverns with mirror lakes and floodlit limestone columns.

ⓘ *Place de la Halle*

▶ *Return to Cénac and go straight on along the D50, through St-Cybranet, then continue as for Siorac-en-Périgord. In Pont-de-Cause bear right for Castelnaud. In Castelnaud, go straight ahead for Fayrac and Les Milandes. Turn left on the D53 as for Siorac then after a 'virages' sign watch for a sharp right uphill signed 'Château des Milandes'.*

9 Les Milandes, Aquitaine
Perched on a terrace giving spreading views over the Dordogne valley, the restored 15th-century castle in the attractive and tucked-away hamlet of Les Milandes was owned from

Domme's spectacular hilltop position has made it a coveted prize throughout France's turbulent history

1949 to 1969 by the American singer Josephine Baker, star of the Paris cabarets between the wars. It was here that she founded a philanthropic foundation to look after children from all over the world.

Beyond the castle, the white courtyard of the farm, which was also part of Josephine Baker's estate, houses a rural museum explaining the improvements in agricultural techniques through the years.

FOR HISTORY BUFFS

On the way from Domme to Les Milandes, on a glorious viewpoint site above the village of the same name, Castelnaud is a restored medieval castle which houses displays on artillery and siege warfare. During much of the Hundred Years' War, the castle was held by the English.

▶ *Continue from the farm museum and bear left as for Veyrines-de-Vergt. Turn right on the **D53** then take the **D50** to Siorac and the **D25** to le Buisson-de-Cadouin. Follow signs to Lalinde, then Bergerac.*

🔟 **Bergerac,** Aquitaine
A cobbled car park which slopes down towards the River Dordogne is a convenient base for a stroll round the restored old town at the heart of present-day Bergerac. There are narrow lanes of part-timbered houses, and tiny squares, one of them shaded by chestnut trees where a statue of Rostand's hero Cyrano de Bergerac, the 17th-century nobleman and soldier famous for his large nose, stands, nobly cloaked.

The impressive Musée du Tabac in the town hall (Maison Peyrarède) illustrates the discovery of tobacco, its sources, and the local tobacco trade, as well as displaying beautifully worked pipes, cigarette holders, snuffboxes and tobacco jars. Its

Medieval houses grace the revived old town in Bergerac

curious second-floor exit leads back down to street level through the town museum (history and regional ethnography).

Near by, the Musée du Vin et de la Batellerie combines several long-standing Bergerac interests – wine, barrel-making and river traffic. The old monastery, built around an elegant courtyard, is the home of the wine council on which all the Bergerac growers are represented.

ℹ️ *97 rue Neuve d'Argenson*

▶ *Leave Bergerac on the **N21** and return to Périgueux.*

SPECIAL TO...

To get a real taste of the culinary delights of the region, visit the famous Château Monbazillac, a few kilometres south of Bergerac. The château, built in the 16th century, presides over its own well-ordered vineyard and about 3,000 bottles are stored in its cellar. You can tour the château (including the cellar), sample the wine, purchase a few bottles – along with such local specialities as *foie gras*, stuffed prunes, conserves and walnut oil – in the shop and then enjoy the Périgord cuisine in the gourmet restaurant.

Through the
High Pyrenees

This is primarily a summer tour, exploring some of the highest roads in the Pyrenees mountains. The Col du Tourmalet usually opens only after the snows clear in June. The mountain roads are exhilarating in fine weather, hair-pinning to great summit view-points. There are pleasant resorts in the foothills.

ITINERARY	
PAU	▶ **Tarbes (38km-24m)**
TARBES	▶ **Bagnères-de-Bigorre (20km-12m)**
BAGNÈRES-DE-BIGORRE	▶ **St-Bertrand-de-Comminges (65km-40m)**
ST-BERTRAND-DE-COMMINGES	▶ **Bagnères-de-Luchon (35km-22m)**
BAGNÈRES-DE-LUCHON	▶ **Col du Tourmalet (87km-54m)**
COL DU TOURMALET	▶ **Gavarnie (37km-23m)**
GAVARNIE	▶ **Cauterets (40km-25m)**
CAUTERETS	▶ **Lourdes (29km-18m)**
LOURDES	▶ **Grottes de Bétharram (13km-8m)**
GROTTES DE BÉTHARRAM	▶ **Pau (28km-17m)**

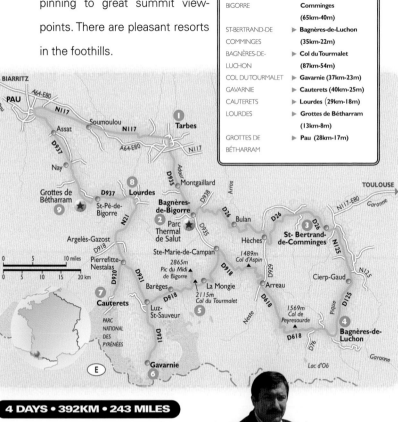

4 DAYS • 392KM • 243 MILES

▶ *Leave Pau on the **N117** to Tarbes, avoiding the autoroute.*

❶ Tarbes, Midi-Pyrénées
With centuries of history as a regional capital behind it, Tarbes is a busy, prosperous and confident city. There is a strong summer programme of musical, theatrical, artistic, floral and sporting events.

Just off the town centre, the Jardin Massey is an attractive woodland park with pools, statues, a bandstand, an open-air theatre and peacocks' outlandish cries echoing over the lawns. Be prepared to give way to families of mallards waddling between the ponds and streams. In the heart of the park, the Musée Massey is an elegant 19th-century mansion with a fine collection of French, Flemish and Italian paintings, and a superb display on the hussars, the élite cavalry corps not only of France, but also of countries all over the world.

Although the present-day hussars stationed at Tarbes are mechanised units, the national stud of Anglo-Arab horses, the Haras National de Tarbes,

founded in 1806, continues to flourish. The stables are regularly open to visitors, and Tarbes hosts several show-jumping and dressage events during the year.

i *3 cours Gambetta*

FOR HISTORY BUFFS

In Tarbes, the boyhood home of the great World War I commander Marshal Foch is a museum with films and photographs, uniforms and honours, and the moving text of his final order of the day in 1918.

▶ *Leaves Tarbes on the **D935** to Bagnères-de-Bigorre.*

❷ Bagnères-de-Bigorre, Midi-Pyrénées
Offering thermal baths, a casino, sports facilities and healthy walks, with industry kept discreetly in the outskirts, Bagnères is a typical southern spa nestling in the forested foothills of the Pyrenees. Occupied in prehistoric times, it was taken over by the Romans, who were the first to build bathhouses over its warm-water

The Col du Tourmalet is an important part of the Tour de France

springs. Its reputation as a spa increased through the years and came to a peak in the 19th century, as the architecture of the thermal establishments shows. The Musée Bigourdan du Vieux Moulin has local displays, while the Musée des Beaux-Arts Saliès is given over mostly to paintings.

Bagnères is well known for its authentic folk-singing concerts. Tennis and the hiring of horses, ponies or all-terrain bicycles can be arranged. As well as fishing, the River Adour running through the town is used for lively white-water canoeing.

i *3 allée Tournefort*

RECOMMENDED WALKS

On the south side of Bagnères, make for the wooded Parc Thermal de Salut. Pathways zigzag to the crest of a beautiful forested ridge, with views down over the spa town in the valley floor.

▶ *Leave Bagnères-de-Bigorre on the **D938** as for Toulouse. Turn right on the **D26**, then right on the **D929** through Hèches. Watch for a left turn, just as you see the 'Rebouc' sign, down over a level crossing and immediately left, following the **D26** again. In St-Bertrand-de-Comminges, go right at the crossroads, uphill on the **D26**.*

❸ St-Bertrand-de-Comminges, Midi-Pyrénées

Here is a most attractively located village whose red-roofed houses climb a modest ridge between the farmlands of the plain and the wooded Pyrenean foothills. The village and its unexpectedly majestic cathedral both take their name from a 12th-century bishop buried here. Pilgrims have been coming in great numbers since the Middle Ages. In the 16th century the cathedral interior was remodelled with stunning carved wood screens around the choir. The splendid organ also dates from that time, and is played at many recitals.

Outside, the beautiful arcaded cloisters look across to the wooded hillsides, which were a refuge for Resistance fighters during World War II.

The village preserves several fine old buildings, such as the 15th-century Maison Bridaut with its stone tower and timber-framed upper storeys.

Below the village stands an isolated 12th-century basilica in Italianate surroundings with tall

The little medieval town of St-Bertrand-de-Comminges can trace its history back to 72BC

cypress trees. Much of its masonry was taken from the ruins of a Roman settlement.

▶ *Return downhill then go straight ahead on the **D26** through Valcabrère. Turn right on the **N125** and follow signs to Bagnères-de-Luchon.*

❹ Bagnères-de-Luchon, Midi-Pyrénées

Most elegant and luxurious of the Pyrenean spas, Luchon (as it is generally known) is centred on a lively tree-lined avenue, with pavement cafés leading to the gardens of the thermal establishment. There is a stylish atmosphere throughout the town.

Walking, rock-climbing, fishing, clay-pigeon shooting, canoeing and rafting, tennis, hang-gliding and horse-riding, archery and golf are all catered for here, and many visitors come to the spa (the largest and most fashionable in the Pyrenees). A telecabin goes to Superbagnères for winter skiing or summer walking.

The history of the town and district is well illustrated in the Musée du Pays de Luchon. This 18th-century mansion has a dozen exhibition rooms also devoted to the wildlife of the Pyrenees, the development of mountaineering and 2,000 years of *curistes* from the time of Pompey and Tiberius, who sojourned at the even then handsomely equipped resort they knew as *Ilixion*.

Visitors can also have a guided tour of the hydroelectric plant (the tourist office handles reservations), which has provided power here since 1921.

SPECIAL TO...

You can see the great Basque game *pelota* being played at Luchon. It is a fast and exciting contest, something like squash, with the racket replaced by a curved wickerwork scoop called a *chistera*.

ℹ 18 allée d'Étigny

FOR CHILDREN

The Col de Peyresourde near Luchon is an area where the children can play place-name games. Ask them to find the villages with no consonants in their names, and the one which sounds singularly unhealthy.

RECOMMENDED WALKS

After Luchon, turn left on the D76 towards the Lac d'Oô. From a car park in this green steep-sided Pyrenean glen, it is a straightforward walk up to the lake, fed by a 275m (900-foot) cascade from Lac d'Espigno higher still.

SPECIAL TO...

The passes of Aspin and Tourmalet are classic stretches of the famous Tour de France cycle race. If you are here on the day of the Tour, forget about driving. Park and join the thousands of spectators to watch the battle for the coveted 'King of the Mountains' title.

BACK TO NATURE

In summer, the foothills of the Pyrenees are carpeted with wildflowers – aconites, asphodel, Pyrenean lilies and many more. The Office de la Montagne in Luchon organises guided visits to some of the best botanical areas. For ornithologists, the area might afford sightings of Alpine choughs, snow finches, golden eagles and griffon vultures.

▶ Leave Luchon on the **D618** over the Col de Peyresourde. In Arreau go right on the **D929** then, opposite the Esso station, not before, bear left uphill over the Col d'Aspin on the **D918**. Turn left in Ste-Marie-de-Campan to follow the **D918** to Col du Tourmalet.

Eating out in the elegant spa town of Bagnères-de-Luchon

5 Col du Tourmalet,
Midi-Pyrénées

At an altitude of 2,114m (6,936 feet), this is the highest through-road summit in the French Pyrenees. The road climbs relentlessly under five avalanche shelters to the ski resort – almost a ghost village at the height of summer – of La Mongie. Hairpin bends then take it up the final stretch, overlooked by colossal granite peaks and pinnacles, to the Col. From the top, the view ahead is magnificent, over peaks and ridges ranged to the horizon.

At a neck-craning angle to the north you will see the still higher observatory buildings and soaring television mast on the 2,865m (9,400-foot) summit of the Pic du Midi. A right turn

just after the actual Col leads along the steep and twisting toll road – to be driven cautiously – which climbs towards the summit and its astounding viewpoint.

BACK TO NATURE

Visitors are welcome to find out about extra-terrestrial (and terrestrial) affairs at the dramatically located Observatoire et Institut de Physique du Globe operated by the University of Toulouse on the Pic du Midi. It has carried out pioneering work on cosmic rays from its huge, arching solar protuberances, and produced some of the finest quality photographs ever taken from Earth. A good way to reach it is by cable car from La Mongie.

▶ *Immediately after the summit of the Col du Tourmalet, bear left through Barèges to Luz-St-Sauveur. Turn left on to the **D921** to Gavarnie.*

6 Gavarnie, Midi-Pyrénées
The narrow road to Gavarnie can be a trial in summer, because it is the busy dead-end approach to one of the most dramatic landscapes in Europe. South of the village lies the sublime Cirque de Gavarnie, a mountain amphitheatre piled with snow, whose rim at over 3,000m (10,000 feet) marks the boundary between France and Spain. Of its many waterfalls, the Grande Cascade, one of Europe's biggest, drops 442m (1,450 feet). You can only get really close to the Cirque on foot or on horseback. A less energetic alternative is to drive the spectacular winding road that climbs through wild country from Gavarnie to finish at a border col further to the west.

Gavarnie itself lies in a fine location with a river crashing through. It has an information centre for the Parc National des Pyrénées (Pyrenees National Park) and, in the heart of a famous climbing area, several monuments to the pioneering mountaineers. Try to be here in

the evening after the press of day visitors has eased – dusk brings a special magic.

ⓘ *Maison du Parc National*

▶ *Return to Luz-St-Sauveur and take the **D921** as for Lourdes. Immediately after leaving Soulom, turn left on to the **D920** to Cauterets.*

7 Cauterets, Midi-Pyrénées
Situated in a narrow river valley, Cauterets is the remotest of the Pyrenean spas. In medieval times it was believed the waters cured sterility. It has sulphur waters, thermal baths, a casino, unexpectedly handsome town houses and hotels, and well-developed winter sports facilities. Victor Hugo and George Sand were among the famous literary figures who came this way and helped to spread its reputation.

There is another information centre here for the Pyrenees National Park, accessible via various roads and footpaths. There is also the small Musée 1900, with seasonal film shows. Waterfalls tumble down near by, especially alongside the road to the Pont d'Espagne.

One of the most engaging features of Cauterets is that,

Excursions into the Pyrenean valleys are possible from Cauterets

although the railway which used to serve it has long since gone, the glorious rustic station, all varnished ornamental wood-work, has been lovingly preserved. Looking at it, you are not quite literally transported back to the 19th century, but the atmosphere remains.

ⓘ *Place Foch*

▶ *Return to the **D921**. Turn left and continue to Lourdes.*

8 Lourdes, Midi-Pyrénées
In 1858, a 14-year-old girl called Bernadette Soubirous, walking by the rocky banks of the river at Lourdes, experienced the first of a long series of visions of the Virgin Mary. During her life-time, pilgrims in increasing numbers, having heard of these wonders, journeyed to Lourdes. Two splendid basilicas were built beside the original grotto. In 1958, a third underground basilica was opened.

The beautiful riverside parkland where this complex is located attracts millions of visitors every year, many of them seeking cures for ailments or disabilities. The Pavilion

Notre-Dame tells the story of St Bernadette and the pilgrimages (Musée Bernadette) and there is also a museum of sacred art (Musée d'Art Sacré du Gemmail). Climbing through woodland, the Chemin du Calvaire passes the 14 Stations of the Cross.

Lourdes itself is often crammed with people and their cars. Overlooking the town from a rocky bluff, the medieval château-fort houses the Musée Pyrénéen, a museum of the arts and traditions of the folk of the foothills. One-tenth scale models show off typical Pyrenean architecture.

Take the funicular railway to the Pic du Jer. It opens up elevated views of the town, the valleys and the mountains.

ⓘ *Place Peyramale*

FOR CHILDREN

Young visitors to Lourdes will be enchanted by 'The Animated Crib'. Re-created biblical scenes tell the story of Jesus' childhood, and there is a 100sq m (1,075sq ft) layout of a Pyrenean village on Christmas Eve, all with animated models, sound and light.

FOR HISTORY BUFFS

Away from the sanctuary area, Lourdes has two museums devoted to showing how it looked in 1858, the year of Bernadette's first vision. The Musée de Lourdes features shops and street scenes, while the Musée du Petit Lourdes is a miniature stonework reproduction of the original simple village, towered over by its château-fort.

▶ *Leave Lourdes on the **D937**, following 'Bétharram' signs. Go through St-Pé-de-Bigorre, then turn left off the **D937** and left*

again to the Grottes de Bétharram.

🟒 **Grottes de Bétharram,**
Midi-Pyrénées

These underground caverns are explored by remarkably varied forms of transport – cable cars, boats and a little 'train' of towed wagons. There are five different levels of caves and stalagmites, stalactites and curious limestone formations such as the Sphinx Window. You are shown old river levels, and taken for a cruise on a subterranean lake in a cavern 50m (165 feet) high. The fourth and fifth levels are linked by the present river dashing over a series of 80m (260-foot) falls.

▶ *Return to the **D937**, turn left and continue to Pau.*

SCENIC ROUTES

After Bagnères-de-Luchon, the D26 is a constantly twisting road round the wooded foothills ending in lovely farming country near St-Bertrand-de-Comminges. The approach to Luchon takes you through an ever-narrowing wedge of valley towards the Pyrenean mountain wall. While the lower Col d'Aspin has more varied views, the Tourmalet is a classic of granite mountain landscape. From Luz-St-Sauveur, the D921 threads its way through a spectacular gorge to Gavarnie.

The grandeur and opulence of Lourdes' enormous basilica

THE SOUTH OF FRANCE

There is no single theme along the littoral of the south of France, nor even a single name for it. West of Marseille lie the flamingo lagoons, the pools, the rice fields and the summer pastures of the Camargue. East of the city stretches a sublime coast of capes and rocky inlets – the beautiful *calanques*. Beyond the great roadstead of Toulon are the islands off Hyères, including, at Port Cros, an entire island nature reserve.

St-Tropez is…quintessentially St-Tropez, and you can have a great deal of fun simply people-watching. On a grander scale are the great resorts of the Côte d'Azur – Cannes, Nice, the immensely wealthy and independent principality of Monaco, and Menton.

Behind Nice and Monaco is the *arrière-pays*, the 'back country', the mountain country. Europe's answer to the Grand Canyon lies there.

Back from the Camargue lie Avignon and the haunting remains of the troubadours' court at Les Baux; Arles and St Rémy with their memories of the artist Vincent van Gogh; and the landscapes made famous in the mocking tales of Alphonse Daudet.

On the Cannes and Nice routes, be ready for hairpinned mountain roads, although most have been improved for tourist traffic.

On the coast, try the seafood restaurants serving Mediterranean mullet, bass and cod, and the great bouillabaisse. Be ready for lots of garlic and olive oil. In Nice, the cuisine reflects the Italian past. Vines were planted here by Greek colonists 2,500 years ago. Most of the modern wines are classified as Côtes de Provence, and the most attractive vineyard country is perhaps around Gassin and Ramatuelle on the St-Tropez peninsula. There is also intense cultivation behind the little resort of Cassis.

Should the coast become too crowded and stylish for you, half an hour inland you will find yourself in a dramatically different world of hills and mountains, forests and river valleys, where time slows down in delightful hilltop villages drowsing beneath a dazzling southern sky.

Marseille

Marseille is the greatest port in France, extending west to the faraway oil refineries of the Golfe de Fos. The yacht harbour, right in the heart of the city, makes a pleasant area for a stroll. The story of Marseille from the days of the Ligurians, Greeks and Romans, by way of the Revolution and the patriotic song which came to be called *La Marseillaise*, is told in four separate museums. Other museums cover art, pottery, furniture, tapestries, marine life etc.

There are many substantial churches, parks, gardens and, at La Canebière, a renowned avenue of shops, hotels, restaurants and pavement cafés. A magnificent view opens up from the hilltop Church of Notre-Dame-de-la-Garde. Offshore lies the sea-bound rock of the Château d'If. You can sail here and recall the story of Dumas' Count of Monte Cristo.

Cannes

In Cannes, the great boulevard de la Croisette stretches eastwards from the casino and the Palais des Festivals. Every May, during the world-famous Cannes Film Festival, the Palais steps are staked out by twitchy television crews. The finest viewpoint is the observatory at Super-Cannes, at 325m (1,065 feet) above sea-level and 2km (1 mile) to the northeast, from which the town is seen in its wider landscape context between the Alps and the sea. Sail to the Îles des Lérins: St-Honorat is a monastery island and on Ste-Marguerite, which offers scented forest walks, was the prison of the real-life Man in the Iron Mask.

Nice

Nice is the capital of the Côte d'Azur. Its Promenade des Anglais recalls the 19th-century British visitors who made its name. The Russian royal family also favoured Nice, and you will see the green and gilded towers of the Orthodox cathedral where they and their court, which transferred here en masse every year, used to worship. There are fine shops, markets (notably the flower market), squares and gardens. Corsica ferries leave from the port. Eastwards, by the Cap de Nice, expensive villas hide above flowery balustrades. In addition to churches, palaces, museums and galleries, there is the Parc des Miniatures, enjoyed by children, which tells the story of Nice itself. The Musée Terra Amata is an imaginative exhibition based on a prehistoric site, whose story starts 400,000 years ago.

Nîmes

Nîmes found favour with the Romans. Their arena, with space for 21,000 spectators, plays host to concerts and bullfights today. The Maison Carrée is a pillared 1st-century BC temple (one of the best preserved in existence) housing a little museum. Archaeology, history, the planets, fine arts and the story of Nîmes are topics covered in other exhibitions. Below a hillside park lies the grand, if somewhat faded, Jardin de la Fontaine. Its 18th-century masonry and water channels were built on the site of the Roman baths, providing a cool retreat from the harshness of the Provençal summer sun.

Opposite: the view west from Les Baux-de-Provence
Below: Marseille's harbour

East From
Marseille

Starting from Marseille, France's second biggest city, this tour visits fishing villages which now have their own substantial holiday clientele, and larger resorts as different in style as Hyères and St-Tropez. All these places have grown up over the centuries, but Port-Grimaud is a modern development. Inland, the tour follows the high wooded ridges of the Massif des Maures as well as visiting an awesomely remote monastic house and the country of a film-maker who captured the soul of Provence.

4 DAYS • 352KM • 221 MILES

ITINERARY

MARSEILLE	►	**Cassis** (23km-14m)
CASSIS	►	**Cap Canaille** (7km-4m)
CAP CANAILLE	►	**Bandol** (25km-16.5m)
BANDOL	►	**Toulon** (35km-22m)
TOULON	►	**Hyères** (25km-16.5m)
HYÈRES	►	**Gassin** (69km-43m)
GASSIN	►	**St-Tropez** (18km-11m)
ST-TROPEZ	►	**Port-Grimaud** (8km-5m)
PORT-GRIMAUD	►	**Grimaud** (6km-4m)
GRIMAUD	►	**Chartreuse de la Verne** (24km-15m)
CHARTREUSE DE LA VERNE	►	**Aubagne** (93km-58m)
AUBAGNE	►	**Marseille** (19km-12m)

_i_ 4 La Canebière, Marseille

▶ Leave Marseille on the **D559**
to Cassis.

❶ Cassis, Provence-Alpes
With cream and ochre-washed
buildings overlooking the
harbour, bars, cafés and seafood
restaurants, and convenient
beaches, Cassis has the obvious
look of a holiday resort. But it is
a fishing port too, and boats take
visitors to the beautiful _calan-
ques_, the rocky inlets in the
roadless coastline to the west.
    Cassis has a life and history
independent of the summer
tourist crush. A ruined castle
(not accessible to the public) on
a cypress-clad hill watches over
it. A modest but informative
local museum shows how the
settlement dates back to Roman
times and before. The town hall
is also worth a visit; illustrations
show how it was rebuilt from a
shambolic ruin in the 1980s.

_i_ Quai des Moulins

▶ Head out of Cassis on the
D559 then right following
'Route des Crêtes' signs on to
the **D41a** and the **D141** to
Cap Canaille.

❷ Cap Canaille,
Provence-Alpes
Less a conventional cape than a
wall of towering sea-cliffs – at
395m (1,300 feet) Europe's
highest cliff – this is one of the
most superb viewpoints in

France. It looks west to the
mazy coastline of the _calanques_,
with offshore islands and rock
pinnacles seeming to float in the
air, like dreamy hills in old
Chinese paintings.

▶ Continue into La Ciotat. Go
right at the T-junction on to
Avenue Victor Hugo, then left
and left again along the
seafront, following signs for
Bandol.

Painters such as Matisse and Dufy
enjoyed the Provençal charm of
Cassis – and probably its wine, too

3 Bandol, Provence-Alpes
This is Cassis writ large, a resort with a marina, a fishing port and even more seafood restaurants. Boats sail from Bandol on cruises along the coast, but the most popular trip is to Bendor, a rocky island crammed with hotels and restaurants, beaches, sailing, diving and tennis clubs, an art gallery and an exhibition on wines and spirits from nearly 50 countries. There is a zoo, and along the coast is a maritime museum.

[i] *Allées Vivien*

▶ *Continue on the **D559** through Sanary-sur-Mer, then go left on the **D63** and follow signs to Toulon.*

is well documented in the Maritime Museum.
   Toulon has perhaps the most amazing suburban background of any city in Europe. The hillside districts behind the town centre suddenly rear up in the colossal limestone cliffs of Mont Faron. A one-way road system reaches the summit, the climb being up a steep incline with forbidding drops. As an option, a cable-car runs from Super Toulon. There are wonderful views from Mont Faron, pinewood picnic sites, a children's playground, a zoo and a comprehensive memorial exhibition on the 1944 liberation of Provence.

[i] *334 Avenue de la République*

▶ *Leave Toulon on the **N98** to Hyères.*

5 Hyères, Provence-Alpes
Hyères is a town of colourful gardens. This is the oldest of all the modern Riviera resorts, although standing back more than most of them from the sea. The old quarter, reached through its original medieval gateways, is full of cool narrow streets, historic buildings and an authentic atmosphere of people going about their daily business. Hyères is mature enough not to be any kind of tourist trap.
   The town's history goes back to the times of the Greeks and Romans – as *Olbia* it was a Greek colony, established by settlers from Marseille. The

4 Toulon, Provence-Alpes
With its interlocking harbours and a busy dockyard, Toulon is a famous and historic naval port. In World War II, in 1942, much of the French fleet was scuttled here, so that it would not come under German control. There is a great deal of civilian activity too. Ferries sail to Corsica and Sardinia, cargo ships use the freight quays, and smaller boats run scheduled services to the offshore islands as well as making shorter trips round the harbour. The story of the port

FOR HISTORY BUFFS

As Captain Bonaparte, Napoleon first made a name for himself at the age of 24, when the Republican army attacked British-held Toulon in 1793.
Under withering enemy fire, his artillery battery bombarded a British strong-point at the fort now named after him, forcing the British ships to withdraw.

Toulon, France's second-largest naval base, is surprisingly lively

excavations are currently closed, due to reopen in 2012. There are some handsome old churches (St Louis associated with King Louis IX who landed at Hyères after crusading, and St Paul with its Romanesque front), and from the castle ruins in a hilltop park a panoramic view is revealed.

[i] *Forum du Casino, 3 avenue Ambroise Thomas*

The cathedral of St Paul dominates the old town of Hyères

BACK TO NATURE

From Hyères-Plage, on the D97 south of town, ferries run to the beautiful nature reserve island of Port Cros. Footpaths explore its bays and forests, and there is even an underwater nature trail for divers and swimmers with flippers and masks. The neighbouring islands of Île du Levant and Île de Porquerolles are also worth a visit. Both have small resort villages and good beaches.

▶ *Leave Hyères on the N98 as for Le Canadel. Watch for a left turn following the N98 signed 'La Môle'. Turn right on the D41 as for Bormes then, at a blind bend on a brow, left on the RF32, the Routes des Crêtes. Go straight on along this road, always on a tarred surface. Turn right at the Col du Canadel, away from La Môle, then left on the D559 through La Croix-Valmer. Watch for 'Auberge les Sarments' sign, then immediately bear right off the D559 to Gassin.*

6 Gassin, Provence-Alpes
Sensitively restored in recent years, this hilltop village often attracts cooling breezes on hot summer days. There are lanes and stairways, houses with potted flowers and pocket-handkerchief gardens, a parish church barely illuminated by the modern abstract stained glass in its three tiny original windows, restaurants on a shaded terrace and, above all, views to the delicious miniature landscapes of the St-Tropez peninsula.

▶ *Leave Gassin for Ramatuelle, turn left at a stop sign, right at a second stop sign, then left towards the D98a. At traffic lights, turn right on that road into St-Tropez.*

BACK TO NATURE

On the left after Gassin, the Chemin du Radio Phare passes three old stone windmills on the way to a short circular walk outside the perimeter fence of a radio beacon. This is a splendid viewpoint, but the great attraction is the number and variety of brightly-coloured butterflies which flit around.

7 St-Tropez, Provence-Alpes
Publicity about the personalities – from the writers Guy de Maupassant and Colette to artists Henri Matisse, controversial writer, designer and film director Jean Cocteau and 'sex kitten' actress Brigitte Bardot – who have settled here, has always tended to hide the fact that this red-roofed town clustered beside a bay is an interesting place in its own right.

St-Tropez shops ask high prices, and the resort is full of deeply tanned characters in high summer fashion, who may be wealthy residents or simply day-trippers putting on an act – it can be fun to try to classify them. Needless to say, café and nightlife is abundant if you can afford the price and keep the pace.

An old chapel has been turned into a museum – the Musée de l'Annonciade – featuring paintings and sculptures by some of the notable artists who have lived here including Bonnard, Braque, Dufy and Utrillo, while lesser lights try to sell their canvases in an unofficial gallery by the harbour rails. The hexagonal 16th-century citadel is now a naval museum (Musée de la Citadelle) on several floors, where you can peruse the exhibits (which include a reconstructed Greek galley) to the accompaniment of unearthly cries from the local peacocks.

The fine sandy beaches are 4 to 5km (2½–3 miles) from St-Tropez town, on the far side of the headland on which it stands. They are varied and very popular. Parking can be difficult.

ℹ️ *Quai Jean-Jaurès*

FOR HISTORY BUFFS

Two processions, called *bravades*, are held every year in St-Tropez. The first, in May, honours St Torpes, the town's patron saint. A month later, the second *bravade* celebrates the defeat of a strong Spanish fleet which tried to capture the town in 1637. Fierce resistance by the local militia drove it away. Participants wear splendid uniforms and carry blunderbusses – which are fired (blanks only) at every opportunity.

▶ *Return along the **D98a**. At a roundabout join the **N98** as for Fréjus, then under the bridge take the right lane for Port-Grimaud and left at the roundabout to the 'Visiteurs' car park.*

8 Port-Grimaud, Provence-Alpes

In the 1960s this was simply a wasteland of marsh and gravel pits. Then the architect François Spoerry created a brand-new village on a lagoon by the sea – a kind of Provençal Venice with canals and peninsulas, bridges and water-buses, shops, cafés, restaurants and colour-washed houses, each with its own boat mooring right outside the door. Everything was to be a modern expression of traditional Provençal design. In the wrong hands, Port-Grimaud could have been a tacky disaster. Instead, it is a resounding triumph.

▶ *Return to the roundabout, go over the bridge then turn right at the T-junction. Continue straight on at the next junction then left on the **D14** to Grimaud.*

9 Grimaud, Provence-Alpes

Further inland, the medieval hillside town which gave Port-Grimaud its name retains many old buildings, notably the houses in the arcaded street of the Knights Templar, and the massive Romanesque church of St-Michel.

Above all, Grimaud, which takes its name from the powerful Genoese Grimaldi family (now rulers of Monaco), is dominated by the hilltop ruins of an 11th-century castle. It provides a wonderful viewpoint.

ℹ️ *1 boulevard des Aliziers*

▶ *Leave Grimaud on the **D558** then turn left on the **D14**. Turn left on the mostly unsurfaced **D214** signed 'La Verne'.*

10 Chartreuse de la Verne, Provence-Alpes

The road is lonely, slow and dusty to this remote and impressive monastery established by the Carthusians as long ago as 1170. At the time of the French Revolution it was deprived of its revenues, and the monks left secretly, disguised as peasants. The buildings then passed through several hands, and are now owned by a trust and are being renovated. In 1983 another order of monks – the Order of St Bruno – moved in. There are guided tours (for visitors who are discreetly dressed) showing the historic buildings and the breathtaking view of high ridges and deep valleys, covered by the forest of the Massif des Maures.

▶ *Rejoin the **D14** and follow it through Collobrières to Pierrefeu. Turn right on the **D12** through Puget-Ville and Rocbaron to Forcalqueiret.*

*Go left on the **D554** and continue to Méounes-les-Montrieux, then right on the **D2** via Signes, and right at Le Camp on the **N8** to Aubagne.*

⑪ Aubagne, Provence-Alpes
At the heart of this town, surrounded by a cat's-cradle of motorway bypasses, there are public gardens and cool tree-shaded squares. In one of them the tourist office pavilion houses a colourful display – using the painted clay-model figures called *santons* which are made in great numbers by craftsmen in the town – of

scenes from the films of the writer and director Marcel Pagnol, a native of Aubagne. After the world-wide screening in the 1980s of new versions of his stories *Jean de Florette* and *Manon des Sources*, interest in Pagnol, who died in 1974, spread widely. Guided tours are organised round the real-life locations he used in the countryside near Aubagne. In the

St-Tropez owes its popularity to its sheltered harbour and marina

western outskirts of the town, the Musée de la Légion Etrangère (Foreign Legion Museum) has displays on its years of service in the baking Sahara sands.

ℹ️ *8 cours Barthélémy*

▶ *Leave Aubagne on the **D2** and return to Marseille.*

The Riviera & its Hinterland

From Cannes and other coastal resorts, by way of artists' and craft-workers' villages, this tour climbs into the glorious mountain scenery that forms the backdrop to the Côte d'Azur. Limestone cliffs and ridges, spectacular valleys and ranges of faraway mountains reach a landscape climax in the magnificent Gorges du Verdon.

4/5 DAYS • 440KM • 273 MILES

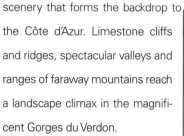

ITINERARY		
CANNES	▶	Cap d'Antibes (14km-9m)
CAP D'ANTIBES	▶	Antibes (5km-3m)
ANTIBES	▶	Biot (7km-4m)
BIOT	▶	Grasse (20km-12m)
GRASSE	▶	Gourdon (12km-8m)
GOURDON	▶	Plateau de Caussols (14km-9m)
PLATEAU DE CAUSSOLS	▶	Castellane (52km-32m)
CASTELLANE	▶	St-André-les-Alpes (22km-14m)
ST-ANDRÉ-LES-ALPES	▶	Riez (60km-37m)
RIEZ	▶	Moustiers-Ste-Marie (15km-9m)
MOUSTIERS-STE-MARIE	▶	Gorges du Verdon (42km-26m)
GORGES DU VERDON	▶	Draguignan (72km-45m)
DRAGUIGNAN	▶	Fayence (38km-24m)
FAYENCE	▶	Mons (15km-9m)
MONS	▶	Cannes (52km-32m)

i Palais des Festivals, 1 la Croisette, Cannes

▶ Leave Cannes on the **N7** towards Golfe-Juan, then bear right on the **N98** signed 'Antibes par Bord de Mer'. In Juan-les-Pins watch carefully for all the 'Cap d'Antibes' signs and join the Cap d'Antibes coast road, **D2559**.

❶ Cap d'Antibes,
Côte d'Azur

There are tiny family-style beaches and boat moorings on the east side of the Cape, which also includes security-guarded millionaires' retreats and, at the Hôtel du Cap and the Eden Roc restaurant, two of the most exclusive establishments of their kind on the coast. A fine museum devoted to Napoleonic and naval history – Musée Napoléonien – occupies an old gun battery, perhaps surprising visitors from the United Kingdom with contemporary cartoons showing the British as the enemy. Around the Villa Thuret there is a botanical garden. Right on the summit of the Cape is the Sanctuaire de la Garoupe, a seafarers' chapel beside the lighthouse tower, which is a marvellous viewpoint, housing a collection of simple but affecting thanks-offerings, often for a safe return from a voyage.

American writers and artists were attracted to the Cape from the 1920s onwards. F Scott Fitzgerald's novel *Tender is the Night* had its real-life setting here. It is possible to trace the exact course of the disastrous car journey described in James Thurber's *A Ride with Olympy*. And Orson Welles once arrived in a hurry for a cash-raising meeting in the Hôtel du Cap, having come by taxi all the way from Rome!

▶ Continue on the **D2559** into Antibes.

❷ Antibes, Côte d'Azur
The old town here, with its narrow streets, cafés and restaurants, is one of the most attractive and least pretentious on the coast. Antibes' connection with the ancient Greeks – it was founded as *Antipolis* by Greek colonists from Marseille in the 4th century BC – attracted the Cretan writer Nikos Kazantzakis, author of *Zorba the Greek*, to settle here, as did the British novelist Graham Greene. While the archaeological museum in the old fortification of the Bastion St André may look gloomy from the outside, it has a wonderful collection of thousands of exhibits going back to Etruscan, Greek and Roman times, many recovered from the sea. The old castle was a stronghold of the powerful Genoese Grimaldi family. With the little 'cathedral', it watches over the bustling market place, and was long since turned into the Musée Picasso. The artist used part of it as a studio for six amazingly fruitful months in 1946, and now it contains many of his – and other artists' – paintings and ceramics, making it one of the most important Picasso collections anywhere. The so-called cathedral is, in fact, a church, with a Romanesque tower and east end, and a 17th-century façade.

i 11 place du Général-de-Gaulle

Paintings in Notre Dame de Bon Port, Cap d'Antibes

RECOMMENDED WALKS

On the south side of the Cap d'Antibes, turn off the Boulevard J F Kennedy for the Sentiers des Douaniers – the Excisemen's Path. Starting alongside the wall of a private estate, it leads to a beautiful little park set among rocks above the sea, with a lovely bay stretching to the west.

▶ Leave Antibes on the **N98** as for 'Nice par Bord de Mer'. Take the left-hand lane, turn left at the traffic lights for Biot, then right and left on the **D4** to Biot.

FOR CHILDREN

Marineland, to the right of the D4 on the way to Biot, has penguins, seals, sea lions and an impressive orca and dolphin show. Also in the complex are the Far West Farm with rides and shows, Aqua-splash and adventure mini-golf.

---

❸ Biot, Côte d'Azur
On the approach road to Biot, a road to the right leads to the Musée National Fernand Léger, unmistakable thanks to the huge abstract in multi-coloured

tiling which decorates its frontage. With more than 300 works on display, it celebrates the life of one of France's major 20th-century artists, and was opened in 1960 with fellow-artists Picasso, Braque and Chagall as its honorary presidents. The charming little town of Biot is largely given over to the shops and studios of painters, potters, woodworkers, embroiderers and craftworkers of many other kinds. Even the town maps are on painted ceramic tiles. Glassmaking is important here nowadays and can be observed at the Écomusée de Verre near the southeast exit from town. Gates and ramparts of the medieval town survive, and away from the tourist bustle there is a pleasant arcaded square beside a 15th-century parish church. The museum features mementoes of the days when the Romans and, later, the Knights Templar, were established here, and has a dazzling pottery display.

ℹ️ *46 rue St-Sébastien*

▶ *Continue on the D4 via Valbonne to Grasse, turning right at a T-junction on the outskirts to follow the D4 towards the town centre.*

4 Grasse, Côte d'Azur
Spread over a south-facing hill-side with splendid views over a lovely plain towards the sea, Grasse enjoys a year-long calendar of concerts, drama, dance and exhibitions of every kind. The old town, crammed with 14th- to 18th-century buildings, is Italian in appearance and atmosphere. Around it, Grasse expanded with exuberant 19th-century architecture in typical French Riviera style.

Grasse has the most famous perfume industry in the world, and one museum, Musée International de la Parfumerie, traces its history as well as the processes by which huge amounts of flower petals are distilled down to tiny volumes of the ultimate essence. The Musée Jean-Honoré Fragonard, named after the painter who was born in the town, is a perfume factory open to the public. The Musée d'Art et d'Histoire de Provence, in an 18th-century mansion, celebrates the art and history of Provence.

Another museum, the Musée de la Marine, has gathered an intriguing collection of ship models to illustrate the career of the 18th-century Admiral de Grasse, an ally of George Washington in the American

Biot is set attractively on a small hill rising in the centre of a valley

War of Independence. A statue on one of the town's outlook terraces recalls Washington's gratitude to him.

ℹ️ *22 cours Honoré-Cresp*

FOR CHILDREN

There is no need for parents to worry that their offspring might get bored at the Musée International de la Parfumerie in Grasse because they organise special activities for children. As soon as they can gather 10 or more youngsters together, they have them making bubble bath, hand cream and Egyptian jewels.

▶ *Leave Grasse on the **D2085** as for Nice. At Pré-du-Lac turn left at the roundabout and immediately bear left on the **D3** to Gourdon. Turn right for the car park at the entrance to the village.*

5 Gourdon, Côte d'Azur
Some writers sneer at Gourdon for being a tourist trap, but this old Saracen stronghold, set on

the edge of a cliff which gives it tremendous views down into the valley of the Loup, goes about its business quietly. In the narrow lanes of restored and impeccably kept buildings, shops sell lavender, honey, herbs, perfumes, pottery, wines, basketwork and glassware, many of them produced locally.

The historic Château de Gourdon (closed until 2011 for construction work), with terraced gardens on the edge of the cliff, dates from the 12th century and has valuable furnishings, collections of arms and armour, and 'naive' paintings by European and American artists.

ℹ️ *Place Victoria*

▶ *Leave Gourdon on the D12 as for Caussols. In about 8km (5 miles) watch for a junction sign. Go sharp left under a sign giving advice to 'Visiteurs'.*

6 **Plateau de Caussols,** Côte d'Azur

A notice at the turning off the D12 warns that gathering stones, mushrooms and snails is forbidden. Do not worry about the mild potholes on the early stretch of the road; the surface never deteriorates too badly. Here on the high limestone plain is a countryside not many casual tourists know: clumps of pines and rock outcrops, occasional sheep farms, isolated holiday homes, groups of beehives and, here and there, a survivor from the days of the *bories*, the stone-built shepherds' huts.

BACK TO NATURE

On the Plateau de Caussols, the rich limestone soil allows the growth of a riot of wildflowers. They flourish all over the natural pastureland, and colour the crevices of the hundreds of rock outcrops which are characteristic of the plateau. Orchids are abundant from April to June.

There are mountain ridges to north and south, with the remote white buildings of the CERGA observatory high on the northern rim. A two-hour guided tour takes in the historic observatory buildings and its olive groves.

▶ *Turn right at a T-junction beside a postbox, following an old sign 'St-Lambert'. This is the D12 again. Turn sharp left as for Thorenc on the D112, then follow 'Thorenc' signs on the D5. Go left on the D2, left on the D2211, then right on the N85 to Castellane.*

7 **Castellane,** Côte d'Azur

A modest little town on the Route Napoléon, Castellane lies in a constricted location where the River Verdon elbows its way through the hills. Directly overlooking the square is a massive

cliff, 184m (604 feet) high, on which the original settlement, dating from Gallo-Roman times, was built.

When the population decided, eventually, to settle in the valley, plague, floods and occupation in this time of the 16th-century religious wars was their reward. Now the classic outing at Castellane is a walk up the steep and occasionally rough pathway to the 18th-century Chapel of Notre Dame du Roc, a magnificent clifftop viewpoint.

ℹ️ *8 rue Nationale*

▶ *Continue on the N85, go right on the D955. Then left on the N202 to St-André-les-Alpes.*

Perched high above the River Loup, Gourdon has stunning views of the coast

8 St-André-les-Alpes,
Côte d'Azur

This is a quiet little inland resort a world away from the hustle of the coast. But St-André was once a busy enough place. The village had four cloth mills, but all that remains of the industry is the canal which supplied their water power. In the latter part of the 19th century it became the railhead of a line from Nice, and the place from which stagecoaches took passengers further on. This railway, now extended to Digne, is the last survivor of the old inland lines. St-André station is a halt on the year-round railcar service, and there are summer excursions on the steam-hauled Train des Pignes (the Pine Cone Train).

St-André lies in an attractive valley that has helped it achieve its present-day renown as a centre for hang-gliding and free-fall parachuting.

i *Place Marcel Pastorelli*

▶ *Continue on the N202 to Barrême, then turn right on to the N85 and left on the D907, then in La Bégude-Blanche take the D953 to Riez.*

9 Riez, Provence-Alpes

Two structures show how old the settlement of Riez is. A group of columns now standing isolated at the edge of the field was once part of a 1st-century Roman temple; and there is an early Christian baptistery (dating from some time in the 4th to 7th centuries), complete with the original font, inside a 19th-century building set up to preserve it. The old town may have a faded look, but its streets contain medieval doorways and

Surely one of nature's most delightful harvests – fields of perfumed lavender at Riez

Renaissance frontages, some in the course of restoration. In pre-Roman times, the settlement stood on the summit of the St-Maxime hill overlooking the present-day town in the valley below. St-Maxime, which is the site of an attractive chapel, is a pleasant place for a stroll. A popular Riez industry is the production of *santons*, characteristic Provençal painted clay figurines, originally made for the traditional Christmas crib, but now sold as souvenirs.

Moustiers has been famous for its pottery since the 17th century

[i] *Place de la Mairie*

▶ *Leave on the D952 to Moustiers-Ste-Marie.*

10 Moustiers-Ste-Marie,
Provence-Alpes
Any history of Moustiers pales before its amazing situation, clustered round the banks of a tumbling mountain stream at the foot of a huge gash in towering limestone cliffs. Footpaths climb to a spectacularly located church, Notre Dame de Beauvoir, set on a high rocky terrace. Across the break in the cliffs, and silhouetted against the sky, a chain supporting a gilded star was, according to tradition, first placed there by a crusader knight, who had sworn to do it when released from weary years of imprisonment.

The town is famous for its glazed pottery, or faïenceware. The industry established in the 17th century died out for a generation or two, and restarted in the 1920s, but without equalling the delicacy of the early designs. There are more than a dozen potters who welcome visitors to their *ateliers*.

[i] *Place de l'Église*

▶ *Continue on the D952 to La Palud. Go straight on through La Palud, then bear right on the D23, the Route des Crêtes. If you enjoy exposed and narrow roads with steep, unguarded drops, follow the D23 all the way back to La Palud and turn right to rejoin the D952. If you do not enjoy this kind of road, go along the D23 to the first two or three belvederes, then retrace your route and turn right again on to the D952. Only the later part of the D23 is difficult.*

11 Gorges du Verdon,
Provence-Alpes
Landscape superlatives are needed here, because this is France's equivalent, on a smaller scale, to the Grand Canyon in Colorado. The River Verdon, on its way to Castellane, runs through a huge ravine in the limestone mountains, with colossal drops, vertigo-inducing views, exciting low-level footpaths and the possibility of organised expeditions on foot and by canoe, raft or rubber dinghy, right through the heart of the gorge. There are magnificent, high-level roadside views from railed-off belvederes (look-out points), some of which, on the Routes des Crêtes, have warnings not to throw stones off the edge – they might fall on walkers 715m (2,350 feet) below!

▶ *Continue eastwards on the D952. After a stretch of overhanging cliffs, turn right on the D955 to Comps-sur-Artuby and Draguignan.*

12 Draguignan,
Provence-Alpes
Down from the mountains, and the vast military training area of Canjuers which occupies the scrubland plateau south of the River Verdon, Draguignan marks a return to the milder landscapes of mid-Provence. There is a dignified old town here, and a fine museum, with thousands of exhibits connected with local industries, including a reconstructed olive oil mill. There is also an artillery museum, reflecting the military presence. Shaded squares and gardens fend off the sun. On the boulevard John Kennedy, the American military cemetery commemorates the mostly Franco-American Provençal landings of August 1944. In front of the memorial there is an imaginative tribute in the form of a massive relief map, in bronze and copper, illustrating the campaign.

[i] *2 avenue Carnot*

FOR HISTORY BUFFS

After Mons, Roche Taillée, to the left of the D56, is a fine example of Roman civil engineering, a deep cutting in a limestone outcrop to take part of the 40km (25-mile) aqueduct which supplied the town of Fréjus near the coast. The aqueduct is still in use today.

▶ *Leave Mons on the **D56** as for Callian, then go left on the **D37**. Follow the **D37** to the left for Montauroux at a T-junction where the right turn is signed 'Callian 0.5km'. Follow the 'Grasse' sign in Montauroux, still on the **D37**, cross the **D562**, then go left on the **D38** through Tanneron. At a five-road junction after Tanneron bear right for Mandelieu-la-Napoule, then watch for an abrupt left turn avoiding a road straight ahead signed 'Poney Club'. Take the **D92** to Mandelieu. Turn right on the **N7** then take the fourth exit at a roundabout signed 'Les Plages'. Go right at the T-junction as for Napoule, then keep in the right lane and return to Cannes.*

▶ *Leave Draguignan on the **D562** as for Grasse. Go left on the **D563** to Fayence.*

13 Fayence, Provence-Alpes
Here is a classic back-from-the-coast village, facing southwards into the sun with its red-roofed houses stacked up a hillside that rises from the plain. Fayence has a very well-maintained 18th-century church, a good selection of craft studios and galleries, and terraces which act as splendid viewpoints. One very pleasant pastime here is to laze around them, look out over the plain and watch the gliders soaring from one of France's most important launching fields far below.

▶ *Continue on the **D563** to Mons.*

14 Mons, Provence-Alpes
The colonists from Ventimiglia in what is now Italy, who founded this little hilltop village in the 13th century, picked the location well. The spacious square, in fact a semi-circle, looks out over an extensive view from the islands off

The Gorges du Verdon offers a range of activities and natural beauty to take your breath away

Cannes to the Italian Alps, with suggestions that, on a really clear day, Corsica appears as a smudge on the horizon. Mons survived two outbreaks of plague and the fact that all its citizens deserted after a brigands' raid in 1468. It then dozed in the sun for centuries before it recently decided to emphasise its situation as one of the 'belvederes of the Côte d'Azur'. There is a maze of cool, narrow alleyways. The historic ramparts are still partly in place. Local arts and crafts are displayed in the museum. And the streets usually bear two names – in French and Provençal.

i Place St-Sébastien

FOR CHILDREN

In Mons, ask them to find the electricity meter for the house at 22 Su Lou Coustihoun.

SPECIAL TO...

From the Lac de St-Cassien to Mandelieu, the beautiful Tanneron massif is planted out with mimosa. In summer there is no trace of the brilliant yellow blooms which light up the winter hillsides.

SCENIC ROUTES

Approaching Gourdon, the D3 looks deep into the valley of the Loup, then reveals a stunning view of the village in the eagle's-eyrie location on the summit of a plummeting cliff.

Exploring the
Côte d'Azur

Often using steep and hairpinned roads, the route climbs spectacular valleys and wooded mountain ridges. Far from the hustle and
bustle of holiday crowds, the valley of the Gordolasque is a cleft in
the wildest part of the Maritime Alps, and the pilgrimage church of
Madone d'Utelle crowns a remote and atmospheric hilltop.

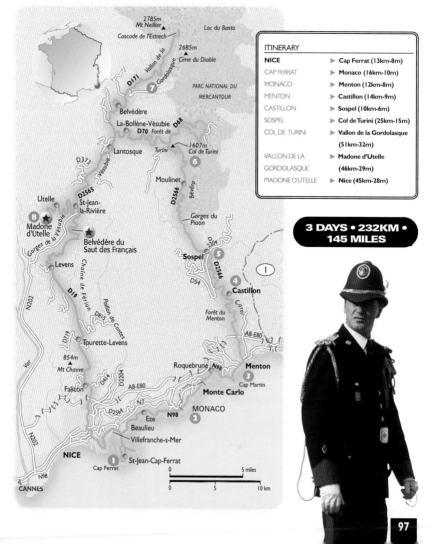

ITINERARY		
NICE	▶	**Cap Ferrat** (13km-8m)
CAP FERRAT	▶	Monaco (16km-10m)
MONACO	▶	Menton (12km-8m)
MENTON	▶	Castillon (14km-9m)
CASTILLON	▶	Sospel (10km-6m)
SOSPEL	▶	Col de Turini (25km-15m)
COL DE TURINI	▶	**Vallon de la Gordolasque**
		(51km-32m)
VALLON DE LA	▶	**Madone d'Utelle**
GORDOLASQUE		**(46km-29m)**
MADONE D'UTELLE	▶	**Nice** (45km-28m)

**3 DAYS • 232KM •
145 MILES**

---

i *5 Promenade des Anglais, Nice*

▶ *Leave Nice following the N98, the Corniche Inférieure, to Villefranche. Bear right for St-Jean-Cap-Ferrat.*

❶ Cap Ferrat, Côte d'Azur
Cap Ferrat is a cape extending about 3km (2 miles) south of Beaulieu. All the capes along the Côte d'Azur are favoured residential areas, with imposing villas in discreet well-wooded grounds. At Cap Ferrat one of the most majestic of these, once the home of the Baroness Béatrice Ephrussi-de-Rothschild, was built in 1905 to house a massive collection of costumes, furnishings, tapestries, paintings and porcelain.

The house and contents were left to the Académie des Beaux Arts and now form the Musée 'Île de France'. It stands among 7 hectares (17 acres) of gardens, and the collection, although it has a strong bias to the 18th century, includes Impressionist paintings and oriental *objets d'art*.

St-Jean-Cap-Ferrat, the resort village facing the towering cliffs that march to Monaco

and the Italian frontier, is on an arm of the cape going off to the east. It has two promenades looking out to the yachts and cruisers bobbing in the harbour.

i *59 avenue Denis Seméria, St-Jean-Cap Ferrat*

FOR CHILDREN

Take the children on an exciting trip on a sailing ship from St-Jean-Cap-Ferrat with SOS Grand Bleu's marine experts. It's educational and fun, and dolphin sightings are part of the experience.

RECOMMENDED WALKS

On Cap Ferrat, the Maurice Rouvier walk is a 2.3km (1.5-mile) round trip from the harbour to Beaulieu, while the slightly longer Pointe St-Hospice walk from Paloma beach circles a rocky peninsula below the villa gardens.

▶ *Return to Villefranche and bear right on the D125, then follow signs through Beaulieu for Monaco.*

FOR HISTORY BUFFS

On a rocky promontory in Beaulieu, which lies between Cap Ferrat and Monaco, the Villa Kérylos is a modern replica of a Greek palace of the 5th century BC, created early in the 20th century by archaeologist Théodore Reinach. Its pillars, mosaics, frescoes and furnishings, marble and alabaster benefit from their location by the deep blue Mediterranean, and there are some granite antiquities among the reproductions.

❷ Monaco
If you are a first-time visitor to Monaco, forget any idea that it is some kind of comic-opera place where only high-society millionaires feel at home. This is an ancient and sovereign

Spectacular view over Monaco from the Jardin Exotique

The bustling harbour in the town of Menton

state, ruled by the Grimaldi family for over 700 years. The Grimaldis originated in Genoa in Italy, one of their number seizing the Rock of Monaco in 1297.

Despite being so tiny – no larger than many a farm – the vastly wealthy principality is divided into four main districts: Monte Carlo, where the casino and the sumptuous Hôtel de Paris are located; La Condamine, around the harbour with its tens of millions of pounds' worth of yachts; the lovely old town on Le Rocher, the original Rock of Monaco, and Fontvieille, a new suburb.

Prince Rainier III's palace is reached from La Condamine up a steep ramp. It is mostly of the 16th and 17th centuries, and has several magnificent rooms open to the public, as well as a museum devoted to Napoleon, who was related to the Grimaldis. A fascinating archive collection documents centuries of Monagasque history. Throughout the palace and Monaco itself there are reminders of Princess Grace, the former film actress Grace Kelly whose fairytale marriage to Prince Rainier delighted the world.

Also in the old town are the elegant cathedral, built in neo-Romanesque style in the 19th century and containing the tomb of Princess Grace, and the Musée Océanographique, rising dramatically from the sea-cliffs. The latter, with an aquarium as well as fascinating museum exhibits, was directed by the famous underwater explorer Jacques Cousteau. Around it lie the beautiful St Martin gardens. They look down on the marina and Fontvieille, which is packed with housing and industry but has a large sports stadium and marina to its credit.

ℹ️ *2 boulevard des Moulins, Monte Carlo*

▶ *Leave Monaco on the **N98** as for Menton. In Roquebrune bear right for Cap Martin.*

BACK TO NATURE

Monaco's Jardin Exotique has a wonderful collection of sub-tropical plants, able to grow successfully because of the very warm microclimate. There is also a museum of anthropology, and below ground there are impressive limestone caverns at the Grotte de l'Observatoire.

SPECIAL TO...

Monte Carlo's Casino is the most famous in the world, with lush interior decorations and a gloriously baroque architectural style. Visitors may enjoy the public rooms without gambling, but a passport or some other identification is necessary, and no one under 21 is admitted.

▶ *Follow 'Menton' signs to the shore road, then keep right along the seafront to Menton.*

❸ **Menton,** Côte d'Azur

An old rhyme about the Riviera resorts claimed that 'Menton's dowdy, Monte's brass, Nice is rowdy, Cannes is class'. For years, Menton did have rather a faded air, brought about partly because its most faithful visitors were invalids and elderly people, from all corners of Europe. Now Menton has revitalised itself, but, nevertheless retains a less hectic pace than most other Côte d'Azur resorts. In addition, it has a lovely climate and Italian-style architecture; the Italian border is in its eastern outskirts.

Menton has beautiful gardens including the Jardin de la Serre de la Madone, laid out by Lawrence Johnston, the creator of Hidcote Manor gardens in Gloucestershire. In the town centre are a casino and fine museums, one of which is dedicated to the work of Jean Cocteau, and churches, promenades and squares. Around it lie the lemon groves – susceptible to very rare winter frosts – which give the town its most famous product. A Lemon Fair, the Fête du Citron, is held in February, when the air is scented with lemons and oranges.

ℹ️ *Palais de l'Europe, 8 avenue Boyer*

▶ *Leave Menton on the D2566 as for Sospel. Watch for the sharp right turn into Castillon.*

4 Castillon, Côte d'Azur
The original Castillon was wrecked in a 19th-century earthquake, and the rebuilt town destroyed during World War II. Their replacement is a charming modern village with

lanes and stairways, a tiny square and a beautiful southern outlook. Shops and studios offer paintings, sculptures, ceramics, leatherwork, stained glass and jewellery.

▶ *Return to the D2566, bearing right to the Col de Castillon. Go through the tunnel and turn right to Sospel.*

5 Sospel, Côte d'Azur
Sospel is situated at the junction of two river valleys and is surrounded by exhilarating mountain scenery, yet still appears scruffy. However, there is an intriguing old quarter with houses alongside the River Bévéra which is crossed by an

Sospel has a bohemian charm that inspires one to reach for a paintbrush and canvas or a camera

11th-century toll bridge, and in the Église St-Michel the town has a former cathedral complete with grand baroque interior.

On the outskirts, Fort St Roch is an astonishing underground artillery installation, part of the Maginot Line of defences built in the 1930s between the Belgian border and Corsica and now a museum of the alpine fortifications.

ℹ️ *19 avenue Jean Médecin*

▶ *Leave Sospel on the D2566 via Moulinet to the Col de Turini.*

6 Col de Turini, Côte d'Azur
In the high pine and larch forests at 1,607m (5,270 feet) above sea-level, Turini is a winter sports resort and a cool bolt-hole in summer from the heat of the coast. Four roads radiate from the hamlet at the summit, one to the still-higher circuit of l'Authion, just inside the huge Parc National du Mercantour. There are magnificent viewpoints here, as well as ruins of military fortifications battled over during the Revolution and in the last bitter days of fighting in 1944.

> ### SPECIAL TO...
>
> The Col de Turini is the most famous stage, every January, in the Monte Carlo Rally. You may see messages painted on the road – encouragement to top drivers from their fans.

> ### BACK TO NATURE
>
> Reached from the Col de Turini, the mountainous Parc National du Mercantour is home to chamois, ibex, ptarmigan and eagles. Alpine flowers and butterflies are at their best from June to August.

▶ *Leave the Col de Turini on the D70 through La Bollène-*

Vésubie, where you should turn sharp right following 'St-Martin' sign. Go right on the D2565 as for St-Martin-Vésubie, then sharp right on the D71, follow signs to Belvédère and go right at the T-junction for Gordolasque. This is the narrow D171. Follow it to a car park before the bridge where the public road ends.

7 Vallon de la Gordolasque, Côte d'Azur

This dead-end valley road follows a rocky mountain stream past steep scree-slopes, crags and boulder-runs where the woodland cover peters out in scattered pines and larches. The public road ends at the 1,700m (5,575-foot) Pont du Countet, beside a relief map of the bare,

RECOMMENDED WALKS

In the valley of the Gordolasque, a long distance footpath on the east bank can be split into individual stretches for shorter walks. Look for the footbridges which cross the river and take you past scree-runs, boulder fields and thinning pinewoods on the other side.

impressive upper valley still to come. An easy stroll gives a grand view of the dashing falls at the Cascade de l'Estrech.

▶ *Return through Belvédère to the D2565 and turn left as for Nice. At St-Jean-la-Rivière take the D32, the hairpinned climb past Utelle. Go left on the D132 to Madone d'Utelle.*

8 Madone d'Utelle, Côte d'Azur

The silence, air of tranquillity and tremendous views make the journey to this remote hill-top well worthwhile. Madone d'Utelle has been a place of pilgrimage since the 9th century. The present church, with its many thanks-offerings, was built in 1806 and is the goal of four major pilgrimages every year. It shares the hilltop with a mountain 'refuge' and a domed orientation table which identifies the major summits among the all but unaccountable mountain peaks included in the glorious 360-degree skyline view.

▶ *Return to St-Jean-la-Rivière and turn right on the D2565. After a 'Nice par Levens' sign, bear left on the D19 and follow it back to Nice.*

La Bollène-Vésubie is an enchanting village in the Col de Turini region. For all its sophisticated reputation, villages like this are the real south of France

SCENIC ROUTES

From the immaculate villas of the Cap de Nice, the N98 swings round to open up a gorgeous view of Villefranche bay. Leaving Menton, the D2566 climbs past woodlands and soaring limestone ridges which stretch to the Italian border. After the tunnel at the top of the Col de Castillon, be ready for a striking northwards view past dramatic wooded ridges to lonely skyline peaks.
Beyond Sospel the D2566 cuts through a seemingly impenetrable mountain wall by hairpinning up the Gorges du Piaon. There is a remarkable view back down the ravine from the little Chapel of Notre-Dame de la Menour, reached by an arched staircase bridge across the road.
The Col de Turini descends a forested mountainside towards the red-roofed village of La Bollène-Vésubie.
As it rises, the winding climb to Madone d'Utelle opens up more and more dramatic views.

Through
Historic Provence

The Romans left some of their most imposing monuments in the region they called *Provincia* – at Nîmes, Arles and Pont du Gard. Avignon retains the architectural grandeur given it by popes in voluntary exile from Rome. In the south, one of France's finest regional nature parks includes most of the Camargue.

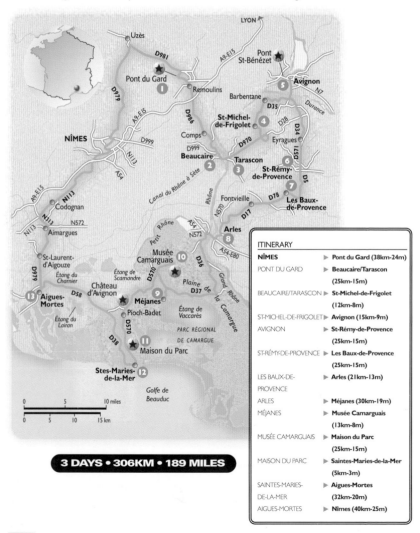

3 DAYS • 306KM • 189 MILES

ITINERARY

NÎMES	▶ **Pont du Gard (38km-24m)**
PONT DU GARD	▶ **Beaucaire/Tarascon** (25km-15m)
BEAUCAIRE/TARASCON	▶ **St-Michel-de-Frigolet** (12km-8m)
ST-MICHEL-DE-FRIGOLET	▶ **Avignon (15km-9m)**
AVIGNON	▶ **St-Rémy-de-Provence** (25km-15m)
ST-RÉMY-DE-PROVENCE	▶ **Les Baux-de-Provence** (25km-15m)
LES BAUX-DE-PROVENCE	▶ **Arles (21km-13m)**
ARLES	▶ **Méjanes (30km-19m)**
MÉJANES	▶ **Musée Camarguais** (13km-8m)
MUSÉE CAMARGUAIS	▶ **Maison du Parc** (25km-15m)
MAISON DU PARC	▶ **Saintes-Maries-de-la-Mer** (5km-3m)
SAINTES-MARIES-DE-LA-MER	▶ **Aigues-Mortes** (32km-20m)
AIGUES-MORTES	▶ **Nîmes (40km-25m)**

☐ *6 rue Auguste, Nîmes*

▶ *Leave Nîmes on the **D979** as for Uzès. Turn right on the **D981**, then watch for a right turn to Pont du Gard.*

❶ Pont du Gard, Languedoc-Roussillon

In civil engineering the Romans thought big. Their settlement at Nîmes needed water, and the magnificent three-tiered aqueduct at Pont du Gard, built around 20BC, was the most spectacular section of the 50km (30 miles) of channels which brought it from faraway springs. The first and second levels of arched bridges are simply supports for the topmost water channel; an excellent exhibition shows each stage of construction. In the modern world, few utilitarian structures have such abiding elegance. There's also a cinema presentation, a children's area and various walks at the site.

▶ *Continue to Remoulins. Go straight on along the **N86**, then follow signs for Beaucaire.*

❷ Beaucaire, Languedoc-Roussillon

Road traffic here defers to the Canal du Rhône à Sète (Rhône-Sète canal). Beaucaire's one-way street system circles an attractive canal basin where barges and holiday cruisers are moored. Beaucaire was where the Camargue style of bullfighting began, free from weapons and any taint of 'blood on the sand'. One statue in the town celebrates 'Clairon' – not a famous bullfighter, but a bull! Classical and jazz concerts are held at various venues in summer.

Beaucaire's part-ruined hilltop castle offers a good view over the lower Rhône and hosts falconry displays, while the town museum holds many reminders of the days when traffic on the Roman highway – the *Via Domitia* – passed through between Italy and Spain. The town hosted a famous fair from

1217 to the mid-19th century and the museum has exhibits illustrating this.

☐ *24 cours Gambetta*

▶ *Leave Beaucaire following signs to Tarascon.*

❸ Tarascon, Provence

The twin, and often the rival, of Beaucaire across the Rhône, Tarascon is famous for two fictional characters – the river monster called the Tarasque, which is paraded through the town during the annual fair on the last Sunday in June, and Tartarin of Tarascon, the protagonist of *Aventures Prodigieuses de Tartarin de Tarascon* by Alphonse Daudet. The hero of these 'prodigious adventures' features in L'Espace Tartarin in

the Cloître des Cordeliers. Tarascon has cool tree-lined avenues where the sun is held at bay. Its 15th-century castle on a dramatic riverside site displays 17th-century tapestries and houses regular art exhibitions. Close by, the church dedicated to St Martha has a very impressive crypt which is the traditional burial place of Martha herself, the sister of Mary and Lazarus in the Bible story.

☐ *16 boulevard Itam*

▶ *Leave Tarascon on the **D970** as for Avignon. Turn right for St-Michel-de-Frigolet, looping over the **D970** on an elevated bridge.*

Practical and beautiful: the Roman aqueduct at Pont du Gard

4 St-Michel-de-Frigolet, Provence

Among the trees, the spires and towers of a complex of abbey buildings suddenly come into view. A religious community has lived here among the sweet scents of herbs and pinewood since as early as 1133, although there were some years in the 20th century when the monks were dispersed elsewhere. In the public areas of the abbey the buildings include a beautifully decorated basilica completed as recently as 1866. The old abbey farm is now a café; and items in the shop include the modern version of Père Gaucher's Elixir, which featured in one of Daudet's best-known stories.

▶ *Continue to Barbentane, where you should ignore the 'Toutes Directions' sign and go straight on, following the 'Château' sign, then turn right and follow signs into Avignon.*

5 Avignon, Provence

Avignon's heyday was in the 14th century, when the papacy moved the court here from Rome. The heart of the city is dominated by the grand 14th-century palace complex built by Popes Benedict XII and Clement VI and the towers, chapels, churches, cloisters and elegant courtyards which grew up to support it. What matters here is the architecture, since the restored buildings are mostly unfurnished, although Gobelin tapestries hang in the banqueting hall. Near by, the famous bridge of St-Bénézet stretches its remaining arches across the Rhône. Visitors from all over the world come to stroll 'sur le pont d'Avignon'.

The modern town has museums of all kinds, and a hectic summer programme of concerts, plays, dance, painting and sculpture exhibitions.

📄 *41 cours Jean-Jaurès*

▶ *Return from Avignon on the N570 as for Arles. Turn left on the D571, then right for St-Rémy-de-Provence on the D34, entering the town on the D571.*

6 St-Rémy-de-Provence, Provence

St-Rémy is a place that knows how to cope with the relentless summer sun of Provence. There are virtual tunnels of shady plane trees, and cooling water

The well-preserved Château de Tarascon, sitting on the bank of the River Rhône

runs down channels in the alleyways of the old town. The Musée des Alpilles, named after the limestone sierra that rises to the south, contains exhibitions on St-Rémy's history and domestic life. Among townspeople commemorated is the 16th-century seer Nostradamus, whose birthplace can still be seen, but not visited. There is, however, a Nostradamus Museum in the nearby village of Salon de Provence.

On the outskirts of St-Rémy one road leads to a woodland lake at the foot of the Alpilles, another to the former Monastère de St-Paul-de-Mausole, converted into the mental home where Vincent van Gogh spun out his last demented days. In the countryside you may see amateur artists painting their own versions of the Van Gogh scenes.

South of the town lie the extensive ruins of the Greek and Roman settlement of *Glanum*. Many of the artefacts discovered here are displayed in the Musée Archéologique in town.

ⓘ *Place Jean-Jaurès*

RECOMMENDED WALKS

From the tourist office in St-Rémy there is a walk through the outskirts of the town (finishing back on the main Boulevard Mirabeau), which visits the scenes of many of Vincent Van Gogh's paintings – farms, poppy fields, plane and olive trees, and the quarry which appealed to him because of the Japanese-style arrangement of the rocks.

BACK TO NATURE

All over the Camargue you will see the characteristic white horses, often ridden by *gardians* – the Camargue equivalent of cowboys. But look out for the foals. They are born black or grey, and may take as long as five years to grow a fully white coat.

FOR CHILDREN

The easiest thing to arrange in the Camargue is an escorted ride on one of the mysterious Camargue white horses, with a *gardian* to act as guide. Sessions as short as half an hour are offered, and many visit farms where bulls are reared for the ring.

▶ *Leave St-Rémy on the **D5**, then go right on the **D27a** to Les Baux-de-Provence.*

☷ Les Baux-de-Provence, Provence

On a ridge that towers above the southern plain, this hill settlement is split into two distinct parts, each of limestone masonry hard to distinguish at a distance from the living rock. The inhabited quarter, dating mostly from the 16th and 17th centuries, crams shops, museums, galleries, cafés, hotels and restaurants into its narrow lanes. The eerie 'Ville Morte' ('dead city') on the crown of the ridge was the medieval stronghold, which became famous for its 'Courts of Love', courtly rituals in which troubadours vied in composing ardent, flowery verses for aristocratic ladies. It is a now a ruin, brought back to life in summer with daily weaponry demonstrations, including shooting a full-size replica *trebuchet* (catapult), and re-enactments such as the 2010 'assault on the castle', with 1,000 participants.

Just outside the town, on the D27, the Cathédrale d'Images offers a majestic audio-visual presentation. In halls cut into the old bauxite quarries (Les Baux was where aluminium ore was first discovered), 40 projectors continuously show historical and nature-based films.

ⓘ *Maison du Roy*

▶ *From Les Baux-de-Provence, follow the signs to Arles, entering the town on the **N570**.*

☸ Arles, Provence

Phoenicians, Greeks and Romans all established themselves here, but it is the Romans who made Arles the capital of *Provincia*, who have left the most abiding monuments. The elliptical amphitheatre (Arènes) built by the Emperor Hadrian in the 1st century AD still survives, used, alas, for bullfights in the Spanish style as well as the bloodless style of the Camargue; and you can attend concerts and festivals in the semi-circular Augustan theatre (Théâtre Antique). The town's summer calendar is crammed with events having an international flavour as well as those firmly rooted in the traditions of Provence. One of these is the parade of *gardians* – the

Carving on the main doorway of the Romanesque cathedral of St-Trophime, in Arles

Camargue 'cowboys' – on their white horses.

Arles is well supplied with museums strong on paintings, sculptures, antiquities, and Provençal life. The former cathedral and cloisters of St-Trophime, one of the finest cloisters in the south, contain beautiful stone carvings. A favourite walk is along the tree-lined avenue of Les Alyscamps, flanked by ancient tombstones, the remains of Arles' once widespread necropolis.

The Fondation Vincent van Gogh is a magnet for art lovers; it was in Arles that, after a fight with his friend Gauguin, he slashed off his own ear. A memorial to his tormented spirit stands in the quiet and shaded public gardens.

ⓘ *Boulevard des Lices*

▶ *Leave Arles on the **D570** as for Saintes-Maries-de-la-Mer. Go left on the **D36**, right on the **D36b**, then right on the **D37**. Turn left on the **C5** to Méjanes.*

9 Méjanes, Provence

In the very heart of the Camargue, and including some of the shoreline of the lagoon called Étang de Vaccarès, this estate doubles as a leisure centre and a farm. It has its own bullring, in which events are held every weekend during the summer, a restaurant, and stables where horses may be hired for short or full-day rides.

▶ *Rejoin the **D37**. Turn right on the **D570** to the Musée Camarguais.*

10 Musée Camarguais, Provence

Based on an old sheepfold, the Camargue Museum is the best place to find out about the geology and history of this curious area and about the lives of the farmers and how intensive draining turned great areas of previously useless marsh into productive grazing and arable land. A walk from the museum follows the banks of a drainage canal dug as long ago as 1543, and shows the difference between reclaimed land and the original marsh. The museum is

one of the main centres of the Réserve Zoologique et Botanique de la Camargue (Camargue Regional Nature Park) which covers more than 83,000 hectares (205,000 acres) of the Rhône delta.

▶ *Return along the **D570** and watch for the Maison du Parc on the left of the road at Pont du Gau.*

11 Maison du Parc, Provence

Complementary to the Musée Camarguais, this centre (may be closed) explains and illustrates the fascinating wildlife of the park, with an audio-visual theatre and a display on all the brands used on the Camargue horses. Throughout, the emphasis is on the fragility of this marvellous habitat. The good advice is offered that anti-mosquito creams are a wise precaution for anybody exploring the Camargue, particularly in September and October; but to avoid the insects, there is indoor wildlife watching here too. The

picture windows at the rear of the centre overlook a pool where flamingos are often seen.

Close by, there is a privately owned Parc Ornithologique where many species of resident and migrant birds are on show.

▶ *Continue to Saintes-Maries-de-la-Mer.*

12 Saintes-Maries-de-la-Mer, Provence

Often packed with summer visitors, the former fishing village of Saintes-Maries takes its name from the tradition that the three Marys from the Bible story, together with Martha (the sister of Mary and Lazarus), sailed here from Palestine and began evangelising the Camargue.

But, for the gypsy people of Europe, the significant figure in the story is Sarah – in one version an Egyptian or Ethiopian servant who accompanied the Marys; in another, a local woman who helped them ashore. Sarah is venerated as the patron saint of gypsies. Her statue, dressed in rich robes,

is paraded through the town during two festivals in May and October. For the rest of the year it rests in the claustrophobic undercroft of the 9th-century church, illuminated by candles which also throw an eerie glow on a head of Sarah sculpted from Silesian coal.

Just south of the church, the Musée Baroncelli concentrates on local and natural history and folklore.

i 5 avenue Van Gogh

FOR CHILDREN

Just beyond Saintes-Maries-de-la-Mer, look for the sign to the pier where *Tiki III*, a little Mississippi-style sternwheeler, starts its cruises around the mouth of the Petit Rhône. This is an ideal way to wander past the grazings of Camargue horses and bulls.

Les Baux-de-Provence, one of France's most famous hill villages

▶ Follow 'Aigues-Mortes' signs from Saintes-Maries, keeping on the **D38**, **D38c** and **D58**.

SPECIAL TO...

The watery landscape of the Camargue and the Mediterranean climate combine to offer perfect conditions for the cultivation of rice, in fact most of the rice consumed in France is grown here. Each September, the area celebrates the harvest with a Rice Festival, complete with a procession of *Gardians* and folk dancing.
The Bouches-du-Rhône delta also produces 'solar' salt, so named because the sea water is collected in evaporation pools and dried by the sun.
Honey is another speciality, with 75 per cent of France's production coming from this area. Lavender is just one of many varieties.

B Aigues-Mortes,
Languedoc-Roussillon
This town is an amazing survival, extended hardly at all beyond the original rampart walls constructed in the 13th century by Louis IX of France who called here on the seventh and eighth crusades. The walls, towers and fortified gateways remain in place. Inside them, a pleasant town retains the old medieval grid pattern of streets. A statue of St Louis looks down on the activity round the central square, just as his gilded statue graces the arcaded interior of the church. The best view of Aigues-Mortes is from the gallery of the Tour de Constance, once a political and religious prison, which overlooks the town and also puts it in a geographical context among the low-lying lagoons and lakes of the Camargue. But where is the sea? Over the years the Mediterranean has receded, stranding the town. In terms of the sea, Aigues-Mortes became what its name implies – the 'Dead Waters'.

i Place Saint-Louis

▶ Return from Aigues-Mortes following 'Nîmes' signs on the **D979**, **N313** and **N113**, avoiding the 'péage' signs, to Nîmes itself.

SPECIAL TO...

Not only in the Camargue itself, but also in the inland towns, are regular and well-attended bullfights. However, these are not usually of the bloodstained Spanish variety that so many visitors find distasteful. Here the aim of the bullfighter (the *rasetteur*) is not to kill the bull but to get away unscathed with a rosette or some other favour that is tied to its horns. Bulls thus live to fight many times and become skilled operators. Some become as well known as the bullfighters.

SCENIC ROUTES

North of Nîmes the D979 crosses the limestone scrubland of the Garrigues, then descends to the gorges of the Gardon and continues through totally different country of fields and vineyards. On the way to Frigolet and Barbentane, to the south of Avignon, the road runs through pleasant pinewoods with long stretches of picnic sites.

BACK TO NATURE

Of the many species of birds that live in the southern part of the Camargue, the most often illustrated are the flamingos. Watch out also for herons and egrets standing motionless in the water before darting down to spear their prey. Bee-eaters are perhaps the most colourful – look for them perched beside roadsides.

Alsace, Savoie, Burgundy, Lorraine – these towns include four provinces, each with its own independent heritage, separate for centuries from that of France. On the French-German border, Alsace and Lorraine were long contended territories, and even after they merged with France, they were lost again during the years of German occupation following the disastrous war of 1870 until the Allied victory in 1918. The battlefields around Verdun and St-Mihiel were the scene of indescribable carnage during World War I.

For 2,000 years and more, the Rhône/Saône valleys have been major highways, and it is still easy to drive quickly and unseeingly through them. However, off the main route, there is a jigsaw of medieval fishponds, and small towns of great interest.

East of Grenoble lie the majestic passes of the Alps and one of the highest roads in Europe. An exploration of the country of the lost duchy of Savoie shows how France's extensive hydro-electric schemes are landscaped so as not to spoil the glorious mountain scenery in which they are set.

Alsace is a different country once again, France with German names, sweeping vineyards and a strong preoccupation with storks. The Vosges mountains here may pale beside the Alps, but their forests and often cloudy upland ridges have an individual appeal.

Driving conditions are very varied. There are roads across the plains, among great acreages of arable land. Others wind through the vine-clad foothills. But on the Col de l'Iseran and the upper reaches of the Col de la Croix de Fer, you are in genuine Alpine country. The first of these passes can be swept by icy winds, the second can create a curious vertigo. All the roads, though, cope with summer tourist traffic.

There is splendid vineyard country here, producing wines as different as Burgundy and the Rieslings of Alsace. Many sophisticated gourmets consider that the country's finest 'table' is in Lyon.

Nancy

If you are expecting some modest provincial town, Nancy will come as a surprise. At the heart of this historic capital of Lorraine, richly gilded Place Stanislas is one of the most elegant squares in France. Look for the lovely late Gothic Palais Ducal containing the Musée Historique Lorrain, for the Église des Cordeliers with the tomb of the dukes of Lorraine, for the superb medieval gateway and former prison of the Porte de la Craffe, and for the beautiful buildings of the old town. The Musée de Fer illustrates the history of iron, for generations a major industry in Lorraine. You can watch the glass-blowers in the crystal works of Daum.

Lyon

Lyon is a handsome city. It has grand, sweeping quays on two rivers, the Rhône and the Saône, whose waters converge in the southern suburbs. Many notable buildings stand on the Presqu'île, the peninsula between the rivers. Here is the Musée des Beaux Arts with others devoted to textiles and decorative arts, printing and the history of banknotes. The 19th-century Basilica of Notre-Dame-des-Fourvière stands on the skyline above the streets of the old quarter in the loop of the Saône. A funicular links it with the lower town. Another climbs to twin Roman theatres still in use today.

The Lumière brothers, pioneers of moving film, worked in Lyon. There is a decorative mosaic, featuring famous figures such as Buster Keaton, near the Institut Lumière, which regularly shows vintage films.

Grenoble

Grenoble, at the confluence of the Rivers Isère and Drac, is dominated by the soaring cliffs of the Massif de la Chartreuse. Cable-cars whisk you to the viewpoint Fort de la Bastille, looking to the mountain ranges of Chamrousse and Vercors.

Beautifully sited, and with extensive parks and gardens, Grenoble offers music and drama, the prestigious Musée de Grenoble which contains paintings and sculpture, and has well-presented museums of automata, natural history, the Resistance and the region of Dauphiné.

Explore the gracious old quarter, admire Grenoble's modern architecture, and note its revived enthusiasm for the urban tram.

Strasbourg

Seat of the Council of Europe and the European Parliament, Strasbourg is also where, in the 15th century, Gutenberg invented modern printing. His memory is still revered.

The heart of the city is a river island. Look for the intriguing quarter called La Petite-France, where lovely old houses stand by the restored navigation canal.

Strasbourg has beautiful Renaissance and half-timbered buildings, a glorious cathedral and a cluster of museums in the 18th-century Palais Rohan. You can take a river cruise, stroll through botanic gardens and enjoy the Parc de l'Orangerie created in 1804 for Napoleon's Josephine.

Opposite: the cathedral of St-Etienne, in Toul, has a splendid Flamboyant frontage
Below: Nancy prides itself on its classical townscape

Visions of
War & Peace

Except for part of the valley of the Moselle, this tour avoids the industrial districts of Lorraine in favour of the agricultural south around Nancy. There are peaceful rural landscapes here, but they have bitter memories. The Franco-Prussian War of 1870 ravaged Lorraine, as did the battles of the 20th century.

3 DAYS • 300KM • 187 MILES

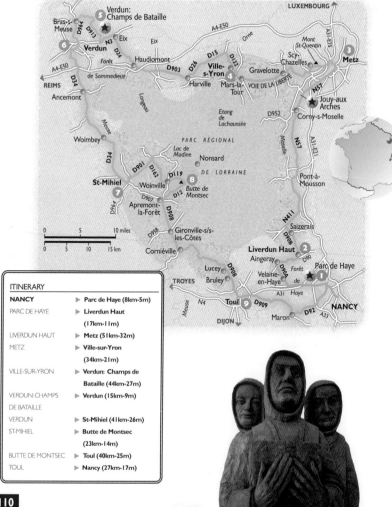

ITINERARY	
NANCY	▶ **Parc de Haye (8km-5m)**
PARC DE HAYE	▶ **Liverdun Haut**
	(17km-11m)
LIVERDUN HAUT	▶ **Metz (51km-32m)**
METZ	▶ **Ville-sur-Yron**
	(34km-21m)
VILLE-SUR-YRON	▶ **Verdun: Champs de**
	Bataille (44km-27m)
VERDUN: CHAMPS	▶ **Verdun (15km-9m)**
DE BATAILLE	
VERDUN	▶ **St-Mihiel (41km-26m)**
ST-MIHIEL	▶ **Butte de Montsec**
	(23km-14m)
BUTTE DE MONTSEC	▶ **Toul (40km-25m)**
TOUL	▶ **Nancy (27km-17m)**

ⓘ *14 place Stanislas, Nancy*

▶ *Leave Nancy as for Paris on the **A31**. Take the 'Parc de Haye' exit.*

❶ Parc de Haye, Lorraine
This extensive leisure park is laid out on the site of a World War II American army camp; so it is appropriate that its motor museum has both civil and military displays. You will see examples of Bugatti, Delahaye and Jaguar among the cars.

▶ *Turn right from the park exit following the **D400** sign, then right through Velaine-en-Haye and Aingeray. Go left over the bridge on the **D90b**, through traffic lights, then left for Liverdun Haut.*

❷ Liverdun Haut, Lorraine
Crowning a bluff above a wooded curve of the Moselle, and providing lovely views over the river, this little medieval town was once the favoured summer residence of the bishops of Toul. Many old buildings survive. The tourist office is in the 16th-century fortified gateway, and there is an arcaded square of the same period. Dedicated to St Euchaire, the church is basically 12th century. Look for the saint's tomb with his beheaded effigy. Euchaire was martyred at nearby Pompey in AD362.

ⓘ *5 place de la Fontaine*

┌─────────────────────────┐
│ **BACK TO NATURE**

See how the currents of air sweeping up the wooded ridge from the Moselle suit the birds of Liverdun Haut. Kestrels nest in the old buildings and hunt above the woodlands. Kites are here too, as well as swifts, swallows and martins darting around the streets.
└─────────────────────────┘

Medieval Liverdun, once favoured by the bishops of Toul

▶ *Return to the **D90b** and continue through Saizerais. Go right on the **D907** then, immediately after the 'Saizerais' board, turn left along Route de Villers. Go right at a give way sign, then left on the **N57** to Metz.*

┌─────────────────────────┐
│ **FOR HISTORY BUFFS**

Jouy-aux-Arches on the N57 takes it name from the high masonry arches, built almost 1,900 years ago in the reign of the emperor Trajan as part of the Roman aqueduct to Metz. Metz was already an old town when Julius Caesar conquered Gaul. The Romans fortified it, their walls forming the battlefield fortifications.
└─────────────────────────┘

❸ Metz, Lorraine
Old fortifications are a reminder that Metz has been besieged, captured and relieved many times over the centuries. Two memorials commemorate its return to France following World War I, after 47 years of German rule, and yet again in 1944.

and the simple château built in 1762 by the Bishop of Metz.

FOR HISTORY BUFFS

Along the D903 near Verdun are certain kilometre stones which nominate the road the 'Voie de la Liberté' (Freedom Way). Allied troops swept the German forces along it in 1944.

FOR HISTORY BUFFS

Turn left along the rue Robert Schuman in Scy-Chazelles, on the way from Metz to Ville-sur-Yron, to visit the modest home, now a museum, where the great French statesman (1886–1963) worked out his plans for a united Europe. Schuman played an important role in the creation of NATO, the Council of Europe and the European Coal and Steel Community, the first step towards the EU. It is still used as a meeting place for groups and organisations concerned with Europe's development.

Despite being an industrial centre, Metz has colourful parks and gardens, a lake and attractive riverside areas, and 45 hectares (110 acres) of the centre have been redeveloped as the Quartier Amphitheatre. The cathedral (St-Étienne) features a soaring interior with intricate stained glass. Archaeology, art and history are all under one roof at La Cour d'Or Musée d'Art et d'Histoire. The Renaissance section is particularly enchanting, as is Roman Metz, displayed through sarcophagi, pottery and architecture.

Opened in 2010, the stunning Centre Pompidou-Metz is a cultural centre incorporating performance spaces and the Musée National d'Art Moderne, an annexe of the Centre Pompidou in Paris.

ℹ️ *Place d'Armes*

▶ *Leave Metz by the N3 through Longeville. At traffic lights in Le Ban-St-Martin, turn right on the D103w for*

Metz has been the prize of armies since Roman times

Mont St-Quentin, following the hairpinned rue Fort. Down from Mont St-Quentin, turn right at the 'stop' sign in the village (this is Scy-Chazelles), go left down rue Leduchat and continue downhill at the next 'stop' sign. Pass rue Robert Schuman on your left. At traffic lights turn right and follow 'Verdun' signs to Gravelotte, then go straight on along the D903 through Mars-la-Tour. Turn right on the D952, then left on the D132 to Ville-sur-Yron.

4 Ville-sur-Yron, Lorraine
In 1990, a fascinating trail was laid out in this village, which allows you to 'read' the architecture, building materials, history and way of life of a typical Lorraine agricultural settlement. It leads over the 19th-century bridge to the watermill, a landlord's and a labourer's farm, the 12th-century church

▶ *Continue on the D132, then go left on the D15, which becomes the D26 to Harville. Rejoin the D903 as for Verdun. Go right on the D24, then left on the D24a and left on the N3 into Verdun. Turn right at the traffic lights as for Paris, then watch for a sharp right turn following 'Champs de Bataille' boards. This is the D112. Go left at the crossroads on to the D913, follow 'Ossuaire' signs, then go left as for Verdun.*

5 Verdun: Champs de Bataille, Lorraine
In 1916 the Germans launched a ferocious attack against the French lines northeast of Verdun: colossal artillery bombardments, mines, flame-

TOUR 17

throwers and poison gas were all employed. In the next few months, literally hundreds of thousands of troops died in the trenches, but the French essentially held the line. After the war, the ground of the battlefields was so ravaged that it was forested over.

Along the D112 and the D913 you will find forts, trenches, memorials and utterly devastated villages. The hilltop Ossuaire (Ossuary) de Douaumont is the last resting place for the bones of 130,000 soldiers on both sides, and offers a regular audio-visual programme on life in the trenches. As you walk to the Fort de Douaumont, you might wonder why the French high command in 1915 decided to leave this greatest underground stronghold in Europe virtually unguarded.

▶ *Continue to Bras-sur-Meuse and turn left to Verdun.*

6 Verdun, Lorraine
Linked with other 'martyred towns' such as Hiroshima, Nagasaki, Coventry and Warsaw, Verdun is the World Capital of Peace. Its vast underground citadel has tableaux of

wartime scenes, and of the sombre moment in 1920 when France's Unknown Soldier was chosen. He now lies under the Arc de Triomphe in Paris.

Attractively sited on a curve of the Meuse, Verdun enjoys riverside quays, a fine Romanesque cathedral and the former bishop's palace, gardens and sports grounds, as well as prehistoric displays, paintings, furnishings and ceramics in the 16th-century Musée de la Princerie. Try the *dragées* – the sugared almonds which have been made in Verdun to a secret recipe since the 13th century.

[i] *Pavillon Japiot, avenue du Général Mangin*

▶ *Leave Verdun on the D34 through Dugny, then go left on the D901 to St-Mihiel.*

7 St-Mihiel, Lorraine
Best known in history for its strategic position in the St-Mihiel salient – the defensive ring created by the Germans in 1918 – this little town also has the notable Benedictine abbey church of St Michel, with a 12th-century Romanesque portal and, in its light and airy interior, 80 beautifully carved choir stalls

from the and in the look for wo century scul a pupil of Mi Benedictines' ...y, itself a masterpiece of Lorraine design, survives with 8,000 valuable books and illuminated manuscripts.

[i] *Rue du Palais de Justice*

▶ *Leave St-Mihiel as for Chaillon. Go right on the D162 and left on the D119 through Woinville to Montsec. Turn right on the D12 then follow 'American monument' signs.*

FOR CHILDREN

Turn left off the route at Woinville for Nonsard on the northeast shore of the reservoir called Étang de Madine. Here youngsters can enjoy mini golf, cyclocross and pedaloes, as relief from the grim memories of war all around.

The impressive Benedictine library in St-Mihiel

8 Butte de Montsec, Lorraine

It was the Americans who smashed through the St-Mihiel salient in September 1918. The US 1st Army's memorial is a massive rotunda on this beautiful viewpoint summit overlooking the Étang de Madine, with a relief map illustrating the course of the battle. Ironically, American troops had to fire on the memorial to subdue a German machine-gun post here in 1944. It was later completely restored.

▶ *Return to the **D12** and turn right. Go left on the **D908** to Toul.*

9 Toul, Lorraine

Almost ringed by the Moselle, the Canal de l'Est and the canal linking the Marne with the Rhine, the fortress city of Toul once had the status of an independent enclave within the dukedom of Lorraine and, as the heart of a diocese and a free imperial city, was very important in medieval times. Old town gateways survive, as do the 17th-century walls, and the cathedral (St-Étienne) shows a splendid 15th-century Flamboyant frontage to the Place Charles de Gaulle.

You should look at the decorated cloisters of the town's other principal church, St Gengoult. With all the water near by, Toul welcomes anglers, and the yacht basin is enlivened by the spray of a fountain in the centre.

i *Parvis de la Cathédrale*

▶ *Leave Toul on the **N4** as for Nancy. Go under the bridge, then right on the **D909** to Maron. Turn left on the **D92** and return to Nancy.*

The town centre of Toul

Secrets of the
Rhône Valley

The landscape changes from level plains scattered with ponds to beautiful vineyards in the foothills and gentle forest passes. Wildlife parks display waterfowl and birds of prey. There is a spa, and one of the loveliest towns in the Lyonnais commemorates a saintly man whose life's work relieved the sufferings of the poor.

4 DAYS • 352KM • 219½ MILES

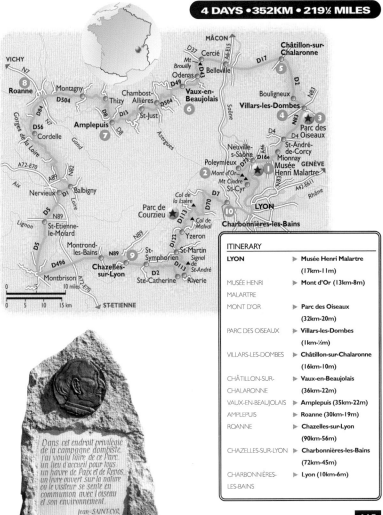

ITINERARY		
LYON	▶	**Musée Henri Malartre** (17km-11m)
MUSÉE HENRI MALARTRE	▶	**Mont d'Or** (13km-8m)
MONT D'OR	▶	**Parc des Oiseaux** (32km-20m)
PARC DES OISEAUX	▶	**Villars-les-Dombes** (1km-½m)
VILLARS-LES-DOMBES	▶	**Châtillon-sur-Chalaronne** (16km-10m)
CHÂTILLON-SUR-CHALARONNE	▶	**Vaux-en-Beaujolais** (36km-22m)
VAUX-EN-BEAUJOLAIS	▶	**Amplepuis** (35km-22m)
AMPLEPUIS	▶	**Roanne** (30km-19m)
ROANNE	▶	**Chazelles-sur-Lyon** (90km-56m)
CHAZELLES-SUR-LYON	▶	**Charbonnières-les-Bains** (72km-45m)
CHARBONNIÈRES-LES-BAINS	▶	**Lyon** (10km-6m)

Dans cet endroit privilégié de la campagne dombiste, j'ai voulu faire de ce Parc un lieu d'accueil pour tous, un havre de Paix et de Repos, un livre ouvert sur la nature où le visiteur se sente en communion avec l'oiseau et son environnement.

Jean SAINT-CYR

*St-Cyr, go right on the **D65**. Continue straight on uphill at the 'stop' sign, then keep right on the **D92** for Mont Cindre. After Mont Cindre, go straight on at a crossroads on the **D90** signed 'Fortin du Mont Thou'. Return to the cross-roads and turn right, then go right on the **D73** to Poleymieux-au-Mont-d'Or.*

2 Mont d'Or, Rhône Valley
Follow the main route to Poleymieux over Mont d'Or ('Golden Hill') above Lyon, but be sure to stop off for occasional strolls, and to admire the views. There are several pleasant villages on the hillsides, as well as farms and woodlands. Mont Cindre, beside a telecommunications tower, is a favourite place for people from Lyon who take to the hills at weekends. Many of them enjoy the walk that starts at the hermitage.

The best 360-degree panoramic view is from Mont Thou, as you walk over the grasslands beside a hilltop military camp.

i Place Bellecour, Lyon

Lyon is a handsome city in the valley of the Rhône

FOR CHILDREN

The Parc de la Tête d'Or, on the banks of the Rhône in Lyon, has a lake, a zoo with 1,000 animals, go-cart track and pony rides.

▶ *Leave Lyon on the **D433** as for Neuville. Go through Caluire-et-Cuire, then turn right at 'Musée de l'Automobile' sign and follow 'Musée' signs along a complicated route to the Musée Henri Malartre.*

1 Musée Henri Malartre,
Rhône Valley
In the attractive, high-set Château Rochetaillée and the exhibition halls in its grounds, is an impeccably maintained collection of really rare cars. The Hugot, Thieulin, Noël Beret and the very early steam-

powered Secretand, displayed in the Musée Henri Malartre, are the only survivors of these makes in the world. A separate hall displays several Gordini racing cars, built by the dogged but perpetually broke French constructor after whom it is named.

Hitler's Mercedes is here, and so is Pope John Paul II's Renault Espace, as well as Edith Piaf's Packard. Look for the bizarre gyroscope-equipped 1926 Monotrace tandem car, and the huge battery-powered Stela which ran as a taxi in Lyon till 1953. There is also a strong collection of cycles and motorcycles (1898–1954).

▶ *Return by the same route to the **D433** and turn left. Go right over the suspension bridge into Couzon, then left on the **D51** into St-Romain. Turn right on the **D89**. In*

FOR CHILDREN

At the Musée Ampère in Poleymieux children are encouraged to try 18 of Ampère's original electrical experiments, including some with magnets. This is fun as well as a fine learning experience, and perfectly safe at the power levels employed.

FOR HISTORY BUFFS

In Poleymieux the Maison d'Ampère is devoted to the brilliant and engagingly eccentric Lyon-born physicist André-Marie Ampère (1775–1836), who gave his name to the standard unit of electric current. It also has an amazing display of historic electrical equipment.

▶ In Poleymieux-au-Mont-d'Or bend right after gantry traffic lights, still on the **D73**, and continue via Curis-au-Mont-d'Or to Neuville-centre on the **D16**. Go straight on along the **D16e** through Montanay, then left at the T-junction (this is the **N83**) through Mionnay. Turn right into the Parc des Oiseaux.

3 Parc des Oiseaux, Rhône Valley

This is one of the foremost bird parks in Europe, with a strong commitment to endangered species. It lies within a public estate near Villars-les-Dombes that takes full advantage of its situation in woodland circling an attractive lake.

Eagles, vultures, parrots and parakeets have enclosures in the woods, and there is a tropical bird house, while pelicans, swans, geese and flamingos favour the water. At the large arena you can watch bird-in-flight presentations, featuring around 20 species. The guided tour, by 'tourist train', takes 30 minutes. A walk round to see the park in all its details might occupy two hours. There is an adventure playground and a picnic area.

▶ Continue to Villars-les-Dombes, eventually leaving the village on the **D2** as for Châtillon.

4 Villars-les-Dombes, Rhône Valley

With a fine Gothic church, a road system which craftily keeps through traffic away from the narrow streets of the pleasant and colourful centre, and an excellent natural history bookshop, Villars is where to start any exploration of the curious plateau district known as Les Dombes.

Here there are a thousand pools, lakes or meres dug as fishponds from the 12th century onwards. They are now split between angling waters and commercial fisheries for carp, tench, roach and pike. Around 2,000 tonnes are taken every year, to make this one of the great inland fishery districts of France. Ask locally about dishes such as fillet of royal carp.

ℹ️ *3 place Hôtel de Ville*

▶ Continue on the **D2** to Châtillon-sur-Chalaronne.

Baby ostriches at the Parc des Oiseaux – Villars-les-Dombes

BACK TO NATURE

Beyond Villars, the lakes and ponds of Les Dombes are havens for wildlife. On the Étang Forêt and the Étang du Château at Bouligneux you can expect to see teal and mallard, coots, herons and grebes.

5 Châtillon-sur-Chalaronne, Rhône Valley

Few small towns in France have been awarded four stars in the national *villages fleuris* ('villages in bloom') competition, but Châtillon deserves every one. You should spend time admiring the blaze of blossoms in parks and gardens, beside the banks of the River Chalaronne and its tributary streams, in window boxes and hanging baskets, and decorating all the bridges.

Châtillon cherishes some beautifully maintained buildings to match the flowers. The covered market hall of 1670 is a gem, some of the old town ramparts survive, and the brickwork Church of St André dates from the 16th century. The famous Châtillon triptych of 1527 is displayed in the dignified town hall. Its three biblical

scenes – the sleeping apostles, Christ taken from the cross and the Resurrection – are beautifully painted and restored.

The old Apothecairerie has a fine collection of earthenware pots from which 18th-century pharmacists concocted their herbal remedies. You can see where some of the prescribed salts ate away the painted surface of the pots!

[i] *Place du Champ de Foire*

RECOMMENDED WALKS

Three walks, mostly on country roads with occasional farm tracks, are suggested by the tourist office at Châtillon. One visits four of the little lakes for which the district is famous. The others go to the old castle ramparts and the banks of the Relevant stream.

wine *cave*. The village even has signs for both names at its boundaries. A little automaton theatre acts out scenes from the book, and there's a small Gabriel Chevallier museum with books and documents. This is one of the most beautifully located of the Beaujolais wine-growing villages, and much of it may be tasted locally.

However, *Clochemerle* is perhaps best remembered for the ceremonial inauguration of the public toilet. La Pisotière de Clochemerle stands on a terrace above the beautiful vine-planted valley.

▶ *Take the Lamure road, leaving Vaux on the 'Le Sottier poids lourds' road, the* **D49***. Follow 'Lamure' signs – ignoring a left turn for Les Buissières. Go left on the* **D44** *to St-Cyr. Turn right on the* **D504** *to Allières, left on the* **D485***, then right on the* **D98** *and over the level crossing. Go straight on through St-Just, then follow signs to Amplepuis.*

SPECIAL TO...

The slopes of Mont Brouilly, between Vaux-en-Beaujolais and Amplepuis, are packed with vineyards whose geometrical lines, at different angles, create a beautiful pattern on the hillsides. Available locally, *Côte de Brouilly* is one of the fine *crus* of Beaujolais wine, with many individual producers.

FOR HISTORY BUFFS

In Châtillon you can see the house where, in 1617, 'Monsieur Vincent' lived as the parish priest. Born in 1580, Vincent de Paul led an eventful early life, having been captured by corsairs on a voyage in 1605 and sold into slavery in Tunis. He was employed by the French royal family after his escape and before he came to Châtillon. Touched by the plight of the poor people of the town, he founded the first of his many charitable organisations, which led to the great Society of St Vincent de Paul (he was canonised in 1737).

The delightfully fragrant town of Châtillon-sur-Chalaronne

▶ *Leave Châtillon on the* **D17***, which becomes the* **D37** *through Belleville and Cercié, then go left on the* **D43** *and left on the* **D43e** *to Mont Brouilly. Return to the* **D43** *and turn left. Turn right on the* **D19***, then right on the* **D49** *to Vaux-en-Beaujolais.*

6 Vaux-en-Beaujolais, Rhône Valley

Gabriel Chevallier immortalised this village among the hillside vineyards as the fictional setting for his famous satirical novel *Clochemerle*, and several enterprises here continue the *Clochemerle* name, including the

7 Amplepuis, Rhône Valley

In this little industrial town, the Musée Barthélémy Thimonnier celebrates a most heroic failure. Barthélémy Thimonnier was an apprentice tailor here. In 1825, having seen the laborious work of the seamstresses, he invented the sewing machine.

He was spurned in Paris. London businessmen paid him an insulting sum for his design. Soon after his dejected return to France, the sewing machine revolutionised the production of clothes. But by then Thimonnier had died – still poor, and still unknown.

ⓘ *Place de l'Hôtel de Ville*

▶ *Leave Amplepuis on the **D8**. Take the **D504** to Roanne.*

8 Roanne, Rhône Valley
Backing on to the Loire, Roanne is on a well-maintained canal along which visitor cruises are run. It is an historic textile town, and old techniques of spinning and weaving are demonstrated at the Musée du Tissage at nearby Bussières. If you enjoy ceramics, visit the Musée Déchelette, which has beautiful displays of French and Italian ware, in addition to its fine arts and Gallo-Roman collections.

Roanne keeps a foothold in the wine business, although the great days when it shipped barge-loads of barrels to Paris are long since gone. You can taste some of the *Côte Roannaise* wine in the town-centre *caveau*.

ⓘ *Place Maréchal de Lattre de Tassigny*

The countryside round Roanne reflects its heyday as a major producer of wine

---

SPECIAL TO...

Many gourmet centres were originally on the main road from Paris to the Riviera. Roanne, on the N7, is now bypassed by the traffic on the Autoroute de Soleil, but it remains a famous gastronomic town. The restaurant of the Troisgros brothers' hotel is classed as one of the finest tables in France.

▶ *Leave Roanne on the **N7** as for Lyon. Go right on the **D43** as for Varennes then right on the **D84** as for Vernay. As soon as you enter Commelle-Vernay turn left as for Cordelle. Follow the **D56** and **N82** into Balbigny. Go right at the traffic lights to Nervieux, then left on the **D5** through St-Étienne-le-Molard. Go left on the **D8** into Montbrison, left on the **D496**, then straight ahead on the **N89**. Take a right turn to Chazelles-sur-Lyon.*

FOR CHILDREN

The Musée d'Allard on the boulevard de la Préfecture in Montbrison, on the way to Chazelles-sur-Lyon, has several individual themes, but is best known for its collection of dolls and puppets from countries all over the world.

---

9 Chazelles-sur-Lyon, Rhône Valley
Off the main roads in the wooded hills north of St-Étienne, Chazelles owes a great deal to the crusaders who brought back from the east the secret of making felt. Chazelles used this new-found expertise to turn itself into a great hat-making centre. The extensive Atelier-Musée du Chapeau explains, with guided tours, audio-visual presentations and working machinery, all the techniques of preparation, manufacture and fashion. On display is a collection of more than 500 felt hats of all styles, including a collection of chefs' *toques*. The museum also devotes space to the history of the town, from its days as a junction of Roman roads.

ⓘ *9 place Jean-Baptiste Galland*

▶ Leave Chazelles on the **D103**, which becomes the **D2**, to Ste-Catherine. Go straight on as for Mornant, then turn left on the **D63** into Riverie and left on the **D113** via St-André-la-Côte to St-Martin. Follow signs to Yzeron, go left as for Plan d'Eau, left on the **D489** as for Duerne, then right on the **D113**. Continue straight on at Col de Malval, then at Col de la Luère go straight on along the **D24** as for Lyon. Watch for a sudden left turn on to the **D70**. Go through Poillonnay then turn right on the **D7** as for Lyon into Charbonnières-les-Bains, then make a left turn for Charbonnières-centre.

BACK TO NATURE

Turn left at Col de Malval for the Parc de Courzieu. Here, not only are wolves, lynx and wildcats on show, but free-flying displays by eagles, vultures and falcons also take place in a 1,000-seat auditorium.

---

⑩ Charbonnières-les-Bains, Rhône Valley
Lyon is one of several French cities to have a totally different-looking spa town just beyond its outskirts, well away from the familiar busy streets. The first mineral spring here was traditionally discovered by a donkey on its last legs, which regained its vigour by drinking from it.

Whatever its origins, Charbonnières developed into a full-scale spa and health resort with thermal baths, a pump house, a casino and elegant

---

RECOMMENDED WALKS

Stop off on the way from Chazelles to Charbonnières and in St-André-la-Côte, or from a left-hand bend on the route beyond it, take the waymarked path to the Signal de St-André. In clear weather the dramatic view extends from a series of hill villages to the mountain wall of the Alps.

---

villas in discreetly wooded grounds. It has good sports facilities, shaded footpaths and a fine array of shops.

▶ Follow 'Lyon-centre' signs and return to Lyon.

SCENIC ROUTES

From Mont Cindre wonderful views open up of Lyon, the Rhône valley and the Alps.
After Châtillon there is a splendid outlook to the hillside vineyards of Beaujolais.
On the D504 to Roanne, look for the gorgeous hilltop setting of Thizy.
The Lac de Villarest reservoir is very attractive from the D56 between Roanne and Chazelles; a view of wooded gorges with an abandoned castle standing on a flooded rock.
There is a magnificent valley view to the right of the D113 after Riverie, on the way from Chazelles to Charbonnières.

Vineyard in the Beaujolais region

The French Alps

This is essentially a mountain tour among the wild and magnificent landscapes of the French Alps. Check the *ouvert-fermé* (open/closed) signs – in most years the route is not fully open till mid-June – and be ready for some steep gradients and exposed hairpinned climbs.

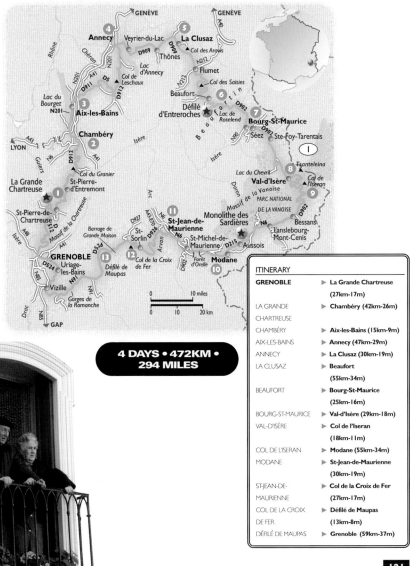

4 DAYS • 472KM • 294 MILES

ℹ️ *14 rue de la République, Grenoble*

▶ *Leave Grenoble for Le Sappey on the **D512**, then continue to St-Pierre-de-Chartreuse. Turn left and follow signs to the Musée de la Grande Chartreuse, using the one-way system.*

1 La Grande Chartreuse, Rhône-Alpes

High on the west side of the Massif de la Chartreuse stands La Grande Chartreuse, the matriarchal house of the Carthusian monks, on ground that is under snow for more than half the year. Its founder, St Bruno, built the first monastery here in 1084.

The monks lead an austere life of study, meditation, solitude and prayer. No visitors are allowed in La Grande Chartreuse itself, and cars may not use the road to it. However, a fine museum has been created at La Correrie, by the end of the public road. It explains and illustrates the monastic life, as well as the history of the Order and the difficulties experienced by the monks here (they were expelled from the monastery during the Revolution, and again between 1903 and 1940).

The famous Chartreuse liqueurs, the profits from whose sales fund the Order's charitable works, are distilled elsewhere.

▶ *Return to St-Pierre-de-Chartreuse and turn left to rejoin the **D512**. Follow this road and the **D912** to Chambéry.*

2 Chambéry, Rhône-Alpes

Why the elephants, you may wonder, on the great fountain in the pleasant centre here? They commemorate the Duc de Boigne, who made his military reputation and his fortune in the East, before retiring to Chambéry to indulge his passion for town planning.

Above the arcaded streets and courtyards of the old quarter stands the castle of the dukes of Savoie, whose territory stretched from Lake Geneva to the Mediterranean and included regions of modern Italy.

The Italian connection persists in the Musée des Beaux-Arts, which has a splendid display of Italian paintings. Local history collections are housed in the Musée Savoisien.

Galerie Eurêka is an exciting science centre, designed to appeal particularly to young

Fontaine des Éléphants, one of the sights of Chambéry

visitors. Three main galleries are devoted to mountains: geology, hazards and man's attempts at taming them.

In the cathedral (look for more elephant motifs), some interior details such as the apparently vaulted ceiling are actually 19th-century attempts at *trompe l'oeil* paintwork.

ℹ️ *5 bis place du Palais de Justice*

▶ *Leave Chambéry for Aix-les-Bains on the **N201**.*

BACK TO NATURE

Approaching Aix-les-Bains, the N201 runs beside the shore of Lac du Bourget. Just before Tresserve, stroll over to look at the reed beds and watch the comings and goings of the great crested grebes. Coots, pochards and little grebes can also be seen on the water, and there are grey herons around the margins.

3 Aix-les-Bains, Rhône-Alpes

Starting at the banks of the Lac du Bourget, the most extensive mountain lake in France, the town rises from a cruise-boat harbour and a lakeside promenade to a very stylish town centre. Aix-les-Bains is an elegant and well-equipped spa resort. Its springs were known to the Romans, and later patrons were Napoleon's family and Queen Victoria.

Colourful gardens, old and new-style fountains and pleasant woodland walks are scattered around. Top-class sports facilities are provided, especially water sports on the lake, and the mountains are always in view. Relics of Roman times include a Temple of Diana and a restored archway facing the Thermes Nationaux. Guided tours – on which you are encouraged to wear a toga – explore the Roman remains, the original baths and the statues preserved in the Musée Lapidaire.

On a hillside boulevard, the Musée Faure houses a valuable art collection. Look for fine paintings and sculpture by Degas, Pissarro, Rodin and Corot.

$\boxed{i}$ *Place Maurice Mollard*

▶ *Continue on the **N201**, then go right on the **D911**. Turn left on the **D31**, right on the **D5** and go straight on as for Le Châtelard on the **D911**. Turn sharp left on the **D912** over Col de Leschaux. Go left on the **N508** to Annecy.*

4 Annecy, Rhône-Alpes
You can see how dearly the Annéciens love their pure and beautiful mountain-rimmed lake (Lac d'Annecy). They have spurned any encroachment on the lakeside parks and gardens which are areas of general relaxation as well as wonderful mountain viewpoints; and they make an attractive feature of the rivers and canals which thread through the lovely old quarter of the town.

Lake cruises are a favourite excursion here, but in a place ideally laid out for aimless

strolling around, or for clip-clopping along in the *calèches* (open carriages) which ply for hire, there are also specific attractions on land. Visit the castle museum, for instance. Go to prison – or, at least, to the Palais de l'Île, the old jail, mint and courthouse (which now houses a small history museum). The restored château houses a local museum.

In the evenings, the old town (pedestrianised) is lively and chattering as its pavement restaurants and cafés fill up. Then the lights reflect in the waters lapping quietly by.

$\boxed{i}$ *I rue Jean-Jaurès*

▶ *Leave Annecy for Veyrier-du-Lac on the **D909**. Continue through Thônes to La Clusaz.*

5 La Clusaz, Rhône-Alpes
Here is the first of many Alpine ski resorts on this tour, occupying a valley site crammed between jagged peaks. In summer when, as throughout the region, the weather can be very changeable, La Clusaz seems to be waiting impatiently until the snows return, bringing with them thousands of winter sports enthusiasts.

However, summer visitors are by no means neglected. The Bureau des Guides will introduce you to rock-climbing in half-day courses, and grass skis are available for hire. You can also, briefly or at length, try your hand at canoeing, fishing, skating, tennis, horse- or pony-

Aix-les-Bains is a great centre for boat trips on the Lac du Bourget

riding, fencing, archery, pistol-shooting and pottery. Folklore groups enliven the evenings.

In among the typical shops, chalets, bars, cafés, hotels and restaurants of a ski resort, La Clusaz has a most attractive modern church. Look for the beautiful stained-glass windows, illustrating work in the mountains, fields and forests.

ⓘ *Place de l'Eglise*

SPECIAL TO...

Before La Clusaz you will begin to see signs to the farms where the delicious traditional Savoie cheeses are produced. Most popular is *Reblochon* – check for the green *'fermier'* label guaranteeing that it is farm-made. Look also for *Tomme de Savoie* and the strong goats'-milk *Chevrotin des Aravis*.

RECOMMENDED WALKS

La Clusaz has a network of summer walks, some from the top stations of cable-car and chairlift lines. Ask at the tourist office, where you can also book for guided walks to lakes and mountain viewpoints, good areas for alpine flowers and the secret trails of the old *contrebandiers* (smugglers).

FOR CHILDREN

La Clusaz has a summer toboggan run called the *luge d'été*. Youngsters (and adults) have a choice of two smooth metal pistes sweeping down the hillside for 800m (2,620 feet). Here also, on summer evenings, there are free shows in the village by jugglers, clowns and puppeteers.

La Clusaz is one of Haute Savoie's oldest and biggest ski resorts

▶ Continue on the **D909** over the Col des Aravis to Flumet, then go straight ahead on the **D218B** over the Col des Saisies and follow signs to Beaufort. Go through Beaufort as for Bourg-St-Maurice.

FOR HISTORY BUFFS

At the breezy summit of the Col des Saisies, on the stretch between La Clusaz and Beaufort, look for the monument to the daring exploit in August 1944, when a daylight wave of RAF planes parachuted arms and ammunition to the Resistance fighters of Savoie.

❻ Beaufort, Rhône-Alpes
At Beaufort, a village in a spruce-clad mountain valley, you may wonder where the road can possibly go next. In fact, it slices through the amazing rock cleft of the Défile d'Entreroches, then up a steep hairpinned pass with magnificent views of the valley left behind.

A good excursion centre, Beaufort is the heart of the Beaufortain district. In its co-operative you can watch the making of 'the prince of Gruyères' – Beaufort cheese, produced with milk from the upland farms – and even help in the process.

Eastwards, the Lac de Roselend reservoir lies in a deep depression among the mountains. Then the road battles up through 10 hairpin bends towards a notch in the skyline. This is an exciting landscape of mountain torrents, scree slopes and high snow-filled gullies. Wildflowers put on their brave summer display.

ⓘ *Grande Rue*

▶ *Continue to Bourg-St-Maurice.*

7 Bourg-St-Maurice,
Rhône-Alpes

Bourg-St-Maurice lies in a spectacular setting overlooked by cliffs and tiers of chalets. Green in summer, the hill slopes to the southeast are in the easily reached skiing area of Les Arcs, upgraded for the 1992 Winter Olympics.

Down in the town itself there is a woodland park beside the compensation reservoir of a hydro-electric scheme. Bourg-St-Maurice is good for sports such as white-water canoeing and rafting. Horse and pony trips can also be arranged. There is a minerals and crystals display, and another co-operative where Beaufort cheese is made.

The satellite village of Vulmis, along a steep road to the southwest, has a chapel with beautiful 15th-century frescoes.

And at Hauteville-Gondon, a couple of kilometres to the south, you will find an unexpectedly baroque 17th-century church.

[i] *Place de la Gare*

FOR CHILDREN

Bourg-St-Maurice has installed a modern funicular railway. Children will enjoy the ride as the train climbs above the river then plunges into a mountain tunnel on its way up to the ski areas of Les Arcs.

▶ *Leave Bourg-St-Maurice on the N90 to Séez. Go right on the D902 to Val-d'Isère.*

8 Val-d'Isère, Rhône-Alpes

The resort of Val-d'Isère lies 1,850m (6,070 feet) above sea level and is one of the most famous locations on the European ski-racing calendar. Cable-cars climb from its narrow valley setting to reach spectacular viewpoint summits such as Bellevarde at 2,827m (9,275 feet). The eastern mountain ridge, marking the frontier with Italy, soars to over 3,350m (11,000 feet).

Val-d'Isère is simply a series of long lines of apartment blocks, chalets, shops, hotels and restaurants. Many of the latest buildings, though, are quite sensitively designed in traditional mountain country idiom.

Summer sports facilities are more for weekly residents than for transients, although horse and pony hire, archery and tennis lessons and mountain biking may be tackled in shorter bursts.

[i] *Val-d'Isère*

▶ *Continue on the D902 to Col de l'Iseran.*

9 Col de l'Iseran,
Rhône-Alpes

When the road over the Col de l'Iseran was opened in 1937, it had taken 20 years to build. At 2,770m (9,088 feet) in the wildest country, it was the highest road in Europe. Today, only a handful surpass it. The Iseran is usually under impenetrable snow till mid-June, but even a month later chill winds may sweep down from the still higher glaciers and snowfields.

In clear weather the Iseran is exhilarating, although the climb is on a broken surface. There is a summit shop. An austere, four-square chapel stands a little way apart. This is the only through road which penetrates the huge nature reserve of the Parc National de la Vanoise. The mountain scenery is magnificent, and the descent is fortunately on a much better-surfaced road.

▶ *Continue on the D902. In Bessans follow the 'Chambéry' sign. Go through Lanslevillard,*

which you will see directly across the valley. Another excursion worth making is to the complex of forts at l'Esseillon, built in the 1820s to defend the forgotten kingdom of Piedmont-Sardinia against possible invasion from France.

▶ Leave Modane on the **N6**, then turn left into St Joan de-Maurienne.

11 St-Jean-de-Maurienne, Rhône-Alpes

Although the world's most modern aluminium factory is sited here, it is well away from the charming heart of St-Jean-de-Maurienne. As you approach, you will see a sweep of pasture land dotted with hamlets and farms, rising above the town.

The town square dips down to a fine modern war memorial outlined against the northern mountains. During the holidays, schoolchildren act as earnest and well-informed guides to the cathedral and the one-time bishop's palace, whose elegant salon and connecting rooms house a comprehensive museum of costume. Displays include traditional women's dresses from villages round about, showing how each place had its individual style. The Opinel company based here exports its wooden-handled clasp knives all over the world. The factory museum shows how its extensive range is produced.

i Place de la Cathédrale

▶ Leave St-Jean for Col de la Croix de Fer on the **D926**.

then, in Lanslebourg-Mont-Cenis, join the **N6** as for Chambéry. In Sollières, turn right on the **D83**. In Sardières, go right as for Hôtel du Parc, then left past La Monolithe. Turn right at the T-junction, rejoining the **D83** to Aussois, then go straight ahead on the **D215** to Modane.

BACK TO NATURE

Pause after Sardières, on your way to Modane, to look at the *monolithe*, a huge isolated limestone pillar soaring to 83m (272 feet) in the heart of a pinewood. This strange weathered feature is not uncommon here. You will see more of them among the pines further on.

10 Modane, Rhône-Alpes
This is where the busy road and rail tunnels to Bardonecchia in Italy begin. The 12.8km

Val-d'Isère has developed into a popular summer and winter resort

(8-mile) road tunnel opened in 1980. Go to the old ornamental rail tunnel entrance above the town, and you will see the coats of arms of the main cities on the Calais–Paris–Rome line.

Modane had a hard time in World War II. It was heavily bombed by the Allies in 1943, in an attempt to disrupt the German-Italian rail supply system, and the Germans fired colossal demolition charges at the rail tunnel entrance in 1944. You can still see a concrete blockhouse, intact but flung askew by the tremendous force of the explosion.

There is a glorious view from here, over Modane in its deep winding valley to the skyline of the Vanoise peaks. The town is an access point to the mountain footpaths of the Vanoise. Local walks include a steep and winding climb to the Fort St Gobain

SPECIAL TO...

Transhumance – the bringing down of sheep from the lush summer mountain pastures – is still practised in the Maurienne. However, nowadays, the flocks arrive by train.

⓬ Col de la Croix de Fer,
Rhône-Alpes

Take care in the five rock tunnels above the stunning Arvan gorge, with the needle peaks of the Aiguilles d'Arves on the skyline. Alpine meadows towards Entraigues, and the little ski resort of St-Sorlin, come and go. Then comes the narrow and dizzying zigzag road up the boulder fields to the summit of the pass. Here you can relax by the restaurant, note the cross of iron which gave the col its name, and marvel at the outlook over a sea of Alpine summits. To the south-south-east, the 3,983m (13,068-foot) peak of La Meije is just in view.

▶ *Beyond the col, turn left as for Grenoble.*

⓭ Défilé de Maupas,
Rhône-Alpes

The final exposed climb to the Croix de Fer may have left you wondering what lies on the other side. In fact, the descent is on a road of a much higher stan-

Grenoble is a modern city dedicated to superlative winter sports

dard, although the grandeur of the mountain scenery and of the majestic gorge which takes the route back down to a lower level is even more impressive.

Pause at the Barrage de Grand'Maison. Displays here explain how this is the top reservoir of the most powerful hydro-electric scheme in France, fed by cascades from the permanent snowfields.

FOR HISTORY BUFFS

On the return route to Grenoble, the 17th-century château at Vizille houses a comprehensive museum of the French Revolution. In 1788, a year before the Revolution, the three Estates – nobles, clergy and commoners – met in this castle to denounce Louis XVI's suppression of parliament and proclaim individual liberty. With tableaux, sculptures, paintings and posters as well as weaponry, the museum stresses the artistic environment of revolutionary France no less than the events and personalities.

▶ *Continue downhill. Avoid the road for Le Verney and take the road signed 'Hydrolec'. Turn left as for Grenoble, then join the N91. Go through Le Péage de Vizille, then turn right to Vizille-centre on the D101. Continue to Uriage on the D524 and return to Grenoble.*

SCENIC ROUTES

From Grenoble to Chambéry the route, runs over a massif of hills, forests, deep-cut valleys and towering limestone cliffs.
On the D34, after Aix-les-Bains, look for the dramatic valley of the Chéran, overlooked by the rock pillars called the Fairies' Chimneys.
The superlative mountain landscapes beyond La Clusaz include glimpses on the eastern horizon of Mont Blanc.
Even the spectacular climb to the Col de la Croix de Fer is surpassed by the descent through precipitous gorges to the N91.

The German
Connection

From the Rhineland plain south of Strasbourg to the viewpoint roads high in the Vosges mountains, this tour explores some of the most beautiful areas of Alsace. There have been vineyards in the eastern foothills of the Vosges since Roman times. At higher altitudes lie forests and upland pastures covered by winter snows.

3/4 DAYS • 420KM • 260 MILES

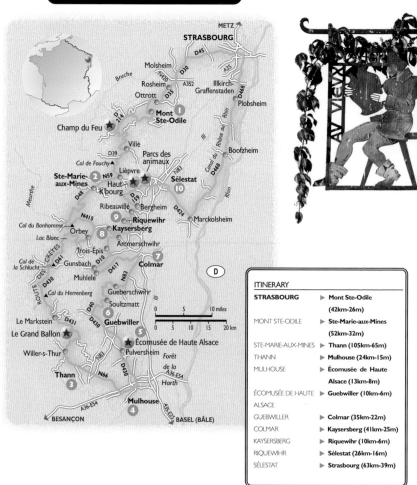

ITINERARY		
STRASBOURG	▶	**Mont Ste-Odile**
		(42km-26m)
MONT STE-ODILE	▶	**Ste-Marie-aux-Mines**
		(52km-32m)
STE-MARIE-AUX-MINES	▶	**Thann (105km-65m)**
THANN	▶	**Mulhouse (24km-15m)**
MULHOUSE	▶	**Écomusée de Haute**
		Alsace (13km-8m)
ÉCOMUSÉE DE HAUTE	▶	**Guebwiller (10km-6m)**
ALSACE		
GUEBWILLER	▶	**Colmar (35km-22m)**
COLMAR	▶	**Kaysersberg (41km-25m)**
KAYSERSBERG	▶	**Riquewihr (10km-6m)**
RIQUEWIHR	▶	**Sélestat (26km-16m)**
SÉLESTAT	▶	**Strasbourg (63km-39m)**

Strasbourg, capital of Alsace and sophisticated seat of government

☐ *17 place de la Cathédrale,
Strasbourg*

▶ *Leave Strasbourg for
Eckbolsheim on the D45.
Continue to Ergersheim, then
take the D30 to Molsheim.
Follow the 'Strasbourg' sign,
then take the D422 and D35
through Rosheim to Ottrott.
Turn right in Ottrott on the
D426, then follow the D426a
to le Mont Ste-Odile.*

SPECIAL TO...

Molsheim, to the southwest of
Strasbourg, was the home of
Bugatti, the marque which
epitomises *pur sang* (the thor-
oughbred ideal) in car design.
Cars are no longer built in
what is now the Messier-
Bugatti factory, but Bugatti
owners regularly make the
pilgrimage to Molsheim.

---

❶ **Mont Ste-Odile,** Alsace
You may be surprised by the
press of traffic on this out-of-
the-way woodland hilltop. The
cluster of buildings here is one
of France's great pilgrimage
centres: the historic convent
which guards the tomb of Saint
Odile.

Odile, abbess of the original
religious house of this splendid
site, died around the year 720.
The present buildings, in fine
order, are from much later
centuries, including the 20th.
With cloister and courtyard
gardens, an excellent paved
walk around viewpoint terraces,
a pilgrims' hall and several individual chapels, this is a place of
beauty, dignity and repose. The
site appealed to earlier civiliza-
tions, too. As you approach the
summit, look for carefully
worked masonry of the imposing Mur Païen (Pagan Wall)
constructed in prehistoric times.

▶ *Return downhill, bear slightly
left and follow signs to le
Champs de Feu. Go straight
ahead there and follow signs
to Villé. Turn right on the D39*

RECOMMENDED
WALKS

At Mont Ste-Odile you can
step into the network of waymarked trails which explore
this beautifully wooded hill.
Some were originally pilgrims'
paths, others follow the Pagan
Wall, and all offer splendid
views to the valleys.

---

*as for St-Dié. In Fouchy, go left
on the D155 to Col de
Fouchy, then follow signs to
Lièpvre and go right to Ste-
Marie-aux-Mines on the N59.
Approaching Ste-Marie, avoid
the tunnel.*

❷ **Ste-Marie-aux-Mines,**
Alsace
From the 16th century onwards,
this little town was famous for
the richest seams of silver in
France. You can join a guided
tour of the old St Bartélemy
mine. Safety helmets and
waterproof capes are provided,
and you start by walking in
through a hillside tunnel to the
levels and galleries beyond.

The Maison de Pays (not
quite the 'country house' which
the local English translation
suggests) houses the Musée
Minéralogique, and also mounts
displays on the mining era and

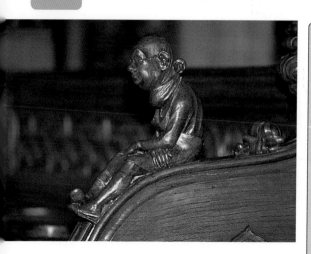

BACK TO NATURE

To the right of the D430 after the Col de la Schlucht, the university-run Jardin d'Altitude du Haut-Chitelet, at nearly 1,228m (4,030 feet), displays hundreds of mountain plant species from all over the world. Beyond the Col de la Schlucht, watch for soaring buzzards. The pine forests are home to the bulky capercaillie. Biggest of the grouse family, it is reduced to something like 160 pairs in the whole of the Vosges. Several species of woodpecker are found in the forests, along with crested tits and Bonelli's warblers.

on the spinning, dyeing, weaving and hosiery which, combined, formed Ste-Marie's other 'boom' industry.

Look for the restrained baroque style of the Church of La Madeleine, for intriguing old buildings such as the towered Pharmacie by the main square, and for the little public gardens which include one, beside the town hall, with a floral peacock on display.

[i] 86 rue Wilson

▶ Leave Ste-Marie-aux-Mines as for Le Bonhomme. Turn right at Col des Bagenelles to Col du Bonhomme. Turn left on the N415. At the roundabout go right on the D48 to Orbey, then follow signs 'Les Lacs' and 'Lac Blanc'. Go left on the D418 to Col de la Schlucht. Turn right on the D417 as for Épinal and almost immediately left on the D430 to Le Markstein. Continue straight ahead on the D431 to le Grand Ballon, then follow signs to Thann.

3 Thann, Alsace
On the banks of the fast-flowing River Thur, overlooked by a hillside Cross of Lorraine, Thann was wrested back from German control by Marshal Joffre's troops in 1914. The text of his emotional proclamation is

Superb carvings on the choir stalls in Thann's Gothic cathedral

carved on a war memorial. Thann's history is even more complex than that of other places in Alsace, as it was Austrian territory from 1324 to 1648.

The splendid collegiate Church of St Thiébaut features immensely detailed sculptured façades and portals, polychrome roof tiling and superb carved-oak choir stalls. Look there for the figures of the gossip, the fiddler and the spectacled man. Thann's local history museum is in the arcaded corn market (Halle aux blés) of 1519. Two towers survive from its medieval ramparts, and several fine buildings from the 16th century onwards remain.

[i] 7 rue de la 1ère Armée

▶ Leave Thann on the N66. Go over the autoroute and continue to Mulhouse.

FOR CHILDREN

At Le Grand Ballon, the highest point in the Vosges mountains, the youngsters will enjoy a whoosh down the luge d'été summer toboggan ride; but in chilly weather make sure they wrap up well.

4 Mulhouse, Alsace
Despite its parks and gardens, zoo and yacht basin and attractive old quarter, 'Moo-loose' is an industrial town which may take some time to grow on you. Look round its museums, and you will realise that this is one of the most amazingly well-endowed towns in Europe as regards museums of technology.

History, fine arts, painted wall-coverings and printed fabrics all have extensive museums of their own, but the Musée des Beaux-Arts is an excellent starting point. Railway enthusiasts should head for the excellent Cité du Train, France's national railway museum, where the glorious century of steam locomotion can be rediscovered, complete with sound effects.

However, the pride of Mulhouse is the Musée National de l'Automobile, the most stupendous motor museum in the world. On display are over a hundred Bugattis, whole collections of Rolls-Royces, Alfa Romeos, Maseratis, Mercedes-Benz, Gordinis and the rest – more than 500 splendid vehicles of almost 100 different makes. The fine tradition continues, as new Peugeots are also made in Mulhouse.

ℹ *9 avenue du Maréchal-Foch*

▶ *Leave Mulhouse as for Guebwiller on the **D430**. Turn on to the **D430bis** and follow 'Écomusée' signs.*

🖪 Écomusée de Haute Alsace, Alsace

Occupying a roomy site on the Alsace plain, here is a fascinating replica village of more than 60 traditionally styled buildings – houses, farms, barns and workshops – created to show the domestic life of past generations, as well as the work of the blacksmith and cart builder, baker, clog-maker and weaver, and all the half-forgotten farming trades.

Favourite local dishes are offered in the restaurants, and Alsace wines are served. There is a keen interest in wildlife conservation: storks, for instance, are encouraged to nest here.

Restoration work and the development of new projects are always under way here, along with special events and other exhibitions.

▶ *Return to the **D430** and continue to Guebwiller.*

🖪 Guebwiller, Alsace

A place full of squares, and bright with window-boxes, Guebwiller is partly built of a soft local stone which gives the Église St-Léger, for instance, a warmer 'feel' than most French churches. St-Léger also has stately arcaded aisles and some worthwhile stained-glass windows.

Overlooked by hillside vineyards, the town enjoys some beautiful parkland. The Parc de la Marseillaise features fine examples of cypress, lime, cedar and sequoia trees.

Guebwiller was the birthplace of the 19th-century ceramic artist Théodore Deck. Examples of his work, and historical mementoes of the district, are on display in the Musée Theodore Deck.

ℹ *Hôtel de Ville*

▶ *Continue on the **D430** as for Le Markstein. Turn right on the **D40** to Soultzmatt, left on*

the **D18bis** to Osenbach, then right on the **D40** again. Bear right to Gueberschwihr, turn left as for Hattstatt, then join the **N83** for Colmar, and enter it on the **D30**.

🖪 Colmar, Alsace

In colour, design, construction, layout and state of preservation, Colmar is one of the world's most beguiling towns. The narrow streets, some darting off at eccentric angles, are lined with colour-washed half-timbered houses of the 16th and 17th centuries, most of them banked with flowers.

Look in particular for the balconied Maison Pfister of 1537, the riverside houses of the quai de la Poissonnerie and 'La Petite Venise' (Little Venice) to which they lead, and for the lovely cluster of buildings by the pastry shop at the corner of Rue Kléber. The 15th-century Koïfhus – the old customs house, used as the town hall – is topped by glorious polychrome roof tiling.

Colmar's fine town hall

Colmar has a museum and art gallery in the old Dominican convent of Unterlinden (Musée d'Unterlinden), noted for its 16th-century altarpiece by Matthias Grünewald – the Isenheim Altarpiece. The sculptor Auguste Bartholdi was born here, in a courtyard house which is now a museum recalling that his most famous work was the Statue of Liberty.

i 4 rue Unterlinden

Take the first left under the archway, follow the 'Toutes Directions' sign, then turn left and continue to Kaysersberg.

8 Kaysersberg, Alsace
As you stroll through this attractive little flower-decked medieval 'city', past the *caves* of wine growers and liqueur distillers, you will encounter many houses, gateways, bridges, towers and chapels of the 13th to 15th centuries.

9 Riquewihr, Alsace
Enclosed in 16th-century ramparts, this charming old town is the 'pearl of the Alsace vineyards'. Wine cellars stock the produce of its Riesling, Muscat, Tokay and Gewürztraminer grapes.

Local history is the concern of the Musée Dolder. The Tour des Voleurs (Thieves' Tower) houses an 'authentic' torture chamber. Installed in a princely palace, the Musée de la

RECOMMENDED WALKS

The hilltop resort of Les Trois-Épis, between Colmar and Kaysersberg, concentrates on sports and open-air activities. Ask at the tourist office about the 50km (31 miles) of footpaths on its invigorating woodland ridges.

The Église Ste-Croix has a magnificent altarpiece of 1518. Other works of religious art are displayed in the local museum.

Kaysersberg is twinned with Lambaréné in Gabon because of the town's links with Dr Albert Schweitzer. He was born in Kaysersberg in 1875 and spent most of his working life at his hospital in West Africa. His birthplace is now the Musée du Docteur Schweitzer.

i 38 rue du Général de Gaulle

► Leave Kaysersberg as for Ribeauvillé on the **D28**. Go left at the roundabout and left on the **D3** to Riquewihr.

Riquewihr, with its clock tower and red-tiled roofs, nestles among the surrounding vineyards

Communication en Alsace includes lavish displays of maps, models, uniforms, electric and wireless telegraphy systems, telephones, teleprinters and a miniature of the *Ariane* space rocket, telling the story of 2,000 years of message deliveries since Gallo-Roman times. The mail coach is housed near by in a former stable block.

► Leave Riquewihr for Ribeauvillé and Bergheim. In Bergheim, go left on the **D42** as for Haut Koenigsbourg.

► Leave Colmar as for Épinal on the **D417**. Turn right to Gunsbach, then right at the crossroads on the **D10**. Go left on the **D11** to Trois-Épis, then right to Ammerschwihr.

Sélestat's greatest glory is its Humanist library

SPECIAL TO...

The population of storks, which have nested for centuries on the rooftops and chimneys of Alsace, dwindled alarmingly in the 1970s. However, the birds are strongly established once again.
After Riquewihr, turn left as for Hunawihr to visit the Parc des Cigognes et des Loutres.

find beautiful medieval, Renaissance and 18th-century houses and public buildings, the Romanesque Church of Ste-Foy and the later Gothic Church of St-Georges. The town's water towers are unexpectedly ornate.

Sélestat is the main centre where modern Alsace artists show their paintings, and its 15th-century Bibliothèque Humaniste, housed in the old corn market (Halle aux blés),

is one of the most valuable libraries of books and manuscripts in France.

ℹ️ 10 boulevard Leclerc

▶ Leave Sélestat on the D424 as for Marckolsheim. At the roundabout, turn left on the D468 and return to Strasbourg.

Turn right on the D159 and continue to Sélestat, entering it on the N83.

FOR CHILDREN

Off the D159 on the way to Sélestat, the Montagne des Singes allows 300 Barbary apes to roam in 20 hectares (50 acres) of forest. At the nearby Volerie des Aigles, in the grounds of a castle, eagles, vultures, kites and falcons give flying displays.

⑩ Sélestat, Alsace
Unremarkable in its suburbs, Sélestat becomes much more interesting as you explore its historic centre. Here you will

FOR HISTORY BUFFS

On the way to Sélestat, turn left off the D159 for the spectacular hilltop castle of Haut-Koenigsbourg. The 12th-century fortress was destroyed in the 17th century, and was completely restored early this century on the orders of Kaiser Wilhelm II. It looks like a film set, and was in fact used by the great director Jean Renoir for *La Grande Illusion*.
On the return route to Strasbourg, turn right into Marckolsheim then left on the D10 to the Musée de l'Abri, recalling the bypassing of the Maginot Line by the Germans in 1940, and the fierce fighting that took place there in 1944.

SCENIC ROUTES

Early on, the D45 opens up long views over villages and vineyards to the forested range of the Vosges.
On the way to Thann, the D48 rises through beautiful miniature landscapes in the valley of the Petite Lièpvre. After the Col de la Schlucht, admire the 'top of the world' views over the deep western valleys from the 'Route des Crêtes', then on to the descent of Le Grand Ballon.
From the approach to Guebwiller, you are in the delicious foothills country of the 'Route du Vin'. The flat return to Strasbourg is enhanced by unexpectedly bright and flower-filled villages.

THE NORTH, BURGUNDY & CHAMPAGNE

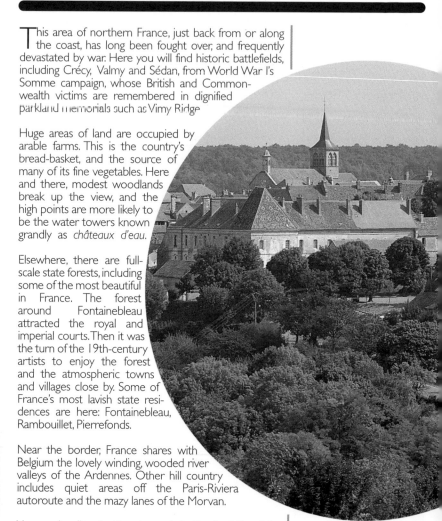

This area of northern France, just back from or along the coast, has long been fought over, and frequently devastated by war. Here you will find historic battlefields, including Crécy, Valmy and Sédan, from World War I's Somme campaign, whose British and Commonwealth victims are remembered in dignified parkland memorials such as Vimy Ridge.

Huge areas of land are occupied by arable farms. This is the country's bread-basket, and the source of many of its fine vegetables. Here and there, modest woodlands break up the view, and the high points are more likely to be the water towers known grandly as *châteaux d'eau*.

Elsewhere, there are full-scale state forests, including some of the most beautiful in France. The forest around Fontainebleau attracted the royal and imperial courts. Then it was the turn of the 19th-century artists to enjoy the forest and the atmospheric towns and villages close by. Some of France's most lavish state residences are here: Fontainebleau, Rambouillet, Pierrefonds.

Near the border, France shares with Belgium the lovely winding, wooded river valleys of the Ardennes. Other hill country includes quiet areas off the Paris-Riviera autoroute and the mazy lanes of the Morvan.

You can hardly miss the vineyards in the foothills of the Côte d'Or and the great champagne estates round Reims. On the coast you will find resorts as different as stylish Le Touquet and simple Le Crotoy by the Somme. Inland towns, such as Pierrefonds, Compiègne and Moret-sur-Loing, have their following too.

You will encounter the long-lost melding of French and English history – Richard the Lionheart conferred with the French king at Vézélay before they set off to lead their joint army in the Third Crusade. And you can learn how Revolutionaries pursued and captured the fleeing Louis XVI, how artists such as Millet shrugged off the studios of Paris and came to paint from real life in the countryside.

Calais

Under English occupation for more than 200 years, Calais has always looked across the Channel. The Dover-Calais route was the first Continental service to be operated by a steamship, the *Rob Roy*, in 1821. One of the most famous sights is Rodin's great statue of the Burghers of Calais, who pleaded with Edward III of England to spare the town after its surrender in 1347. There is a confidently ornate town hall, a fine arts museum displaying the lacework, and a parkland museum of the town's travails in World War II.

Amiens

Amiens is centred on the majestic Cathédrale Notre-Dame, largest of all the Gothic churches in France, with wonderful fretted upper reaches. Inside, there are beautifully carved oakwood choir stalls. Museums and galleries show local art and history and the former home of Jules Verne doubles as a museum of his work. Amiens is the capital of Picardy. Quaysides and inlets of the Somme thread through the northern suburbs, and an area of market gardens first cultivated in medieval times is laced with canals.

Reims

Reims is not just outwardly the city of champagne. Millions of Euros' worth lies in cellars underground. Visitors are welcome at the champagne houses which even commissioned stained-glass panels of the different vineyard areas for the cathedral. Two of the old city abbeys have been turned into museums. You can see where the German capitulation order was signed in 1945. And Reims has a major motor museum devoted entirely to French marques.

Chalon-sur-Saône

Baseball in France? Yes, in a beautiful park at Chalon-sur-Saône, which also features a magnificent riverside garden with 26,000 roses from Europe, America, Japan and the Himalayas.

By the Saône, visit the museum commemorating the pioneer of photography, Nicéphore Niepce. Exhibits range from his first camera of 1822 to the Apollo equipment taken to the moon.

There is an exhibition centre for the 44 vineyard villages known collectively as the Côte Chalonnaise. On the little St Laurent island, the topmost gallery of the Tour du Doyenné is an unusual viewpoint over the town.

Chartres

Chartres is, first and foremost, its cathedral, Notre Dame, whose twin towers are seen for miles across the plain. Connoisseurs consider that the stained-glass windows at Chartres are the finest in the world. The International Stained Glass Centre covers every aspect of the craft, and there are studios where present-day artists work.

Look for the Maison Picassiette with its décor picked out in fragments of glass and china. Admire the paintings, sculptures and tapestries in the fine arts museum, and stroll by the quays, mills and wash-houses on the River Eure.

Opposite: Flavigny sits on a rocky outcrop above wooded valleys
Below: *caves of Moet & Chandon*

The English
Connection

This tour from Calais, busiest of all the French car ferry ports, visits resorts both sophisticated and family-style. The chalk headlands match the white cliffs of Dover, which can be seen on a clear day, glistening in the sun. Behind the coast there are inland river valleys where quiet villages nestle in the shelter of gently wooded hills.

3 DAYS • 272KM • 170 MILES

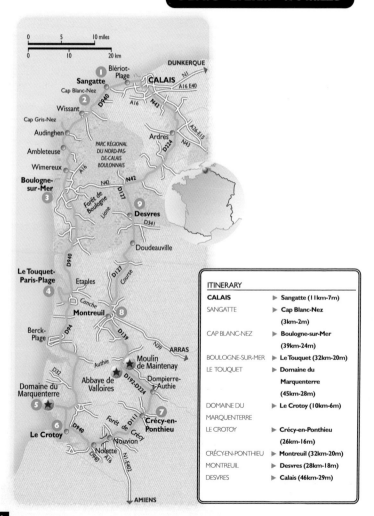

ITINERARY		
CALAIS	▶	**Sangatte** (11km-7m)
SANGATTE	▶	**Cap Blanc-Nez**
		(3km-2m)
CAP BLANC-NEZ	▶	**Boulogne-sur-Mer**
		(39km-24m)
BOULOGNE-SUR-MER	▶	**Le Touquet** (32km-20m)
LE TOUQUET	▶	**Domaine du**
		Marquenterre
		(45km-28m)
DOMAINE DU	▶	**Le Crotoy** (10km-6m)
MARQUENTERRE		
LE CROTOY	▶	**Crécy-en-Ponthieu**
		(26km-16m)
CRÉCY-EN-PONTHIEU	▶	**Montreuil** (32km-20m)
MONTREUIL	▶	**Desvres** (28km-18m)
DESVRES	▶	**Calais** (46km-29m)

Calais' ornate Hôtel de Ville (town hall)

---

i *12 boulevard Clemenceau, Calais*

▶ *Leave Calais on the **D940** through Sangatte.*

SPECIAL TO...

West of Calais there are several smaller fishing ports. One local speciality is *moules* (mussels), often sold from stalls outside the fishermen's homes.

❶ Sangatte, Pas de Calais
Already familiar to anyone who has taken the Channel Tunnel route to France, Sangatte is the huge landward base on the French side.

▶ *Continue on the **D940** to Cap Blanc-Nez.*

❷ Cap Blanc-Nez,
Pas de Calais
This sweeping chalk headland is introduced by a fine windswept statue of the pioneer French aviator, Hubert Latham, who was famous, like Blériot, for his 'audacious flights' above the Channel. Turn right for the splendid viewpoint memorial to the French sailors of the World War I Dover Patrol. The footpath from here to Cap Gris-Nez offers peaceful views of ferries sailing to or from Calais, while concrete bunkers from World War II are silent witnesses from more troubled times.

BACK TO NATURE

The chalk cliffs around Cap Blanc-Nez and Cap Gris-Nez are a nesting ground for gulls and fulmars which skim the waves and soar on the up-currents of air. Kestrels also nest here, and you may be lucky enough to see one hovering over the grassy clifftops before plunging on its prey. The clifftop flora is outstanding during the summer months.

▶ *Continue on the **D940** through Audinghen, where the **D191** on the right leads to Cap Gris-Nez. Beyond Wimereux the left turn signed 'vers A16' leads towards the Colonne de la Grande Armée. The **D940** continues to Boulogne-sur-Mer.*

FOR CHILDREN

Nausicaà (National Marine Centre) in Boulogne, claims to be the largest marine complex in Europe. Its vast array of aquariums contains no fewer than 4,000 fish, and the centre also has film shows and exhibitions, a library, bookshop and café.

❸ Boulogne-sur-Mer,
Pas de Calais
France's most important fishing port has a bustling harbour front. Every morning fishermen's stalls offer the freshest possible produce of the sea.

Turn uphill through the busy shopping streets, and you will come to one of the best-preserved historic citadels in the north of France. The castle museum covers a bewildering variety of subjects including archaeology, ethnology, painting and sculpture and local souvenirs from the time of Napoleon. A pleasant stroll round the towers and fortified gateways of the preserved 13th-century ramparts, which enclose the medieval Haute Ville, gives views of the ferries below discharging and loading.

i *Forum Jean Noël*

FOR HISTORY BUFFS

On the outskirts of Boulogne, the Colonne de la Grande Armée is a towering monument topped by a statue of Napoleon in characteristic pose. He assembled his army here in 1803 for an invasion of Britain which never took place.

▶ *Leave Boulogne on the **N1**, then take the **D940** and **N39** to Le Touquet-Paris-Plage.*

4 **Le Touquet,** Pas de Calais
Le Touquet grew up in the 19th century, largely as a haven for British gamblers taking advantage of the more lenient French gambling laws. Developed jointly by French and British interests Le Touquet has unparalleled facilities for all kinds of sport, including a huge annual motor-sport 'enduro' race on its extensive sands. There are three well-kept golf courses.

Some of the seafront apartment blocks contrast hideously with the few remaining 19th-century buildings there, but the heart of the town has retained a certain elegance. Discreet wooded footpaths are threaded through the pine- and birch-woods of the handsome residential suburbs.

[i] *Palais de l'Europe, place de l'Hermitage*

FOR CHILDREN

Aqualud on the seafront at Le Touquet is a modern swimming pool complex. Its water fountains and curving chute are great fun for the children; adults might enjoy the sauna.

FOR CHILDREN

On the D940 south of Le Touquet, the extensive fun park at Bagatelle features a roller-coaster ride which finishes with a belly-flop into a lake, a monorail, a mirror maze, round-abouts, an aviary and a zoo.

Le Touquet is a fine example of a turn-of-the-20th-century seaside resort

▶ *Leave Le Touquet following Berck and Hesdin signs, and rejoin the **D940** as for Rue. Turn right, following signs to Domaine du Marquenterre.*

5 **Domaine du Marquenterre,** Picardy
Reached by a rough approach road, this private estate is one of the finest bird reserves in Europe. La Parc Ornithologique de Marquenterre was created behind a screen of pine trees on land reclaimed as recently as the 1970s from the estuary of the Somme. Residents and migrants include ducks, geese, swans, gulls and waders, hoopoes, avocets, spoonbills, storks and dozens of other species of shore, lake and salt marsh.

▶ *Return from the Domaine and follow signs to Le Crotoy.*

6 **Le Crotoy,** Picardy
Very much a French family resort, Le Crotoy has a good beach, fishing and yacht harbours by the River Somme. Fresh fish and shellfish are available from roadside stalls and in the restaurants. You should take care before imitating the locals' casual-seeming gumbooted strolls across the tidal inlets. Make sure not to be caught by the incoming tide. The old station is a terminus for the Chemin de Fer Touristique de la Baie de Somme (Bay of the Somme Railway) whose steam-hauled trains explore the pleasant countryside inland.

[i] *1 rue Carnot*

RECOMMENDED WALKS

Local tourist offices have maps of the network of walks inland from Le Crotoy, in the lovely pastureland behind the Somme estuary. They wander past fields, woodlands and water channels in what was unproductive marshland just a few generations ago.

▶ *Leave Le Crotoy by 'Sortie Ville' signs. Turn right on the D940, then left on the D140 to Noyelles. Turn left over a level crossing, then left on the D111 through Nolette to Crécy-en-Ponthieu.*

7 Crécy, Picardy

On the exit from the village a view-point tower (Le Moulin Édouard III) stands at Edward III's traditional vantage point over the battlefield of Crécy in 1346, when his English archers routed the French crossbow-men in one of the most decisive battles of the Hundred Years' War. The Musée Emhisarc contains a relief model of the battle site and related displays.

▶ *Continue on the D111 to Dompierre, then go left on the D224 which becomes the D192. After the Abbaye de Valloires turn sharp right to Moulin de Maintenay, right at a roundabout and left on the D139 to Montreuil.*

8 Montreuil, Pas de Calais

Formerly Montreuil-sur-Mer, the town is now 14km (9 miles) from the sea. It retains many picturesque houses on cobbled and steeply cambered streets; some of the action of Victor Hugo's *Les Misérables* is set here. A statue of Sir Douglas Haig is a reminder that the British commander-in-chief in World War I made his headquarters near by. Montreuil's historic ramparts provide a beautiful hour-long walk, partly edged with trees and giving splendid sunset views. The abbey church dates back to the 11th century.

ⅰ *21 rue Carnot*

▶ *Leave Montreuil on the N39, then take the N1 as for*

Le Crotoy is a bustling fishing and yacht harbour on the River Somme

Boulogne. Bear right off the N1 for Inxent, then follow the D127 to Desvres.

9 Desvres, Pas de Calais

The square here is the site of regular morning markets, but since the 18th century the main business of the town has been in faïence or glazed pottery. Several workshops welcome visitors, and there is a purpose-built pottery museum.

ⅰ *41 rue des Potiers*

▶ *Leave Desvres on the D127. Turn right on the N42 and then take the D224 to Ardres. In Ardres turn left on the N43 and return to Calais.*

FOR HISTORY BUFFS

At Nolette, between Le Crotoy and Crécy, one of the most unusual cemeteries in France commemorates the 96,000 members of the Chinese Labour Force employed by the Allies during World War I. Its base was near by, and 870 of the Chinese, who died in an epidemic, are buried here.

One hero of the Battle of Crécy was the blind King John of Bohemia, brother-in-law of the French king, Philippe VI. A cross marks the spot on the battlefield where he is said to have fallen. A tradition that this king's emblem was adopted by the Black Prince as the Prince of Wales' Feathers is a romantic fiction.

SCENIC ROUTES

After the D940 climbs out of Sangatte it swoops up and down hill through immaculately tended farmland.

Further south, bypassing Rue, the D940 crosses lovely pastoral country given artificial horizons by line upon line of stately poplars.

Towns of
Picardy

Centred on the cathedral city of Amiens, this tour is through districts often missed by visitors to France. It features wide rural landscapes in areas such as the Picardy plateau, goes through the fringes of the northern industrial belt and takes in elegant towns.

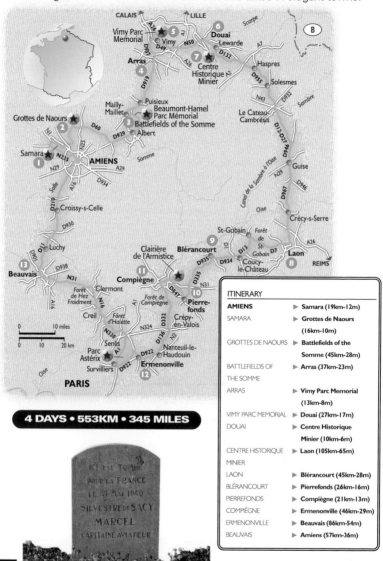

4 DAYS • 553KM • 345 MILES

ITINERARY		
AMIENS	►	**Samara** (19km-12m)
SAMARA	►	**Grottes de Naours** (16km-10m)
GROTTES DE NAOURS	►	**Battlefields of the Somme** (45km-28m)
BATTLEFIELDS OF THE SOMME	►	**Arras** (37km-23m)
ARRAS	►	**Vimy Parc Memorial** (13km-8m)
VIMY PARC MEMORIAL	►	**Douai** (27km-17m)
DOUAI	►	**Centre Historique Minier** (10km-6m)
CENTRE HISTORIQUE MINIER	►	**Laon** (105km-65m)
LAON	►	**Blérancourt** (45km-28m)
BLÉRANCOURT	►	**Pierrefonds** (26km-16m)
PIERREFONDS	►	**Compiègne** (21km-13m)
COMPIÈGNE	►	**Ermenonville** (46km-29m)
ERMENONVILLE	►	**Beauvais** (86km-54m)
BEAUVAIS	►	**Amiens** (57km-36m)

ICI EST TOMBÉ
POUR LA FRANCE
LE 21 MAI 1940
SILVESTRE DE SACY
MARCEL
CAPITAINE AVIATEUR

[i] *6 bis rue Dusevel, Amiens*

▶ *Leave Amiens on the **N235** through Picquigny, then go right on the **D191** to Samara.*

❶ Samara, Picardy
Laid out among scrubland, marsh and ponds, Samara is a fascinating historical park which looks at thousands of years of human life and activity in the valley of the River Somme. There are accurate representations of ancient dwellings and demonstrations of prehistoric trades such as flint cutting. There is a botanical garden and arboretum, an excavated Celtic town and displays covering both the distant past and what life may be like in the future.

[i] *115 place du Général de Gaulle, Picquigny*

▶ *Continue on the **D191** to St-Sauveur, go left on the **D97** at 'Grottes de Naours' sign, left on to the **D933** to Flesselles, straight on along the **D117** to Naours, right on the **D60**, then sharp left to the Grottes de Naours.*

Amiens, a pleasing mixture of ancient riverside streets and modern development

❷ Grottes de Naours, Picardy
Burrowed into a wooded hillside above the village, the Underground City of Naours (Grottes de Naours) is one of the most amazing places in France. About 30 tunnels and 300 separate rooms – including chapels and stables – have been used as refuges in times of danger and invasion from the Gallo-Roman era to the 18th century. They were the haunt of salt smugglers and used as stores for the British Army in World War II.

▶ *Return from the car park, go left at the 'stop' sign and follow the **D60** to Contay. Turn right on the **D919**, immediately left on the **D23** to Franvillers and left on the **D929** through Albert. Go left on the **D20**, right on the **D151** to Thiepval, left on the **D73** and follow signs to Beaumont-Hamel memorial park.*

❸ Battlefields of the Somme, Picardy
The countryside hereabouts is scattered with war graves and monuments recalling the first day of July 1916, the opening of the Battle of the Somme. Among the most impressive are Sir Edward Lutyens's massive

brick-and-stone memorial at Thiepval; the Ulster Tower also near Thiepval; and the Newfoundland Memorial Park at Beaumont-Hamel, where almost the whole of the 1st Newfoundland Regiment were mown down by enemy machine-gun fire and shrapnel. The circuit of Remembrance is a 60km (38-mile) route, taking in all the major sites.

At the Château de Peronne, the purpose-built Historial de la Grande Guerre (Museum of the Great War) illustrates life at the front and behind the lines. Its halls display over 25,000 items, including weapons and military equipment, and there are displays on the civilian war effort and a collection of Otto Dix etchings.

▶ *Continue on the **D53** to Mailly-Maillet. Turn right on the **D129**, then right on the **D919** to Arras.*

❹ Arras, Picardy
Arras, the capital of Artois, has two spectacular squares, lined by elegant architecture, and two UNESCO World Heritage sites – the Citadel, listed in 2008, and the soaring belfry of the handsome Hôtel de Ville, which was listed in 2005. Climb to the top

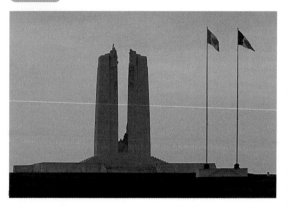

of the latter for a good view. Part of the former Benedictine Abbaye de St-Vaast is now a cathedral (18th- to 19th-century); in the south wing of the abbey is a well-stocked fine arts museum with extensive collections of French and Flemish paintings, medieval wood carvings and a superb display of local porcelain and tapestry.

ⓘ *Place des Héros*

▶ *Leave Arras on the N425, then take the D937 as for Béthune. Turn right on the D55 following the sign for 'Memorial Canadien' to Vimy Parc.*

🄳 Vimy Parc Memorial, Picardy

One of the largest war memorial areas in France, Vimy Parc commemorates, in particular, the tremendous assault on 9 April 1917 when all four divisions of the Canadian Corps stormed the German defences on Vimy Ridge. Keep to the paths, as there is still a chance of encountering unexploded shells and ammunition. Guided tours explore the fascinating underground galleries.

On the crown of the ridge, the Mémorial et Parc Canadien, whose soaring pillars bear the maple leaf of Canada and the fleur-de-lys of France, is the most majestic of all the fine monuments raised after the Great War.

The Vimy Parc Memorial honours the 75,000 Canadians who died in 1917

▶ *From the memorial, return down the D55 as for Arras, then go left at the first junction following the 'Gendarmerie' sign. Turn right on the N17 to Thélus, left on the D49, right on the D33, go under a bridge, then turn left and join the N50 dual carriageway to Douai.*

🄶 Douai, Picardy

An industrial town brightened by judiciously placed gardens, flowery roundabouts and avenues of trees, Douai is, at its heart, an island bounded by the River Scarpe and its associated canals, lined with old quaysides. The most impressive building is the ornate Gothic belltower, completed in 1410. Escorted tours show visitors the view from the top, over the town, and also the fine interior of the historic Hôtel de Ville.

ⓘ *70 place d'Armes*

SPECIAL TO...

The belfry at Douai houses the largest carillon in France, using no fewer than 62 individual bells. Douai's official carillonist is the 34th in a line which started in 1391. Douai also owns the first mobile carillon in France, with 50 bells.

▶ *Leave Douai on the N45. In Lewarde turn right on the D135 and follow 'Centre Historique Minier' signs on to the D132.*

🄷 Centre Historique Minier, Picardy

On the site of the old Delloye pit (Fosse Delloye) near Lewarde, you will find an extensive indoor, outdoor and underground museum dedicated to coal-mining in the north of France. Former miners guide visitors round displays about the geology and exploitation of the coal-seams, the machinery and processing plant used in the mines, and the working conditions of miners through the centuries. Finally, you can descend into one of the original pits where 450m (490 yards) of galleries have been reconstructed as they would have been in their heyday.

▶ *Continue on the D132 to Bouchain. Go right on the D943, left on the N30, then right to Haspres. Go left for Saulzoir and right before the FINA station, leaving Haspres on the D955 to Solesmes. Then follow signs to Le Cateau-Cambrésis. Leave Le Cateau on the D12, which becomes the D27, then follow the D946 and the D967 to Laon.*

🄸 Laon, Picardy

The attractions of Laon are partly in its situation, partly in the architecture of the old city (Ville Haute) surrounded by medieval ramparts and imposing entrance gates. Laon lies on a long narrow ridge which dominates the surrounding plain and is an excellent natural viewpoint. The many-towered 12th- to 14th-century cathedral, one of the great Gothic edifices of France, has a nave of immense grandeur and some beautiful medieval stained-glass windows. Beside an old garden chapel of the Knights Templar (Chapelle des Templiers), the museum holds extensive archaeological and arts collections.

ⓘ *Place du Parvis Gautier de Mortagne*

▶ *Leave Laon on the **D7** for St-Gobain. Go left on the **D13**, then right on the **D5** to Coucy. Join the **D937** as for Folembray, then turn left on the **D934** to Blérancourt.*

🟑 Blérancourt, Picardy
Headquarters during World War I of the American volunteer ambulance corps, the pavilions, ground floor and gardens of the Château de Blérancourt are now the national Museum of Franco-American Co-operation. It honours notable Americans and preserves documents and mementoes of battles in which the two nations fought side by side. The museum is currently closed for restoration, but the gardens remain open.

ⓘ *Maison de St-Just, 2 rue de la Chouette*

▶ *Leave Blérancourt on the **D935**, which becomes the **D335**, to Pierrefonds.*

🔟 Pierrefonds, Picardy
Drive slowly down the hill into Pierrefonds, so as not to miss the first stunning glimpse of the massive castle which towers

over this engaging island resort. Handsome villas in discreet wooded grounds overlook a lake, which rowing boats and pedaloes share with the coots and mallards. The Parc Rainette is home to a herd of stately fallow deer.

However, it is the château which dominates the town. Napoleon I bought it in ruins, but it was Napoleon II who commissioned the great architect Viollet-le-Duc to oversee its transformation into a grand imperial residence. Guided tours show off the whole lavish project; one room is dedicated to the architect himself, but the château itself is his memorial.

ⓘ *Place de l'Hôtel-de-Ville*

▶ *Leave Pierrefonds on the **D973** as for Compiègne. Go right on the **D547** to Vieux Moulin, then left on the **N31** and right on the **V4** to Clairière de l'Armistice. Then follow signs to Compiègne.*

⓫ Compiègne, Picardy
Here is a dignified and spacious town with a fine riverside frontage on the River Oise, spreading parkland, and suburbs to south and west

where villa gardens drift into the glorious Forêt de Compiègne. Louis XV and Louis XVI commissioned the building of a palace here, facing a wide cobbled square. It was completed in the fateful year of 1789. After the Revolution, Napoleon I had it rebuilt, and later still it was the favourite residence of Napoleon III and Empress Eugénie.

Open to the public, the royal and imperial apartments recall all these personages, and there is a separate Musée du Second Empire. A first-class motor and carriage museum (Musée National de la Voiture et du Tourisme) includes splendid exhibits of vehicles from the horse-drawn age, and cars which are a reminder that, although Germany was the birthplace of the automobile, the French were livelier designers and experimenters.

Other memorable museums in Compiègne are the Musée Vivenel, which includes fine collections of archaeological items and classical ceramics, and the Musée de la Figurine.

ⓘ *Place de l'Hôtel-de-Ville*

For 200 years until 987, Laon was actually capital of France

*Parc Astérix take the next autoroute exit as for Senlis. After the toll booths follow the 'Creil' sign on the **N330**, then the Beauvais signs via Clermont into Beauvais itself.*

FOR CHILDREN

Parc Astérix, off the A1, on the way from Ermenonville to Beauvais, is an expensive but massive theme park based on the adventures of the ancient Gauls – Astérix, Obélix and Toutafix – made famous by Goscinny and Underzo. If the Wild West appeals, visit La Mer de Sable at Ermenonville, which has Cowboy and Indian shows, rides, attractions and buffalo.

The elegant town of Compiègne

▶ *Leave Compiègne on the **D332** as for Meaux. In Crépy-en-Valois follow 'Paris' signs and take the **D136** into Nanteuil, ignoring the bypass. Watch the navigation here. About 55m (60 yards) after a Fiat garage, turn right following the sign 'Ermenonville Tourisme'. Go left on the **D922**, then right on the **N330** through Ermenonville.*

12 Ermenonville, Picardy
Ermenonville is besieged by traffic, thanks to signposts recommending it as a way of bypassing other towns. However, to the left of the main road is a park, introduced by a carved stone which translates as 'here begins the course of a sweet and rustic leisure' with woodland paths, ponds and streams.

The Abbey of Chaalis, 3km (2 miles) north of town, is a classical 18th-century château on the site of an old Cistercian monastery. The château has fine paintings, including the Jean-Jacques Rousseau collection. The park contains the old abbey ruins and one of France's finest rose gardens.

ℹ️ *2 bis rue René de Girardin*

▶ *Turn left for Mortefontaine. Join the **D922** and in Plailly follow the blue and white 'A1' signs. Join the **A1** autoroute as for Lille. Parc Astérix is reached by the first exit. After*

RECOMMENDED WALKS

Ask at the tourist office in Pierrefonds for the *Itinéraires circuits pédestres* booklet describing four waymarked walks in the eastern part of the Forêt de Compiègne. One follows an ancient Roman road, another goes past the Empress Eugénie's hunting pavilion.

13 Beauvais, Picardy
One victim of World War II was the tapestry industry at Beauvais, removed elsewhere and never brought back. The Galérie Nationale de la Tapisserie, a gallery of French tapestries from the 15th century onwards, is one of the sights of the town. Stained glass was another Beauvais craft, and much of it survives, both in the Church of St-Etienne and as a feature of the superb interior of the cathedral (St Pierre), which has a tremendous height for the area of its base. The cathedral's astronomical clock, gilded and astonishingly complicated, was completely restored in 1989.

Beside the cathedral, the old bishop's palace houses the Musée Départemental de l'Oise, the principal museum in the *département* of the Oise region. There are wide-ranging displays of classical and contemporary art, art nouveau and art deco, as well as a glorious exhibition of ceramics.

ℹ️ *1 rue Beauregard*

▶ *Leave Beauvais on the **D901** as for Abbeville, then take the **D149** as for Crèvecoeur-le-Grand and the **D11/D210** back to Amiens.*

A Taste of
Champagne

Although Reims itself is the heart of champagne country, in the early part of the tour you will find many vineyards occupying sloping fields on the edge of the Montagne de Reims, south of the city. Arable plains stretch north to the hill and river country which France shares with Belgium in the Ardennes.

3/4 DAYS • 386KM • 240 MILES

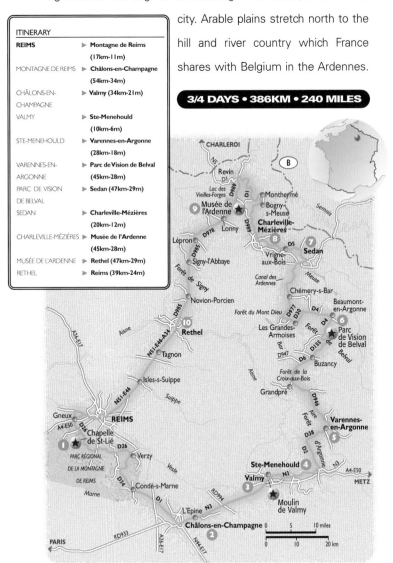

ℹ️ *2 rue Guillaume de Machault,*
Reims

▶ *Leave Reims on the **N31** as*
for Soissons. Turn left on the
***D27** to Gueux, then left on*
*the **D26** through Vrigny. Turn*
right into Ville-Dommange,
follow 'Courmas' sign, then go
right to the Chapelle de St-Lié.

❶ Montagne de Reims,
Champagne-Ardenne
From the viewpoint below the
Chapelle St-Lié there is a lovely
outlook down over the vineyards on the lowest slope of the
wooded hills south of Reims,
and of the city itself, separate on
the plain. Many of the villages
are the home of champagnes
little known abroad – Rilly for
Vilmart, Ludes for *Blondel*,
Villedommange immediately
below for *Champagne de la
Chapelle*. St-Lié, a church on the
summit of a wooded hill sacred
from pagan days, is being
sympathetically restored.

The hilly woodlands and the
villages are all included in the
Parc Naturel Régional de
Montagne de Reims. Many
waymarked walks have been
laid out in it. St-Lié is on the
sentier petite montagne which
meanders along the north-
facing slopes.

▶ *Return to the **D26** and turn*
right. Follow this road, not
always numbered on signs,
through Villers-Allerand, Ludes,
Rilly-la-Montagne and
Verzenay to Verzy. In Verzy,
watch for a right turn on the
***D34** to Louvois and Condé.*
*Go left on the **D1** to Châlons-*
en-Champagne.

BACK TO NATURE

On the way to Châlons, turn
left off the D34 for Les Faux de
Verzy. These are bizarrely
mutated beeches, first
mentioned in monastic writings
of the 6th century, with thin
corkscrewed trunks and
umbrella-like foliage.

---

❷ Châlons-en-Champagne,
Champagne-Ardenne
This is an old established town
whose main street is on the line
of the Romans' Via Agrippa
that runs from Milan to
Boulogne. As its name
suggests, the town does have
extensive champagne cellars to
be visited. The largely 13th-
century cathedral (St Étienne)
with lovely stained glass which
you can easily admire, because
it is at less than the usual neck-
craning angle, has a march of
flying buttresses and a later
north front uncomfortably out
of tune with the rest. You may
find Notre-Dame-en-Vaux just
as interesting. In a cloister
museum reached by a lane
beside this multi-towered
church, more than 50 carved
columns featuring saints,
prophets and medieval personalities are on display. Châlons
has many waterfronts along the
River Marne and the canals
connected with it. Look for the
series of parks and formal
gardens called the Jards.

ℹ️ *3 quai des Arts*

▶ *Leave Châlons on the **N3** as*
for Metz. After Auve, watch for
a left turn signed for Valmy.
*This is the **D284**. Turn right for*
Moulin de Valmy.

FOR HISTORY BUFFS

In the village of L'Épine, on
the N3 after Châlons, the
pilgrimage church is an
astonishing miniature cathedral
in Flamboyant Gothic style.
It houses a statue of the
Virgin found miraculously
unharmed in a burning thorn
bush (*épine*).

---

❸ Valmy, Champagne-
Ardenne
The reconstructed windmill
(*moulin*) on the hilltop at Valmy,
marks the site of the most
significant engagement in the
war which Revolutionary France
fought against the Prussians
and Austrians. Plaques show

the line-up of troops on 20 September 1792, when General Kellermann's inexperienced French army faced the battle-hardened Prussians under the Duke of Brunswick. Expecting an easy victory, the Prussians were in fact repulsed, and the young Revolutionary forces proved they could defend the homeland. Within a few hours, the Republic was proclaimed. The French troops, and Kellermann himself (by a spirited statue) are commemorated in the little village of Valmy.

▶ *Continue on the D284, follow signs to Braux-Ste-Cohière, then follow sign 'Vers N3'. Go left on the N3 to Ste-Menehould.*

4 Ste-Menehould,
Champagne-Ardenne
A statue of Dom Pérignon recalls the fact that this Benedictine monk, to whom we owe the modern method of blending different wines into

champagne, was born here in the 17th century. Incongruously, perhaps, you will find many shops selling a quite different speciality – pigs' trotters.

At the now-restored Maison de Poste, the ill-fated Louis XVI and Marie Antoinette were recognised and subsequently arrested by Revolutionaries.

At Ste-Menehould you will witness the unusual sight of a river flowing in different directions. Thanks to canal works, the Aisne splits into two channels which encircle the town and join up again after it. Since the Auve joins the Aisne here, Ste-Menehould has many pleasant waterways.

Its plateau location and a woodland fringe keep the old upper town almost out of sight, but a good self-guided walk links it with the lower town, whose elegant public buildings were razed after a disastrous fire in 1719.

A picturesque windmill (moulin) still operates in Verzenay

ℹ️ *5 place Général Leclerc*

▶ *Continue on the N3. In Les Islettes turn left for Varennes, following the D2 and then the D38.*

5 Varennes-en-Argonne,
Champagne-Ardenne
In June 1791, when Louis XVI and his family fled secretly from Paris to try to join loyal troops at Metz, it was in Varennes that their coaches were stopped. Arrest, trial and the guillotine followed. The Musée d'Argonne is an excellent local museum, which describes the drama, and gives a balanced account of a king who forcefully supported the Americans in the War of Independence but made many political blunders at home. It also has intriguing displays on the old crafts and industries of the Forest of Argonne, and on the devastating effect of World War I on the district.

French and American flags fly at the entrance to the little grassy park leading to the pillared Pennsylvania Monument. It was troops from that US state who liberated Varennes in 1918.

▶ *Leave Varennes on the D946. Turn right on the D6 to Buzancy, left on the D947, then right and left on the D155 to Fossé, taking care on the bumpy roads. Go left on the D55, left on the D4 and follow it right as for Beaumont, to the Parc de Vision de Belval.*

6 Parc de Vision de Belval,
Champagne-Ardenne
In 350 hectares (865 acres) of woodland and clearings, with a lake to accommodate its ducks and geese, this extensive wildlife park houses around 400 wild animals belonging to species which either still live in the northern forests or are known to have lived in them within the last 2,000 years.

Because the red, roe and fallow deer, the wild boars, the

Sedan, dominated by its fortress, has had a turbulent history

moufflons, the bison and the other animals all live in semi-freedom inside the boundary fence, visitors drive slowly along the viewing roads, follow a fenced-in walking route or travel on the little 'train', whose locomotive is a thinly-disguised tractor. The only animal kept in a separate secure enclosure is a brown bear, which might otherwise become testy if annoyed!

▶ Continue on the **D4** through Beaumont, then go straight on to the **D30** as for Le Chesne. Beyond Les Grandes-Armoises, after the bend sign, take the first right to pass an '8t' sign. Turn right at the 'give way' sign. This is the **D977**. Follow the signs to Sedan.

RECOMMENDED WALKS

After joining the D977 for Sedan, turn right on the D230 into the Forêt de Mont-Dieu. The Circuit de la Chartreuse walk wanders through the forest and overlooks the historic monastery of Mont-Dieu.

---

7 **Sedan,** Champagne-Ardenne

Some quarters of the town are fairly depressing, but Sedan can barely dispel the memories of its past. This is where Napoleon III capitulated to end the Franco-Prussian War of 1870. In World War I the huge Château-Fort, in area the biggest castle in the whole of Europe, was a brutal forced-labour camp. And in the next war, this was where the Germans burst through the French lines in 1940. Now the castle houses a museum on Sedan's military history, and there is a guided tour.

Sedan had royal connections in the 17th century when cloth was woven here for kings. Louis XIV had two fountains built here, and the one on place du Château was filled with wine to celebrate the birth of his son. There are pleasant promenades by the River Meuse.

ℹ *35 rue du Ménil*

▶ Leave Sedan for Floing on the **D5** and continue on this road to Charleville-Mézières. Avoid the autoroute.

8 **Charleville-Mézières,** Champagne-Ardenne

Two once-separate towns, around loops of the River Meuse, have merged here. Mézières to the south is virtually on two islands. Within its 16th-century ramparts, the Flamboyant Gothic Church of Notre-Dame d'Espérance will surprise you with its abstract and geometrical stained-glass windows by René Dürrbach, a collaborator of Picasso's.

At Charleville the elegant, arcaded Place Ducale remains virtually as it was completed in 1628 (pity about the faded and obsolete shop signs).

The grand watermill (Vieux Moulin) on the Meuse is a local museum (Musée Rimbaud), partly dedicated to the poet Arthur Rimbaud, who was born at Charleville.

ℹ *4 place Ducale*

FOR CHILDREN

Charleville-Mézières is the world capital of puppetry. Its Institut International de la Marionette has details of its September 2011 festival.

▶ *Leave Charleville on the D988 and follow signs to Monthermé along the D989. In Monthermé watch for a sharp left turn on the D1 to Revin. Go left on the D989 as for Les Mazures, then Renwez and turn left at the junction with the D140 into the Musée de l'Ardenne.*

9 Musée de l'Ardenne,
Champagne-Ardenne

As much a museum 'in' the forest as 'of' the forest, this 5-hectare (12-acre) area of woodland is devoted to showing – partly with the aid of cheery wooden sculptures – the traditional crafts and harvesting methods of a few unmechanised generations ago. Strolling round, you will see how birchwood brushes were made, how oak bark was peeled, how charcoal burners went about their trade, the kind of huts woodcutters lived in, and a selection of axes and single- and two-man saws.

The museum holds occasional wood-chopping contests, where competitors test their speed and accuracy as they axe their way through felled logs.

▶ *Continue on the D40. Go straight through Lonny. Turn right into Sormonne and left on the D978 as for Laon. Go left on the D985 and continue to Rethel.*

FOR CHILDREN

Before Rethel turn left off the D978 after Lonny for a neat little karting centre with two circuits for children of different ages. Low-powered karts are available for the real youngsters, and first-time drivers are patiently shown how to go about it.

10 Rethel, Champagne-Ardenne

An inscription at the bridge over the River Aisne here is a simple

list of seven years between 1411 and 1940 – the years when war came to Rethel. In the 1930s the town hall was proudly re-created in Renaissance style; then in May 1940 more than three-quarters of the buildings in Rethel were flattened. But the town bobbed up again, as it always has.

The fine old Church of St-Nicholas was restored and the local museum was restocked. Walks along the river and the nearby canal were opened up, including the tree-lined promenade des Isles.

There are sports facilities here for everything from tennis and rugby to show-jumping and archery, and the modern swimming pool is partly under cover, partly in the open air.

Rethel is famous for its local culinary speciality – the *boudin blanc*, a white sausage made from pork, eggs, shallots and seasoning.

SCENIC ROUTES

From the beautifully kept village of Gueux, the D26 runs along the foothills of the Montagne de Reims, through vineyards below the forest ridge.

Beyond Varennes the route follows a pleasant rural landscape, sometimes on the shallow valley floor. The D6 gives long views over fields and wooded hills.

After Monthermé the deep, sinuous and thickly wooded valley of the Meuse gives the finest scenery in the French Ardennes.

ℹ️ *3 quai d'Orfeuil*

▶ *Leave Rethel on the N51 to Reims.*

Monthermé is a popular resort in the Meuse valley

The Heart
of Burgundy

North of Chalon-sur-Saône, this tour runs through the famous Burgundy vineyards. Then it crosses upland areas off the usual tourist track, and wanders through the farm and forest country of the extensive Parc Naturel Régional du Morvan.

3 DAYS • 408KM • 255 MILES

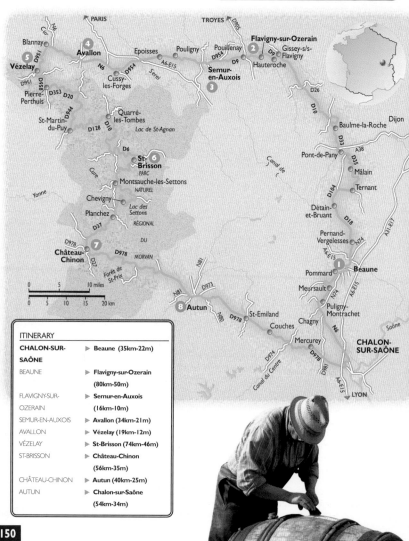

ITINERARY

CHALON-SUR-SAÔNE	▶ Beaune (35km-22m)
BEAUNE	▶ Flavigny-sur-Ozerain (80km-50m)
FLAVIGNY-SUR-OZERAIN	▶ Semur-en-Auxois (16km-10m)
SEMUR-EN-AUXOIS	▶ Avallon (34km-21m)
AVALLON	▶ Vézelay (19km-12m)
VÉZELAY	▶ St-Brisson (74km-46m)
ST-BRISSON	▶ Château-Chinon (56km-35m)
CHÂTEAU-CHINON	▶ Autun (40km-25m)
AUTUN	▶ Chalon-sur-Saône (54km-34m)

ℹ️ *4 place du Port Villiers, Chalon-sur-Saône*

▶ *Leave Chalon on the **N6** as for Beaune. Turn right on the **N74**, left on the **C2** to Puligny-Montrachet, then take the **D113b** to Mersault. Go straight ahead on the **D23**, turn right on the **D17**, continue through Pommard and go left into Beaune.*

❶ Beaune, Burgundy
Thousands of visitors come every year to Beaune. Many go to the Hôtel-Dieu, opened in 1443 as a charitable hospital. Containing displays which show how the nuns looked after their aged patients in years gone by, as well as Rogier van der Weyden's stunning 15th-century altarpiece of the *Last Judgement*, the building is a ravishing mixture of polychrome tiling, intricate window details and appealing galleries. Beaune is honeycombed with wine cellars, some of them in the town walls. The Musée du Vin de Bourgogne occupies an old town mansion of the dukes of Burgundy, while the Athenaeum is a cultural centre linking wine, literature and local history.

Magnificent tapestries hang in the Church of Notre-Dame. Beaune's Musée des Beaux-Arts spans the 12th to 20th centuries, with a particularly fine collection of 16th- to 18th-century Flemish and Dutch paintings.

ℹ️ *6 boulevard Perpreuil*

SPECIAL TO...

Puligny-Montrachet, Meursault and Pommard are vineyard villages of the Côte d'Or, whose white burgundies are held in high regard. More than a dozen *grand crus* and *premiers crus* come from Puligny-Montrachet, while the Meursault growers are keenest on welcoming visitors. Details of wine tours are available from the tourist information office in Beaune.

▶ *Leave Beaune on the **D18** going north, passing Pernand-Vergelesses. Continue on the **D18** through Changey, turn right on to the **D8**, then take the **D25f** and the **D25** to Bruant. Go left on the **D8** again, fork right on the **D104**, right on the **D104b** to*

Magnificent Gothic architecture characterises medieval Beaune

*Ternant, then take the **D35** to Pont-de-Pany. Go left on the **D905**, and immediately after leaving Pont-de-Pany turn right over the autoroute to Mâlain on the **D33**. Continue through Baulme-la-Roche. Turn left on the **D10** to Gissey-sous-Flavigny. Bear left at the roundabout, past Café de l'Oze, on to the **D10e** to Hauteroche. Turn sharp right and follow signs to Flavigny, entering it on the **D9**.*

FOR HISTORY BUFFS

Look for the dolmens in the woodland left of the D104b before Ternant. These great balanced-stone chambers remain impressive and mysterious after 6,000 years.

❷ Flavigny-sur-Ozerain, Burgundy
History has moved on, isolating this little medieval hilltop town. Park outside, study the labyrinthine medieval street plan and feel the centuries drift

away as you stroll through an ancient gateway, along narrow streets and alleyways, to the 13th-century church in the square. Local farm produce is sold here. Guided tours are arranged of an eerie 8th-century crypt. There are farm-track walks on the plateau, one to a site said to be a Roman camp from Julius Caesar's time.

SPECIAL TO...

Though the town was the location for the film *Chocolat*, it is aniseed balls that are Flavigny's most famous product. The old abbey makes aniseed in many forms – sweets, candies and flavourings. The genuine article – *Les Anis de Flavigny* – is on sale in local grocery shops.

▶ *Continue on the D9 and D954 to Semur-en-Auxois.*

3 Semur-en-Auxois, Burgundy

Semur occupies a pinched-in red granite promontory at a hairpin bend on the River Armançon. Its 18th-century Pont Joly looks to banked-up houses and the massive rampart towers of the medieval fortress.

The 13th-century Church of Notre-Dame features an eccentrically narrow nave and good stained-glass windows including a rather frank account of the work of the butchers' guild. There are medieval houses and a rampart walk. From the Pont Joly, Semur probably looks its best floodlit or at sunset.

The Church of St-Lazare, Avallon, has fine carvings on its doorway

ℹ *2 place Gaveau*

▶ *Continue on the D954 and N6 to Avallon.*

FOR HISTORY BUFFS

At Époisses, on the D954 on the way to Avallon, pause to visit the dry-moated château, with its dovecote exhibition and cheese tastings. Madame de Sévigny was a frequent visitor to the château. Even when the château itself is closed, you can visit its grounds, which form a Burgundy village in miniature.

---

4 Avallon, Burgundy

Many of the old rampart walls, towers, bastions and gateways survive in the very agreeable old town. Perimeter walks and stairways look down on the attractive valley of the River Cousin.

Avallon is packed with fascinating old buildings, such as the clock tower of 1456, formerly a town gate, through which a street leads to the well-endowed Musée de l'Avallonnais and the 12th-century Church of St-Lazare. Part of St-Lazare houses the etchings for 20th-century artist Georges Rouault's harrowing but highly regarded series of prints entitled *Miserere*.

At the Musée du Costume you can see exhibitions of period costumes, which are rotated on an annual basis. Over 100 costumes dating from 1800 to 1970 are presented in 12 rooms.

ℹ *6 rue Bocquillot*

▶ *Continue on the N6 as for Auxerre, then turn left on the D951 to Vézelay.*

5 Vézelay, Burgundy

Climbing sinuously to a hilltop, the main street of this little town passes artists' studios, galleries and displays of semi-precious stones before it reaches the Basilica of Ste-Madeleine, one of the all-time glories of Romanesque design. The church, a great pilgrimage goal when it was believed to contain the remains of Mary Magdalen, survived fire, plunder and virtual destruction during the Revolution, to be completely restored in the 19th century. Look for its splendid doorways, intricately carved capitals, impressive crypt and the view from the tower, but most of all for the mellow light that pours into the interior.

Stylised carving over a doorway at the Basilica of Ste-Madeleine

RECOMMENDED WALKS

Ask at the tourist office in Vézelay about the seven waymarked walks in the countryside 'under the hill'. Each is described in an individual leaflet which includes a map, walking directions and information.

ℹ️ *Rue St-Etienne*

▶ *Leave Vézelay on the **D957** to St-Père, then go right on the **D958** to Pierre-Perthuis. Turn left on the **D353** and immediately right following 'Les Ponts' sign. Go through Précy-le-Moult, then turn right on the **D36** which becomes the **D20**. At a crossroads, turn right on the **D944**. In St-Martin-du-Puy, watch for a sharp left turn to Quarré-les-Tombes on the **D128**. In Quarré, turn right through Les Levaults on the **D10**, then right on the **D211**. Go straight ahead on the **D6** to the Maison du Parc.*

6 St-Brisson, Burgundy
On the edge of St-Brisson, a fine old red-roofed farm complex is the headquarters of the Parc Naturel Régional du Morvan, the Morvan being the wooded mountain region between the rivers Loire and Saône. The Maison du Parc illustrates wildlife, crafts, conservation and the rural way

of life. The grounds include a herb garden, animal enclosures, a waterfowl pond, and pathways down to the lake. Also here is the Musée de la Résistance, which tells the story of the Morvan's secret war in World War II.

▶ *Return from Maison du Parc, take the first left, go left at the T-junction through St-Brisson, then bear right on the **C1** and continue to Montsauche-les-Settons. Go left on the **D37**, then left on the **D193**. Keep Lac des Settons on your right, then watch for a sharp right turn following the 'Rive Gauche' sign. At the give way sign turn left on the **D37** and continue to Château-Chinon.*

FOR CHILDREN

Lac des Settons beside the D193 is a fine recreational reservoir with wooded bays, beaches and picnic sites. The youngsters can try out pedaloes and generally splash around.

7 Château-Chinon, Burgundy
Capital of the Morvan, Château-Chinon rises to a parkland with walks and drives and gorgeous views over the surrounding countryside.

The Musée du Costume also has displays on local arts and traditions. In the Musée du Septennat you will find an exhibition of the ceremonial gifts lavished at home and abroad on François Mitterrand during his first term as President of France. Previously a local politician here, he donated them all to the *département*.

ℹ️ *Place St-Christophe*

▶ *Leave Château-Chinon on the **D978** to Autun.*

8 Autun, Burgundy
Founded by the Emperor Augustus as *Augustodunum*, Autun retains Roman archways such as the Porte St-André and the Porte d'Arroux, still used by traffic and pedestrians. The Musée Rolin, housed in a 15th-century mansion, specialises in Roman exhibits, and the original riverside theatre is still in use. Look for the majestic portal of the 12th-century Cathédrale St-Lazare, the medieval rampart walk, the immaculate military academy, and the 18th-century Lycée Bonaparte where Napoleon was a pupil.

ℹ️ *13 rue Général Demetz*

▶ *Leave Autun following signs to Chalon-sur-Saône.*

The Historic
Centre of France

Many strands of French life and history combine in this tour from Chartres – the palace of Fontainebleau, the castle at Rambouillet, Barbizon and Moret-sur-Loing. You will find pleasant roads which run through cool shady woodlands, and others which cross skyline-to-skyline arable plains, wide open to the summer sun.

2/3 DAYS • 312KM • 194 MILES

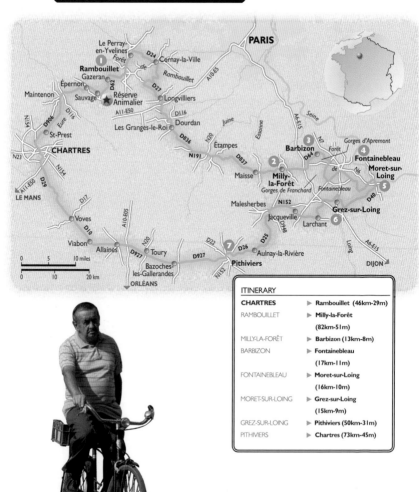

ITINERARY

CHARTRES	▶	**Rambouillet (46km-29m)**
RAMBOUILLET	▶	**Milly-la-Forêt**
		(82km-51m)
MILLY-LA-FORÊT	▶	**Barbizon (13km-8m)**
BARBIZON	▶	**Fontainebleau**
		(17km-11m)
FONTAINEBLEAU	▶	**Moret-sur-Loing**
		(16km-10m)
MORET-SUR-LOING	▶	**Grez-sur-Loing**
		(15km-9m)
GREZ-SUR-LOING	▶	**Pithiviers (50km-31m)**
PITHIVIERS	▶	**Chartres (73km-45m)**

▶ *Leave Chartres on the **N154**. At the traffic lights, turn right for St-Prest and continue on the **D906** to Maintenon. Turn right to Épernon. Turn right on the **D176**, then continue through Droue to Émancé. Go as for Orphin, turn left on the **D62** to Gazeran, then follow the signs to Rambouillet.*

❶ Rambouillet, Île de France
This is France's 'presidential town'. Its elegant château, standing among extensive woodlands, lawns and water gardens, is an official residence of the president, but is open to visitors most of the year. Louis XVI commissioned two buildings in the grounds – the ornamental dairy called the Laiterie de la Reine, and the Chaumière des Coquillages ('Cottage of Shells') with its wall covering of seashells, mother-of-pearl and tiny pieces of marble. Also in the grounds you will see the Bergerie Nationale, famous for its pedigree Merino rams. There is a museum here on the husbandry and breeding of sheep. Rambouillet's racecourse is southeast of town. Beyond it (take the D27), the Espace Rambouillet wildlife reserve shelters wild boar and deer.

ℹ️ *8 place de la Libération*

▶ *Leave Rambouillet as for Paris, join the **N10** dual-carriageway and turn off through Le Perray-en-Yvelines on the **D910**. Go right on the **D24** and continue to Cernay-la-Ville. Turn left on to the **D306**, then sharp right on the **D72**, left on the **D61**, then right on the **D72** again to Clairefontaine-en-Yvelines. Go left on the **D27** and follow 'Dourdan' signs, turning right on the **D149**. Go left on the **D836** to Dourdan, then take the **D116** before rejoining the **D836** and taking the **N191** through Étampes. Go right on the **D837** and into Milly-la-Forêt.*

❷ Milly-la-Forêt, Île de France
Expertly trimmed, shade-providing trees; a 15th-century market hall; red-tiled houses; and a wandering stream with wash-house quays: all these combine to give this village a

Rodin called Chartres Cathedral the 'Acropolis of France'

timeless appearance.
    The artist, poet and dramatist Jean Cocteau is buried in the little 12th-century chapel of St-Blaise-des-Simples, which he had previously decorated. The *simples* are medicinal herbs, which remain a preoccupation of Milly today. On the Nemours road is the Conservatoire National of medicinal and aromatic plants and plants used by industry (see panel below).

ℹ️ *47 rue Langlois*

▶ *Follow 'Fontainebleau' signs on the **D837**. In Arbonne, bear left as for Melun. Turn right on the **D64** to Barbizon.*

❸ Barbizon, Île de France
In the mid-19th century, a group of landscape artists centred on the painter Théodore Rousseau, made this village their base.

They were to become known as the Barbizon School. Greater figures, such as the Realist painter Jean François Millet, whose *Angelus* was painted near by, were also Barbizon men.

The L'Atelier Jean-François Millet is a popular attraction, full of reminders of his life and work (though no original paintings) and staging several temporary exhibitions a year.

The artists' often frugal meals were taken at the village inn run by old Monsieur Ganne. Now the Auberge Ganne houses an atmospheric museum in which it is easy to imagine that the next person at the door is a hungry painter, ready for dinner after a day's sketching in the countryside.

ℹ️ *41 Grande Rue*

▶ *Leave Barbizon by the Grande Rue and enter the Forêt de Fontainebleau. Turn right at a T-junction following the 'Fontainebleau par route forestière' sign. Go right at the stop signs for Franchard (this is the **D301**), then left on the **N152** and at the busy roundabout take the **N6** for the town of Fontainebleau.*

4 **Fontainebleau,** Île de France

Everything else in this elegant town defers to the spectacular palace in its parkland of lakes, woods and formal and landscape gardens. A discreet plaque acknowledges John D Rockefeller Jr's generous funding of the palace restoration. The Musée Napoléon, combined with a guided visit of the small apartments, paints a vivid picture of life under the Second Empire. In the town itself, the Musée d'Art et d'Histoire Militaire features grand displays of the French military through the ages.

ℹ️ *4 rue Royale*

BACK TO NATURE

Planted with pines, birches, oaks, chestnut trees, hornbeams and – especially – glorious beechwoods, the Forêt de Fontainebleau is one of the most beautiful and most carefully protected woodlands in Europe. It covers about 25,000 hectares (61,775 acres), most of them open to the public.

▶ *Return to the busy roundabout and take the **D58** as for Bourron-Marlotte. Go straight ahead on the **D148**, then turn left on to the **D104** to Moret-sur-Loing.*

5 **Moret-sur-Loing,** Île de France

This very appealing little place is an 'ancient and royal city' that once stood on the French frontier, fortified against Burgundy, across a beautiful stretch of the River Loing. Fine medieval gateways, Renaissance and later buildings survive.

Cycle enthusiasts should not miss the Conservatoire du Vélo, a museum sited where the Prugnat factory made spare parts; exhibits from every decade include the most recent racing bikes. Moret also celebrates its connection with the Impressionist painter Alfred Sisley.

ℹ️ *4 bis place de Samois*

▶ *Leave Moret on the **D302**, then immediately turn right at traffic lights for Nemours.*

Napoléon was responsible for Fontainebleau's sumptuous interior

*Watch for another right turn as for Nemours along the **D40**. Go right on to the **D40d**, then left into Grez-sur-Loing.*

FOR CHILDREN

As you approach Grez-sur-Loing, look on the right for Tacot des Lacs, a full-scale railway, with trains like the 1900 steam locomotive *Clémentine* running trips through scrubland and across the River Loing.

6 Grez-sur-Loing, Île de France

Here is a lovely stretch of the Loing with gardens, boathouses, weeping willows and flotillas of geese and mallards. Swallows and damselflies dart above the water, swifts in the higher air. Beyond the old arched bridge rises a pale 12th-century tower.

In the 1870s, Robert Louis Stevenson joined the Bohemian summer colony at Grez. Later, Frederick Delius composed much of his music here.

Stroll to the austere and lofty medieval church, and along the hollyhock lane from the little Place Jolivet. The artists have gone, but the appeal of this charming village never fades.

▶ *Leave Grez as for La Chapelle-la-Reine, taking the **D104**. After the junction sign watch for a left turn to Larchant. Go right as for La Chapelle on the **D16**. Turn left on to the **D36** and follow signs to Jacqueville. Bear right then left following the 'Malesherbes' sign on the **C7**. Take care at the level crossing. At the give way sign, go left on to the **N152** to Malesherbes. Take the **D948** as for Puiseaux, then go right on the **D25** through Pinçon and Briarres. Continue through Aulnay-la-Rivière to Pithiviers.*

FOR HISTORY BUFFS

Malesherbes, on the way to Pithiviers, has a castle worthy of a visit on its outskirts. Off the D132, the many-turreted Château de Rouville overlooks the valley of the Essone. The Château de Malesherbes itself, on the Puiseaux road, is closed to visitors

Moret-sur-Loing is a favourite destination for Parisians

7 Pithiviers, Île de France

Famous for its fine almond cakes, Pithiviers has a very interesting local museum, housed in the former 18th-century Hôtel-Dieu, which explains the local cuisine and its cooks' pioneering use of saffron – the region was once of European importance for saffron-growing.

Historic steam locomotives from as early as 1870 run on the last 4km (2½-mile) stretch of a light railway opened in 1892. The Musée des Transports displays some elegant old coaches and tells the story of France's branch lines.

ⓘ *Mail-Ouest, Maison 'Les Remparts'*

▶ *Leave Pithiviers on the **D927** to Allaines. Now follow the signs to the **D12** and join the **D10** to Voves. Turn right on to the **D17** as for Auneau and enter the one-way traffic system in Voves. At the two-way sign turn into a side road on the left. Go right at the 'stop' sign and return to Chartres on the **D29**.*

MOTORING IN FRANCE

ACCIDENTS

If you are involved in an accident in France you must complete a *constat l'amiable* before moving the vehicle. It must be signed by the other party involved, and in the event of a dispute or a refusal to complete the form, you should immediately obtain a *constat d'huissier*, a written report from a bailiff (*huissier*).

BREAKDOWNS

If your car breaks down, try to move it out of the way of traffic. Place a warning triangle to the rear of the vehicle. It will be necessary for you to seek local assistance as, at present, there is no nationwide road assistance service in France. See also **Warning Triangle**, page 159.

CAR HIRE

Most car-hire firms have offices at airports, main railway stations and in large towns and cities in France. It can be expensive, so consider arranging a fly-drive package from home.

You must be at least 20 years old to hire a car in France, and have held a full driver's licence for at least a year. There may be a maximum age limit, usually 70.

To hire a car you will have to have your licence and passport or national ID card.

Some companies include mileage in the cost, but others may charge extra above a certain distance, so check before you rent.

Make sure you have adequate insurance cover (see **Insurance**).

CHILDREN

Children under 10 are not permitted to travel as front seat passengers, with the exception of babies or very young children in an approved rear-facing child seat. Children under 10 in the rear of the vehicle must use a child seat or restraint if fitted. Note: under no circumstances should a rear-facing restraint be used in a seat that's fitted with an airbag.

DOCUMENTS

To drive in France, a valid full driver's licence is required, and the minimum driving age is 18. Visitors may use temporarily imported motorcycles of up to 80cc at 16 years. An international licence is not required for visitors from the US, UK or Western Europe.

You also need to carry the vehicle's registration document, plus a letter of authorisation from the owner, if they are not accompanying the vehicle, and the current insurance certificate (a green card is not mandatory but remains internationally recognised and can be helpful). You will also need to affix a nationality plate or sticker to the vehicle.

DRINKING AND DRIVING

The laws in Europe regarding drinking and driving are very strict and the penalties severe. They include stiff fines and police escort back to a ferry terminal.

DRIVING CONDITIONS

Keep to the right (*serrez à droite*).

Though main roads have priority (*passage protégé*), right of way is given to vehicles coming in from the right (*priorité à droite*) if there are no stop signs.

The *priorité* rule no longer applies at roundabouts, where you give way to cars already on the roundabout.

Mountain tours call for a properly serviced and not overladen car. Especially in these areas, petrol stations may be far apart.

On the Clermont-Ferrand, Pau and Grenoble tours, roadside notices displaying *Ouvert* (open) or *Fermé* (closed) show road conditions ahead.

FERRY SERVICES

Brittany Ferries
www.brittany-ferries.com
Condor Ferries
www.condorferries.com
Irish Ferries
www.irishferries.com
L D Lines
www.ldlines.co.uk
Norfolk Line
www.norfolkline.com
P&O Ferries
www.poferries.com
Seafrance
www.seafrance.com
Transmanche Ferries
www.transmancheferries.com

FUEL

Some garages may close between noon and 3pm, but fuel is generally available 24-hours on motorways. Prices on motorways will normally be higher than elsewhere; self-service pumps will be slightly cheaper.

Leaded gas (*essence super*) is now only sold in one grade (98 octane), while unleaded is sold in two: 95 octane (*essence sans plomb*) and 98 octane (*super sans plomb*). Diesel (*gasoil* or *gazole*) is much cheaper and readily available.

Credit cards are generally accepted, except in some rural areas. Automatic pumps may not accept international credit cards.

INSURANCE

Fully comprehensive insurance, which covers you for some of the expenses incurred after a breakdown or an accident, is advisable. Proof of insurance may be needed.

LIGHTS

It is obligatory to use headlights, as driving on sidelights only is not permitted. In fog, mist or poor visibility during the day, either fog lamps or dipped headlights must be switched on in addition to sidelights.

It is compulsory for motor-cyclists riding machines exceeding 125cc to use dipped headlights during the day. Failure to comply will lead to an on-the-spot deposit (see **Police Fines**).

Take a set of replacement bulbs. Drivers able to replace a faulty bulb when requested to do so by the police will not avoid a fine, but may avoid the cost and inconvenience of a garage call-out. Yellow tinted headlights are no longer necessary, but beams must be adjusted for right-hand drive – beam deflectors are the easiest option.

PETS TRAVEL SCHEME

The Pet Travel scheme (PETS), which only applies to dogs (including assistance dogs), cats, ferrets and certain other pets, enables pets resident in the UK to enter France without quarantine restrictions and then return to Britain. Thanks to the relaxation of quarantine controls in the UK, they can go straight home on arrival. In order to bring your pet into, or back into, the UK from France, it must be fitted with a microchip, be vaccinated against rabies, pass a blood test at least six calendar months before travel, and be issued with a pet passport (or hold a valid pet certificate dated before 1 October, 2004).

Before entering the UK, the animal will also need to receive both tapeworm and tick treatments from a French vet. Careful thought should be given about the welfare of your pet and whether a holiday abroad is appropriate. When in France, keep your pet under strict control when near livestock, as you would in the UK, and be aware that fiercely protective guard dogs are common in rural areas.

PETS gives information about France's involvement in the scheme, regulations, documentation required, microchip ID tags, help finding a vet, guidance on looking after pets during transportation, bringing your pet from a long-haul country, authorised routes, approved transport companies, charges, a 'what's new' section, and more.

For information on how to achieve all the requirements of the scheme, contact PETS Helpline (tel: 0870 241 1710, lines open Mon–Fri 8–6; email: quarantine@animalhealth.gsi. gov.uk; www.defra.gov.uk/ animalh/quarantine/pets/

POLICE FINES

Police in France impose an on-the-spot deposit for minor traffic offences and subsequently levy a fine which may be the same as, or greater or lesser than, the deposit. If the fine is not paid, legal proceedings will usually follow. Once it has been paid, a fine cannot be recovered, but a receipt should be obtained as proof of payment.

ROADS

France has a very comprehensive network of roads, and their surfaces are generally good; exceptions are usually signposted *Chaussée déformée*.

The *autoroute* (marked by an A on maps) is the French equivalent of the British motorway or American expressway. There are also *Route Nationale* (N) roads, *Route Départementale* (D) roads and, of course, smaller, quieter country roads.

Some roads also have an E number, which denotes a European route.

SAFETY VEST

It is mandatory to carry a yellow reflective safety vest inside the vehicle.

SEAT BELTS

It is compulsory to wear seat belts if a car is fitted with them.

SPEED LIMITS

In dry weather a higher speed limit applies than in wet weather. Unless otherwise indicated, maximum speed limits are as follows, with wet-weather limits in *italics*.

Built-up areas 50kph (31mph). Outside built-up areas on normal roads 90kph (56mph) *80kph (49mph)*; on dual carriageways separated by a central reservation 110kph (69mph); also motorways without tolls.

Toll motorways 130kph (80mph) *110kph (69mph)*.

The beginning of a built-up area is indicated by a sign with the place-name in blue letters on a light background; the end is marked by a sign with a thin red line diagonally across the place-name. Unless otherwise signposted, follow the above speed limits.

The minimum speed in the fast lane on a level stretch of motorway during good daytime visibility is 80kph (49mph); drivers travelling below this speed could be fined.

In fog, when visibility is reduced to 50m (55 yards), the speed limit on all roads is 50kph (31mph).

Visitors to France who have held a driving licence for less than two years, must not exceed 80kph (49mph) outside built-up areas, 100kph (62mph) on dual carriageways separated by a central reservation and 110kph (69mph) on motorways.

TOLLS

Tolls are payable on many motorways in France. Toll booths will not accept travellers' cheques, but some credit cards are accepted.

WARNING TRIANGLE/ HAZARD WARNING LIGHTS

The use of a warning triangle or hazard warning lights is compulsory in the event of an accident or breakdown. It is advisable to carry a warning triangle, even if your car has hazard warning lights.

The triangle must be placed on the road 30m (33 yards) behind the vehicle, or further, if necessary, to allow for bends in the road, and must be clearly visible for 100m (110 yards).

ACCOMMODATION AND RESTAURANTS

Listed below is a selection of hotels (◊) and restaurants (⊕) which can be found along the routes of each tour.

Prices
Hotel charges are divided into three price brackets based on a double room for one night:
€€€ – over €110
€€ – €65–€110
€ – under €65

Restaurant prices are based on two courses, without wine:
€€€ – over €65
€€ – €30–€65
€ – under €30

TOUR I
CAEN Normandy
◊ **Hôtel des Quatrans €–€€**
17 rue Gémare (tel: 02 31 86 25 57; www.hotel-des-quatrans.com).
47 rooms.

◊ ⊕ **Ivan Vautier €€€**
3 avenue Henry Chéron (tel: 02 31 73 32 71; www.ivanvautier.com). *Gourmet Norman cuisine from one of the region's top chefs.*
19 rooms.

⊕ **ArchiDona €€**
17 rue Gémare (tel: 02 31 85 30 30). *Elegant fine dining on creative modern cuisine. Closed Sat lunch, Sun & Mon.*

BAYEUX Normandy
◊ **Le Lion d'Or €€–€€€**
71 rue St Jean (tel: 02 31 92 06 90; www.liondor-bayeux.fr).
25 rooms.

⊕ **Le Pommier €**
38 rue des Cuisiniers (tel: 02 31 21 52 10). *Seasonal Normandy cuisine. Open daily lunch & dinner.*

GRANDCAMP-MAISY
Normandy
◊ **Duguesclin €–€€**
4 quai Crampon (tel: 02 31 22 64 22).
22 rooms.

BAGNOLES-DE-L'ORNE
Normandy
◊ ⊕ **Le Manoir du Lys €€–€€€**
Route de Juvigny, La Croix Gautier (tel: 02 33 37 80 69). *Gourmet & regional cuisine. Open daily lunch, dinner. Closed Sun evening, also Mon Nov–Apr.*
32 rooms.

TOUR 2
HONFLEUR Normandy
◊ **Les Maisons de Léa €€€**
13 place Ste-Catherine (tel: 02 31 14 49 49; www.lesmaisonsdelea.com).
29 rooms.

⊕ **La Terrasse et l'Assiette €€**
8 place Ste-Catherine (tel: 02 31 89 31 33). *Traditional Normandy cuisine. Open Wed–Sun lunch & dinner.*

ROUEN Normandy
◊ **Hôtel de Bourgtheroulde €€€**
15 place de la Pucelle (tel: 02 35 14 50 50; www.hotelsparouen.com).
76 rooms.

⊕ **Auberge Saint Maclou €€**
222 rue Martainville (tel: 02 36 71 06 67). *Traditional cuisine in a historic building with a cobbled terrace. Closed Sun dinner, Mon.*

TOUR 3
LE MONT-ST-MICHEL
Normandy
◊ **Mouton-Blanc €€**
Grande Rue (tel: 02 33 60 14 08; www.lemoutonblanc.fr).
15 rooms.

ST-MALO Brittany
◊ **Ascott €€**
35 rue du Chapitre (tel: 02 99 81 89 93; www.ascotthotel.com).
10 rooms.

⊕ **Bouche en Folie €–€€**
14 rue du Boyer, Intra Muros (tel: 06 72 49 08 89). *Breton specialities include wild boar and herbed salmon. Open Wed–Sun lunch & dinner.*

DINARD Brittany
◊ **Hôtel Printania €€–€€€**
5 avenue George V (tel: 02 99 46 13 07).
55 rooms.

⊕ **Altair €€**
8 boulevard Féart (tel: 02 99 46 13 58). *Traditional French fare with masses of seafood. Open Thu–Sun lunch & dinner, Tue–Wed dinner only. Closed Mon & winter, except school hols.*

ERQUY Brittany
⊕ **La Table de Jeanne €**
60 rue du Port (tel: 02 96 72 32 60). *Specialises in seafood and grills cooked over wood. Open daily lunch & dinner.*

DINAN Brittany
◊ **Hôtel d'Avaugour €€–€€€**
1 place du Champs (tel: 02 96 39 07 49; www.avaugourhotel.com).
24 rooms.

TOUR 4
QUIMPER Brittany
◊ **Océania €€–€€€**
17 rue du Poher, Kerdrézec (tel: 02 98 90 46 26).
92 rooms.

⊕ **Brasserie de l'Epée €–€€**
14 rue du Parc (tel: 02 98 95 28 97). *Traditional brasserie with grills and seafood. Open daily lunch & dinner.*

BREST Brittany
◊ **Hôtel de la Corniche €–€€**
1 rue Amiral Nicol (tel: 02 98 45 12 42; www.hotel-la-corniche.com).
19 rooms.

⊕ **Armen €€€**
21 rue de Lyon (tel: 02 98 46 28 34). *Gourmet restaurant; chef is former student of Paul Bocuse and Joël Robuchon. Open Tue–Sat lunch & dinner.*

ST-THÉGONNEC Brittany
◇ **Ar Presbital Coz** €
18 rue Lividic (tel: 02 98 79 45
62) No Credit Cards.
6 rooms.

⊕ **Auberge St-Thégonnec**
€–€€
6 place de la Mairie (tel: 02 98
79 61 18). *French cuisine. Closed
Sat lunch, Sun dinner (& lunch
Sep–Mar) & Mon.*

TOUR 5
CLERMONT-FERRAND
Auvergne
◇ **Mercure** €€–€€€
82 boulevard François
Mitterrand (tel: 04 73 34 46 46;
www.mercure.com).
123 rooms.

⊕ **Brasserie Danièle Bath**
€–€€
Place du Marché St Pierre (tel:
04 73 31 23 22). *Modern French
cuisine; booking required. Open
Tue–Sat lunch & dinner. Closed 3
weeks Feb & 2 weeks Sep.*

LE MONT-DORE Auvergne
⊕ **Le Pitsounet** €–€€
Ancienne route Le Mont Dore,
La Bourboule, Au Genestoux
(tel: 04 73 65 00 67;
www.lepitsounet.com). *Regional
specialities. Closed Mon, Sun
dinner, mid-Oct to mid-Dec.*

AMBERT Auvergne
◇ **Le Prieuré** €–€€
Le Bourg, Chaumont le
Bourg (tel: 04 73 95 03 91;
www.leprieurehotelrestaurant.
com).
25 rooms.

TOUR 6
LIMOGES Limousin
◇ **Hotel Luk** €–€€
29 place Jourdan
(tel: 05 55 33 44 00;
www.lukhotel-limoges.com).
57 rooms.

⊕ **Domaine de Faugeras** €€
Allée de Faugeras (tel: 05 55 34
66 22). *Traditional French cooking, using fresh local produce. Open
Tue–Sat lunch & dinner.*

UZERCHE Limousin
◇ **Hotel Ambroise** €
34 avenue du Général de
Gaulle (tel: 05 55 73 28 60;
www.hotel-ambroise.com).
14 rooms.

⊕ **Restaurant Teyssier** €–€€
Rue du Pont Turgot (tel: 05 55
73 10 05). *Mediterranean
flavours. Open lunch (excluding
Wed) & dinner daily.*

AUBUSSON Limousin
⊕ **Café des Arts** €
2 place Maurice Dayras (tel: 05
55 66 10 05). *Typical brasserie
menu within arts centre. Open
Tue–Sat, lunch & dinner.*

TOUR 7
LA ROCHELLE
Poitou-Charente
◇ **Les Brises** €€–€€€
1 Chemin de la Digue de
Richelieu (tel: 05 46 43 89 37;
www.hotellesbrises.com).
48 rooms.

◇ **Le Rupella** €–€€
1–3 quai Maubec
(tel: 05 46 41 30 31).
20 rooms.

⊕ **Brasserie Des Dames** €
Place Barentin (tel: 05 46 41
61 17). *French nouvelle cuisine,
seafood, world cuisines, including
Asian. Open daily for lunch.*

COGNAC Poitou-Charente
◇ **Domaine du Breuil** €€
104 rue Robert Daugas
(tel: 05 45 35 32 06; www.hotel-
domaine-du-breuil.com).
24 rooms.

ANGOULÊME
Poitou-Charente
◇ **Mercure Hôtel de
France** €€–€€€
1 place des Halles (tel: 05 45 95
47 95; www.accorhotels.com).
89 rooms.

NIORT Poitou-Charente
⊕ **Le Sorrento** €€
7 avenue de Paris (tel: 05 49 24
58 59). *Typical French cuisine
with an Italian accent, including
pizzas. Light, airy dining room.
Open daily 12–2, 7–11.*

TOUR 8
NANTES Loire Atlantique
◇ **Château de Bois Briand** €€
10 rue de Bois Briand
(tel: 02 51 79 70 25). *Closed 21
Dec–early Jan.*
2 rooms.

◇ **Hôtel Graslin** €€–€€€
1 rue Piron (tel: 02 40 69 72 91;
www.hotel-graslin.com).
47 rooms.

⊕ **La Cigale** €–€€
Place Graslin (tel: 02 51 84
94 94). *Classic French brasserie
menu, plus café and salon de thé.
Open daily for lunch & dinner.*

SAUMUR Loire Valley West
◇ **Anne d'Anjou** €€–€€€
32 quai Mayaud (tel: 02 41 67
30 30; www.hotel-
anneanjou.com).
43 rooms.

◇ **Hôtel St Pierre** €€–€€€
Rue Haute St Pierre
(tel: 02 41 50 33 00;
www.saintpierresaumur.com).
14 rooms.

ANGERS Loire Valley West
◇ **Hôtel d'Anjou Best
Western** €€–€€€
1 boulevard Maréchal Foch
(tel: 02 41 21 12 11;
www.bestwestern.com).
53 rooms.

◇ **Hôtel de France** €€€
8 place de la Gare (tel: 02 41 88
49 42; fax: 02 41 86 76 70).
55 rooms.

⊕ **Grandgousier** €
7 rue St Laud (tel: 02 41 87
81 47). *Regional cuisine of the Pays
de la Loire. Open Mon–Sat lunch &
dinner. Closed Sun.*

TOUR 9
TOURS Loire Valley Central
◇ **Hôtel du Manoir** €€
2 rue Traversière (tel: 02 47 05
37 37; fax: 02 47 05 16 00).
20 rooms.

⊕ **Le Petit Patrimoine** €
58 rue Colbert (tel: 02 47 66 05
81). *Classic French cooking; booking recommended. Open Tue–Sat*

lunch & dinner. Closed last 2 weeks Jul & Christmas.

AMBOISE Loire Valley Central
◇ **Belle-Vue €€**
12 quai Charles Guinot (tel: 02 47 57 02 26; fax: 02 47 30 51 23). Closed Dec–late Apr. 32 rooms.

VALENÇAY Loire Valley Central
◇ **Hôtel le Relais du Moulin €–€€**
95 rue Nationale (tel: 02 54 00 38 00; www.hotel-lerelais dumoulin.com). 54 rooms.

TOUR 10
BORDEAUX Gironde
◇ **Hôtel Continental €€–€€€**
10 rue Montesquieu (tel: 05 56 52 66 00; www.hotel-le-continental.com). 50 rooms.

◇ **Hôtel de Sèze €–€€**
5 rue de Sèze (tel: 05 56 52 65 54; fax: 05 56 48 98 00). 24 rooms.

ARCACHON Aquitaine
◇ **Le Trianon €€–€€€**
161 boulevard de la Plage (tel: 05 56 22 34 00; fax: 05 56 83 10 70). 80 rooms.

MIMIZAN Aquitaine
◇ **Hôtel Atlantis €–€€**
19 rue de l'Abbaye (tel: 05 58 09 02 18; www.atlantis-mimizan.com). 20 rooms.

⑪ **Le Plaisance €–€€**
10 rue des Cormorans (tel: 05 58 09 08 06). Regional specialities, seafood, grills. Closed Tue & Wed.

NÉRAC Aquitaine
◇ **Hôtel Henri IV €**
4 place du Général Leclerc (tel: 05 53 65 00 63; www.hotelhenriIV.fr). 10 rooms.

TOUR 11
PÉRIGUEUX Aquitaine
◇ **Hôtel Bristol €€**
37–39 rue Antoine-Gadaud (tel: 05 53 08 75 90; www.bristolfrance.com). 29 rooms.

⑪ **Hercule Poirot €–€€**
2 rue de la Nation (tel: 05 53 08 90 76). Regional dishes such as magret de canard sauce Périgueux. Closed Wed, Tue dinner in low season, first 2 weeks Jan.

LES EYZIES Midi-Pyrénées
⑪ **Moulin de la Beune €€**
2 rue des Moulins bas (tel: 05 53 06 94 33). Traditional French cuisine is the speciality here. Open Apr–Oct daily. Closed Tue, Wed & Sat lunch.

ROCAMADOUR
Midi-Pyrénées
◇ ⑪ **Grand Hôtel Beau Site €€**
Cité Médiévale (tel: 05 65 33 63 08; www.bestwestern-beausite.com). Regional cuisine, including duck, foie gras, truffles. Closed mid-Nov to mid-Feb. 39 rooms.

TOUR 12
PAU Midi-Pyrénées
◇ **Gramont €€–€€€**
3 place Gramont (tel: 05 59 27 84 04; www.hotelgramont.com). 34 rooms.

GAVARNIE Midi-Pyrénées
◇ **Le Taillon €–€€**
Village Centre (tel: 05 62 92 48 20; www.hotelletaillon.com). Closed Nov–26 Dec. 19 rooms.

⑪ **Le P'Tit Toy €–€€**
At foot of Cirque de Gavarnie (tel: 05 62 92 40 43). Traditional regional specialities. Open daily lunch & dinner. Closed Oct–Nov.

LOURDES Midi-Pyrénées
◇ **Grand Hôtel de la Grotte €€–€€€**
66 rue de la Grotte (tel: 05 62 94 58 87; www.hotel-grotte.com). 80 rooms.

⑪ **Taverne de Bigorre €**
21 place du champs Commun (tel: 05 62 94 75 00). Regional cooking. Open daily lunch & dinner. Closed Jan–early Feb.

TOUR 13
MARSEILLE Provence-Alpes
◇ **Hôtel Saint Louis €€**
2 rue des Récolettes, Cours St Louis (tel: 04 91 54 02 74; www.hotel-st-louis.com). 24 rooms.

⑪ **Toinou €–€€**
3 cours St Louis (tel: 08 11 45 45 45). Seafood and nothing else. Open daily lunch & dinner.

TOULON Provence-Alpes
◇ **La Corniche €€–€€€**
17 littoral Frédéric-Mistral (at Le Mourillon) (tel: 04 94 41 35 12; www.cornichehotel.com). 25 rooms.

⑪ **L'Arbre Rouge €–€€**
25 rue Denfert Rochereau (tel: 04 94 92 28 58). Seasonal Provençal cooking, booking recommended. Closed dinner Mon–Wed, all day Sun

HYÈRES Provence-Alpes
◇ **Casino-Hôtel des Palmiers €€–€€€**
1 avenue Ambroise Thomas (tel: 04 94 12 80 80; www.hyereshotel.com). 15 rooms.

⑪ **Au Bon Coing €**
41 place Massillon (tel: 04 94 35 51 20). Salads, plats du jour, moules frites. Open daily lunch & dinner.

ST-TROPEZ Provence-Alpes
◇ **St Amour–La Tartane €€€**
Route des Salins (tel: 04 94 97 21 23; www.saintamour-hotel.com). Closed Oct–Apr. 28 rooms.

⑪ **Le Girelier €€–€€€**
Quai Jean Jaurès (tel: 04 94 97 03 87). Seafood & Provençal specialities. Open lunch & dinner daily.

TOUR 14
CANNES Côte d'Azur
◇ **Le Florian €**
8 rue Commandant-André
(tel: 04 93 39 24 82).
31 rooms.

◇**Villa de l'Olivier €€€**
5 rue des Tambourinaires
(tel: 04 93 39 53 28).
24 rooms.

JUAN-LES-PINS Côte d'Azur
◇ **Hôtel Cecil €–€€**
Rue Jonnard (tel: 04 93 61 05
12; fax: 04 93 67 09 14).
21 rooms.

⑪ **Le Bijou Plage €–€€**
Boulevard du Littoral (tel: 04
93 61 39 07). *Provençal cuisine
and seafood. Open daily lunch &
dinner.*

ANTIBES Côte d'Azur
◇ **Le Cameo €**
5 place Nationale (tel: 04 93 34
24 17; fax: 04 93 34 35 80).
8 rooms.

GRASSE Côte d'Azur
◇ **Les Arômes €€**
115 Route de Cannes (tel: 04
93 09 08 01).
5 rooms.

FAYENCE Provence-Alpes
⑪ **Le Castellaras €€–€€€**
Route de Seillans (tel: 04 94 76
13 80). *Gourmet French cuisine.
Closed Mon & Tue.*

TOUR 15
NICE Côte d'Azur
◇**Villa Eden €–€€**
99 bis promenade des Anglais
(tel: 04 93 86 53 70; www.hotel-
villaeden.com).
11 rooms.

⑪ **La Petite Maison €–€€**
11 rue St François de Paule
(tel: 04 93 92 59 59). *Niçoise
cuisine. Open Mon–Sat lunch &
dinner.*

MENTON Côte d'Azur
◇**Aiglon €€–€€€**
7 avenue de la Madone
(tel: 04 93 57 55 55;
www.hotelaiglon.net).
29 rooms.

SOSPEL Côte d'Azur
⑪ **Auberge Provençale €€**
Route du Col de Castillon (tel:
04 93 04 00 31). *Provençal rustic
cooking. Open daily lunch &
dinner. Closed mid-Nov to
mid-Dec.*

LEVENS Côte d'Azur
◇**Vigneraie €**
82 route St-Blaise (tel: 04 93 79
77 60; fax: 04 93 79 82 35).
Closed mid-Oct to mid-Feb.
18 rooms.

TOUR 16
NÎMES Languedoc-Roussillon
◇ **Hôtel des Tuileries €€**
22 rue Roussy
(tel: 04 66 21 31 15;
www.hoteldestuileries.com).
11 rooms.

AVIGNON Provence
◇**Angleterre €–€€**
29 boulevard Raspail
(tel: 04 90 86 34 31;
www.hoteldangleterre.fr).
39 rooms.

ST-RÉMY-DE-PROVENCE
Provence
◇ **Hôtel du Soleil €€**
35 avenue Pasteur (tel: 04 90 92
00 63; www.hotelsoleil.com).
24 rooms.

⑪ **La Gousse d'Ail €–€€**
6 boulevard Marceau (tel: 04
90 92 16 87). *Provençal dishes,
including vegetarian. Open
Fri–Wed lunch & dinner. Closed
mid-Nov to early Mar.*

AIGUES-MORTES
Languedoc-Roussillon
⑪ **Les Arcades €–€€**
23 boulevard Gambetta
(tel: 04 66 53 81 13). *Regional
specialities. Closed Mon, Tue
lunch, Thu lunch.*

TOUR 17
NANCY Lorraine
◇**All Seasons €€**
3 rue de l'Armée-Patton
(tel: 03 83 40 31 24;
www.accorhotels.com).
85 rooms.

⑪ **Les Pissenlits €–€€**
25 bis rue des Ponts (tel: 03 83
37 43 97). *Good value traditional
brasserie. Open Tue–Sat lunch &
dinner.*

METZ Lorraine
⑪ **Le Loft €–€€**
5 place du Général de Gaulle
(tel: 03 87 50 56 57).
*International and traditional
French cuisine. Closed Sat lunch,
Sun lunch.*

VERDUN Lorraine
◇ **Le Coq Hardi €€–€€€**
8 avenue de la Victoire
(tel: 03 29 86 36 36;
www.coq-hardi.com).
35 rooms.

TOUR 18
LYON Rhône Valley
◇ **Bayard €€–€€€**
23 place Bellecour (tel: 04 78 37
39 64; www.hotelbayard.fr).
15 rooms.

⑪ **Bistrot de Lyon €€**
64 rue Mercière (tel: 04 78 38
47 47). *Traditional Lyonnais
cuisine. Open daily lunch & dinner.*

⑪ **Café des Fédérations €**
8 rue Major Martin (tel: 04 78
28 26 00). *Classic bistro fare;
booking recommended. Open daily
lunch & dinner.*

ROANNE Rhône Valley
◇ **Hôtel des Lys €€**
133 avenue de la Libération,
Le Coteau (tel: 04 77 68 46 44).
18 rooms.

TOUR 19
GRENOBLE Rhône Alpes
◇**Angleterre €€€**
5 place Victor-Hugo
(tel: 04 76 87 37 21; www.hotel-
angleterre-grenoble.com).
62 rooms.

AIX-LES-BAINS
Rhône Alpes
◇ ⑪ **Hôtel Thermal €€€**
2 rue Davat (tel: 04 79 35 20 00;
www.hotelthermal.fr).
Traditional cuisine of Provence.
80 rooms.

ANNECY Rhône Alpes
◇ **Hôtel du Nord** €€
24 rue Sommelier (tel: 04 50 45
08 78; www.annecy-hotel-du-
nord.com).
30 rooms.

⑪ **Le Clos des Sens** €€–€€€
13 rue Jean Mermoz (tel: 04 50
23 07 90). *Regional Savoyard
cooking; booking recommended.
Open Tue dinner, Wed–Sat lunch &
dinner.*

VAL D'ISÈRE Rhône-Alpes
⑪ **Les Clochetons** €–€€
Vallée du Manchet (tel: 04 79
41 13 11). *Grills, pasta, fondue.
Closed dinner Sun–Tue.*

TOUR 20
STRASBOURG Alsace
◇ **Cardinal de Rohan** €€–€€€
17 rue du Maroquin
(tel: 03 88 32 85 11;
www.hotel-rohan.com).
36 rooms.

⑪ **Brasserie de l'Ancienne
Douane** €–€€
6 rue de la Douane (tel: 03 88
15 78 78). *Local dishes. Open
daily lunch & dinner.*

MULHOUSE Alsace
⑪ **Auberge du Vieux
Mulhouse** €–€€
Place de la Réunion (tel: 03 89
45 84 18). *Classic & regional.
Open daily lunch & dinner.*

COLMAR Alsace
◇ **Hostellerie le Maréchal**
€€€
4–5 place des Six-Montagnes-
Noires (tel: 03 89 41 60 32;
www.hotel-le-marechal.com).
30 rooms.

RIQUEWIHR Alsace
⑪ **Winstub la Diligence** €
11 rue du Général de Gaulle
(tel: 03 89 49 05 21). *Alsace
cuisine. Open daily for lunch &
dinner.*

TOUR 21
CALAIS Pas de Calais
◇ **Mercure** €€€
36 rue Royale (tel: 03 21 97 68
00; www.accorhotels.com).
41 rooms.

LE TOUQUET Pas de Calais
◇ **Résidence Hippotel** €–€€
Avenue de la Dune aux Loups
(tel: 03 21 05 07 11).
72 rooms.

MONTREUIL Pas de Calais
⑪ **Auberge la Grenouillère**
€€–€€€
La Madeleine-sous-Montreuil
(tel: 03 21 06 07 22). *Traditional
French cuisine. Open Feb–Dec
Thu–Mon, lunch & dinner.*

TOUR 22
AMIENS Picardy
◇ **Le Carlton** €€
42 rue de Noyon
(tel: 03 22 97 72 22).
24 rooms.

ARRAS Picardy
⑪ **Le Rapière** €
44 Grand Place (tel: 03 21 55 09
92). *Traditional French cuisine.
Open daily noon–2, 7–9.15.
Closed Sun evening.*

LAON Picardy
◇ **Hôtel de la Bannière de
France** €€
11 rue Franklin-D.-Roosevelt
(tel: 03 23 23 21 44). *Closed last
2 weeks in Jul.*
18 rooms.

TOUR 23
REIMS Champagne-Ardenne
◇ **Grand Hôtel du Nord** €€
75 place Drouet-d'Erlon
(tel: 03 26 47 39 03).
50 rooms.

**CHÂLONS-EN-CHAM-
PAGNE** Champagne-Ardenne
⑪ **Jacky Michel** €€–€€€
19 place Monseigneur Tissier
(tel: 03 26 68 21 51). *Classic
French gastronomic cuisine. Closed
Sat lunch, Sun & Mon lunch, late
Jul to mid-Aug, 23 Dec to mid-
Jan.*

SEDAN Champagne-Ardenne
⑪ **Au Bon Vieux Temps** €–€€
1–3 place de la Halle (tel: 03 24
29 03 70). *Traditional and
regional specialities. Closed Sun
dinner, Mon, Wed dinner, mid-Feb
to early Mar, 1 week late Aug/early
Sep, 26 Dec–1 Jan.*

TOUR 24
BEAUNE Burgundy
◇ **Hostellerie de Bretonnière**
€€
42 rue du Faubourg
Bretonnière (tel: 03 80 22 15 77;
www.hotelbretonniere.com).
32 rooms.

AVALLON Burgundy
◇ **Moulin des Ruats** €€–€€€
9 rue des Iles Labaumes
(tel: 03 86 34 97 00;
www.moulin-des-ruats.com).
25 rooms.

VEZELAY Burgundy
⑪ **Le St-Etienne** €€
39 rue St-Etienne (tel: 03 86 33
27 34). *Regional specialities. Open
Fri–Tue lunch & dinner. Closed
mid-Jan to mid-Feb.*

AUTUN Burgundy
◇ ⑪ **Hostellerie du Vieux
Moulin** €–€€
Porte d'Arroux (tel: 03 85 52 10
90; fax: 03 85 86 32 15).
*Excellent dishes featuring classic
ingredients. Open daily lunch &
dinner. Closed Dec–late Mar.*
16 rooms.

TOUR 25
CHARTRES Île de France
⑪ **Le Geôrges** €€–€€€
Hôtel Grand Monarque, 22
place des Epars (tel: 02 37 18 15
15). *Classic French cuisine; booking recommended. Open Tue–Sat
lunch & dinner, Sun lunch.*

BARBIZON Île de France
⑪ **Le Relais de Barbizon** €–€€
2 ave Charles de Gaulle (tel: 01
60 66 40 28). *Traditional French
cuisine. Book at weekends. Closed
Tue dinner, Wed. Also 15–31 Aug
and 2 weeks at Christmas.*

FONTAINEBLEAU
Île de France
◇ **La Demeure du Parc** €€
6 rue d'Avon
(tel: 01 64 22 24 24).
31 rooms.

⑪ **La Caveau des Ducs** €–€€
24 rue de Ferrare (tel: 01 64
22 05 05). *Rustic French fare,
seafood, snails. Open daily lunch
& dinner.*

PRACTICAL INFORMATION

TOUR INFORMATION

The addresses, telephone numbers and opening times of the attractions mentioned in the tours, including the telephone numbers of the Tourist Information Offices are listed below.

TOUR 1

i Place St-Pierre, Caen. Tel: 02 31 27 14 14; www.tourisme.caen.fr.

i 2 rue Maréchal Joffre, Arromanches. Tel: 02 31 22 36 45; www.ot-arromanches.fr.

i Pont St-Jean, Bayeux. Tel: 02 31 51 28 28; www.bayeux-tourism.com.

i Place du Château, Valognes. Tel: 02 33 40 11 55; www.ot-cotentin-bocage-valognais.fr.

i 10 rue des Écoles, Barneville-Carteret. Tel: 02 33 04 90 58; www.barneville-carteret.fr.

i 4 cours Jonville, Granville. Tel: 02 33 91 30 03; www.ville-granville.fr.

i 8 place des Costils, Villedieu-les-Poêles. Tel: 02 33 05 05 69; www.ot-villedieu.fr.

i Place du Marché, Bagnoles-de-l'Orne. Tel: 02 33 37 85 66; www.bagnolesdelorne.com.

i Place du Tripot, Clécy. Tel: 02 33 69 79 95; www.ot-suisse-normande.com.

1 Pegasus Bridge
Mémorial Pegasus
Avenue du Major Howard, Ranville. Tel: 02 31 78 19 44; www.memorial-pegasus.org. *Open daily, Feb–Mar 10–5; Apr–Sep 9.30–6.30; Oct–Nov 10–1, 2–5. Closed Dec–Jan.*

2 Arromanches
Arromanches 360
Chemin du Calvaire. Tel: 02 31 22 30 30; www.arromanches360.com. *Open daily, Jun–Aug 9.40–6.40; Feb, Dec 10.10–4.40; Mar, Nov to 5.10; Apr–May, Sep–Oct to 5.40. Closed 24–25 Dec, Jan.*
Musée du Débarquement
Place du 6 Juin. Tel: 02 31 22 34 31; www.musee-arromanches.fr. *Open daily, Jan–Feb, Nov–Dec 10–12.30, 1.30–5; Mar, Oct 9.30–12.30, 1.30–5.30; Apr 9–12.30, 1.30–6; May–Aug 9–7; Sep 9–6. Closed 24–25, 31 Dec, 1 Jan.*

3 Bayeux
Musée de la Bataille de Normandie
Boulevard Fabian-Ware. Tel: 02 31 51 46 90. *Open daily, May–Sep 9.30–6.30; Oct–Apr 10–12.30, 2–6. Closed last 2 weeks in Jan.*
Musée de la Tapisserie
Centre Guillaume le Conquérant, rue de Nesmond. Tel: 02 31 51 25 50; www.tapisserie-bayeux.fr. *Open daily, Mar to mid-Nov 9–6.30/7; mid-Nov to mid-Mar 9.30–12.30, 2–6. Closed 24–26 Dec, 31 Dec–2 Jan, Mon–Fri 2nd week in Jan.*
Musée Baron Gérard
Hôtel Doyen, rue Lambert Leforestier. Tel: 02 31 92 14 21. *Closed for restoration until Jun 2012.*

4 Plage d'Omaha
Musée Mémorial d'Omaha Beach
Avenue de la Libération, St-Laurent-sur-Mer. Tel: 02 31 21 97 44; www.musee-memorial-omaha.com. *Open daily, mid-Feb to mid-Mar 10–12.30, 2.30–6; mid-Mar to mid-Nov 9.30–6.30 (7.30 Jul–Aug).*

5 Valognes
Hotel de Beaumont
Rue Barbey d'Aurévilly. Tel: 02 33 40 12 30. *Open Jul to mid-Sep Mon–Sat 10.30–noon, 2.30–6.30, Sun 2.30–6.30.*

Musée de l'Eau de Vie et des Vieux Métiers
Rue Pelouze. Tel: 02 33 40 26 25. *Open Apr–Sep Mon, Wed–Sat 10–noon, 2–6, Sun 2–6; also Tue Jul–Aug.*
Musée Régional du Cidre et du Calvados
Rue du Petit Versailles. Tel: 02 33 40 22 73. *Open Apr–Sep Mon, Wed–Sat 10–noon, 2–6, Sun 2–6; also Tue Jul–Aug.*

7 Granville
Musée du Vieux Granville
2 rue Le Carpentier. Tel: 02 33 50 44 10. *Open Apr–Sep Wed–Mon 10–noon, 2–6; Oct–Mar Wed, Sat, Sun 2–6. Closed 22 Dec–31 Jan.*
Musée Richard Anacréon
Place de l'Isthme. Tel: 02 33 51 02 94. *Open Jun–Sep Tue–Sun 11–6; Oct–May Wed–Sun 2–6. Closed Jan.*
Musée Christian Dior
Villa Les Rhumbs. Tel: 02 33 61 48 21; www.musee-dior-granville.com. *Open mid-May to late Sep daily 10–6.30.*

8 Villedieu-les-Poêles
Atelier du Cuivre
54 rue du Général Huard. Tel: 02 33 51 31 85; www.atelierducuivre.com. *Open Mon–Fri 9–noon, 1.30–5.30, Sat 9–noon.*
Maison de l'Étain
15 rue du Général Huard. Tel: 02 33 51 05 08. *Open May–Jun, Sep Mon–Fri tours at 11, 3, 4.30, Sat 11; Jul–Aug tours hourly 10–5.*
Fonderie de Cloches
10 rue du Pont Chignon. Tel: 02 33 61 00 56; www.cornille-havard.com. *Open mid-Feb to mid-Nov Tue–Sat 10–12.30, 2–6; also daily from 9am Jul–Aug.*
Musée de la Poeslerie and Maison de la Dentellière
25 rue du Général Huard. Tel: 06 80 45 51 08. *Open Apr to mid-Nov Tue 2–6.30, Wed–Sat 10–12.30, 2–5.30, alternate Sun 2–6.30 (every Sun Jul–Aug).*

10 Clécy
Musée Hardy
Place du Tripot. Tel: 02 31 69 79 95. *Open Apr–Sep*

Tue–Sat 10–12.30, 2.30–6.30 (also Sun am and Mon Jul–Aug).

Back to Nature
Maison de la Mer
Place du 6 Juin, Courseulles-sur-Mer. Tel: 02 31 37 92 58. *Closed for refurbishment.*

For History Buffs
Musée Airborne
Rue Eisenhower, Ste-Mère-Église. Tel: 02 33 41 41 35; www.musee-airborne.com. *Open Feb–Mar, Oct–Nov, Christmas hols 9.30–noon, 2–6; Apr–Sep 9–6.45.*

For Children
Le Village Enchanté
Route du Moulin, Bellefontaine. Tel: 02 33 59 01 93; www.village-enchante.fr. *Open Easter week daily 11–6; May–Jun, Sep Wed 11.30–5.30, Sat–Sun 11–6; Jul–Aug daily 10.30–7; Oct Sat–Sun, school hols noon–5.*
Chemin de Fer Miniature
Les Fours à Chaux. Tel: 02 31 69 07 13; www.chemin-fer-miniature-clecy.com. *Open Mar Sun 2–5.30; Apr–Jun, early Sep Tue–Sun 10–noon, 2–6 (10–6 hols); Jul–Aug daily 10–6; mid- to end Sep Tue–Sun 2–6; Oct–early Nov Sun, hols 2–5. Closed early Nov–Apr.*

Special to…
Musée des Sapeurs-Pompiers
16 boulevard Christophe, Bagnoles-de-l'Orne. Tel: 02 33 38 10 34. *Open Apr–Oct daily 2–6.*
Maison de la Pomme et de la Poire
La Logeraie, Barenton. Tel: 02 33 59 56 22. *Open Apr to mid-Oct daily 10–noon/12.30, 2–6/6.30.*

TOUR 2

i Pont Ango, quai du Carenage, Dieppe. Tel: 02 32 14 40 60; www.dieppe-tourisme.com.

i Quai Sadi Carnot, Fécamp. Tel: 02 35 28 51 01; www.fecamptourisme.com.

Practical Information

ℹ 9 place Maurice-Guillard, Étretat. Tel: 02 35 27 05 21; www.etretat.net.

ℹ 186 boulevard Clémenceau, Le Havre. Tel: 02 32 74 04 04; www.lehavretourisme.com.

ℹ Place du Général de Gaulle, Caudebec-en-Caux. Tel: 02 32 70 46 32; www.tourismecauxseine.com.

ℹ Quai Lepaulmier, Honfleur. Tel: 02 31 89 23 30; www.ot-honfleur.fr.

ℹ 25 place de la Cathédrale, Rouen. Tel: 02 32 08 32 40; www.rouentourisme.com.

❶ Varengeville-sur-Mer
Parc Floral des Moutiers
La Haie des Moutiers. Tel: 02 35 85 10 02. *Open mid-Mar to mid-Nov daily 10–noon, 2–6.*
Manoir d'Ango
Town centre. Tel: 02 35 83 61 56. *Open mid-Apr to Sep daily 10–12.30, 2–6; Oct Sat–Sun 10–12.30, 2–6*

❷ Fécamp
Palais Bénédictine
110 rue Alexandre-le-Grand. Tel: 02 35 10 26 10. *Open daily, early Feb–late Mar, mid-Oct to Dec 10.30–12.45, 2–6; late Mar–early Jul, Sep to mid-Oct 10–1, 2–6.30; mid-Jul to Aug 10–7. Closed Jan–early Feb.*
Musée des Terre-Neuvas et de la Pêche
27 boulevard Albert 1er. Tel: 02 35 28 31 99. *Open Jul–Aug daily 10–7; Sep–Jun Wed–Mon 10–noon, 2–5.30*

❸ Étretat
Nungesser and Coli Museum
Tel: 02 35 27 07 47. *Open spring weekends; mid-Jun to mid-Sep daily 10–noon, 2–6.*

❹ Le Havre
Musée Malraux
2 boulevard Clemenceau. Tel: 02 35 19 62 62. *Open Wed–Mon 11–6 (7 Sat–Sun).*
Musée du Havre
1 rue Jérôme Bellarmato. Tel: 02 35 42 27 90. *Open Wed,. Fri–Sun 10–12.30, 2.30–6.*

Natural History Museum
Place du Vieux Marché. Tel: 02 35 41 37 28. *Open Tue–Wed, Fri–Sun 9.30–noon, 2–6, Thu 2–6.*

❺ Caudebec-en-Caux
Musée de la Marine de Seine
Avenue Winston Churchill. Tel: 02 35 95 90 13. *Open daily 2–6.30 (5.30 Oct–Mar).*

❻ La Haye-de-Routot
Four à Pain
Tel: 02 32 57 07 99. *Open Mar–Jun, Sep–Nov Sun 2–6; Jul–Aug daily 2–6.30.*
Musée du Sabot
Tel: 02 32 57 59 67. *Open Mar–Jun, Sep–Nov Sun 2–6; Jul–Aug daily 2–6.30.*

❽ Honfleur
Musée Eugène Boudin
Place Erik Satie. Tel: 02 31 89 54 00. *Open mid-Mar to Sep, Wed–Mon 10–noon, 2–6; other months Mon–Fri 2.30–5.30, Sat–Sun 10–noon, 2.30–5.30 (closed Jan to mid-Feb).*
Musée d'Ethnographie et d'Art Populaire
Rue de la Prison. Tel: 02 31 89 14 12. *Open mid-Feb to Mar, Oct to mid-Nov Tue–Sun 2.30–5.30; Apr–Sep Tue–Sun 10–noon, 2–6.30*
Musée de la Marine
Quai St-Étienne. Tel: 02 31 89 14 12. *Open mid-Feb to Mar, Oct to mid-Nov Tue–Sun 2.30–5.30; Apr–Sep Tue–Sun 10–noon, 2–6.30*

❾ Le Bec-Hellouin
Abbaye du Bec-Hellouin
Tel: 02 32 43 72 60; www.abbayedubec.com. *Guided tours Mon, Wed–Sat from 10.30; Sun from noon onwards.*
Les Ateliers du Bec
Monastère Ste-Francoise-Romaine. Tel: 02 32 43 72 60. *Open daily 2–5.45 (4.15 Sun and religious festivals).*

❿ Rouen
Musée de Cire Jeanne d'Arc
33 place du Vieux Marché. Tel: 02 35 88 02 70; www.jeanne-darc.com. *Open daily, mid-Apr to mid-Sep 9.30–1, 1.30–7; mid-Sep to mid-Apr 10–noon, 2–6.30*

Musée des Beaux-Arts
Esplanade Marcel Duchamp. Tel: 02 35 71 28 40. *Open Wed–Mon 10–6.*

For Children
Forêt de Montgeon
Access via the Jenner Tunnel to the north of Cours de la République. *Open all year.*
Petit Train de Rouen
Place de la Cathédrale. *On the hour 10–noon, 2–5 Apr–Oct.*

Back to Nature
Réserve Naturelle des Mannevilles
Tel: 02 35 37 23 16. *Open Sun in Jul–Aug.*

Special to...
Maison de la Pomme
Ste-Opportune-la-Mare. Tel: 02 32 20 27 11. *Open weekends 2–6.30.*

TOUR 3

ℹ 11 rue St-Yves, Rennes. Tel: 02 99 67 11 11; www.tourisme-rennes.com.

ℹ Place Général-de-Gaulle, Vitré. Tel: 02 99 75 04 46; www.ot-vitre.fr.

ℹ 2 rue Nationale, Fougères. Tel: 02 99 94 12 20; www.ot-fougeres.fr.

ℹ Corps de Garde des Bourgeois, Le Mont-St-Michel. Tel: 02 33 60 14 30; www.ot-montsaintmichel.com.

ℹ Esplanade St-Vincent, St Malo. Tel: 08 25 13 52 00; www.saint-malo-tourisme.com.

ℹ 2 boulevard Féart, Dinard. Tel: 02 99 46 94 12; www.ot-dinard.com.

ℹ Place de Chambly, Fréhel. Tel: 02 96 41 53 81; www.paysdefrehel.com.

ℹ 3 rue du 19 Mars 1962, Erquy. Tel: 02 96 72 30 12; www.erquy-tourisme.com.

ℹ 9 rue du Château, Dinan. Tel: 02 96 87 69 76; www.dinan-tourisme.com.

❶ Vitré
Musée de la Faucillonnaie
Montreuil-sous-Pérouse.

Tel: 02 99 74 41 29. *Open May–Sep Wed–Mon 10–12.45, 2–6; Oct–Apr Mon, Wed–Sat 10–12.15, 2–5.30, Sun 2–5.30*
Château-Musée des Rochers-Sévigné
Route d'Argentré du Plessis. Tel: 02 99 96 76 51. *Open as for Musée de la Faucillonnaie.*

❷ Fougères
Château de Fougères
Place Pierre Symon. Tel: 02 99 99 79 59. *Open daily, Feb–Mar, Oct–Dec 10–noon, 2–5; Apr to mid-Jun 9.30–noon, 2–6; mid-Jun to mid-Sep 9–7.*
Musée Emmanuel de la Villéon
51 rue Nationale. Tel Tourist Office: 02 99 94 12 20. *Open Wed–Sun 10–noon, 2–5.*

❸ Le Mont-St-Michel
Abbaye, Archéoscope and Museums
Tel: 02 33 89 80 00; www.au-mont-saint-michel.com. *Open Abbey: daily, May–Aug 9–7, Sep–Apr 9.30–6; Archeoscope: early Feb–early Nov, Christmas hols, daily 9–5.30 (to 6.30 Jul–Aug, Christmas); museums: daily 9–6.*
Maison de la Baie du Mont St-Michel
Route de la Roche Torin, Courtils. Tel: 02 33 89 66 00; www.maison-baie.com. *Open daily 9–12.30, 2–5.30 (closed winter weekends).*

❺ St-Malo
Musée d'Histoire
Château. Tel: 02 99 40 71 57. *Open daily 10–noon, 2–6; closed Mon in winter.*
Tour Solidor
Tel: 02 99 40 71 58. *Open daily 10–noon, 2–6 (closed Mon Oct–Mar).*

❼ Cap Fréhel
Fort la Latte
Plevenon. Tel: 02 96 41 57 11. *Open daily Apr–Sep 10–12.30, 2–6; Oct–May weekends and school holidays 2–6.*

❾ Dinan
Château and museum
Porte de Guichet. Tel: 02 96 39 45 20. *Open daily, Jun–Sep 10–6.30; Oct–Dec, Feb–May 1.30–5.30.*

Tour de l'Horloge
Rue de l'Horloge. Tel: 02
96 87 02 26. *Open Jun–Sep
10–6.30; Apr–May 2–6.30.*

10 Tinténiac
Château et Parc
Zoologique de la
Bourbansais
Pleugueneuc. Tel: 02 99 69
40 07; www.labourbansais.
com. *Chateau tours:
Apr–Sep daily 11.15, 2, 3, 4,
5; Oct Sun 3, 4; Nov–Feb
school hols 3, 4. Zoo and
gardens: Apr–Sep daily
10–7; Oct 1.30–5.30;
Nov–Feb school hols 10–6.*

Musée de l'Outil et des
Métiers
5 quai de la Donac. Tel: 02
99 23 09 30. *Open Jul–Sep
Tue–Sat 10–noon, 3–6, Sun
3–6.*

For History Buffs
Manoir de l'Automobile
Rte de Lieuron, Loheac.
Tel: 02 99 34 02 32;
www.manoir-automobile.fr.
*Open Tue–Sun 10–1, 2–7
(Jul–Aug daily 10–7).*

For Children
Alligator Bay
Beauvoir. Tel: 02 33 68 11 18;
www.alligatorbay.com.
*Open Apr–Sep daily 10–7;
Oct–Mar 2–6 (weekends
and school hols only
Dec–Jan).*

Special to...
Ferme Marine
Route de la Corniche,
Cancale. Tel: 02 99 89 69 99.
*Open French mid-Feb to Oct tours
in French Mon–Fri 3pm
(also Sat, Sun Jul to mid-
Sep); tours in English Jul to
mid-Sep daily 2pm.*

TOUR 4

i Place de la Résistance,
Quimper. Tel: 02 98 53 04
05; www.quimper-
tourisme.com.

i 2 rue Docteur Mével,
Douarnenez. Tel: 02 98 92
13 35; www.douarnenez-
tourisme.com.

i 15 quai Kléber,
Camaret-sur-Mer. Tel: 02 98
27 93 60; www.camaret-sur-
mer.com.

i Mairie, Landévennec.
Tel: 02 98 27 78 46.

i Place de la Liberté,
Brest. Tel: 02 98 44 24 96;
www.brest-metropole-
tourisme.fr.

i 18 place Aristide
Briand, Huelgoat. Tel: 02 98
99 72 32; http://tourisme
huelgoat.fr.

2 Douarnenez
Le Port-Musée
Place de l'Enfer. Tel: 02 98
92 65 20; www.port-
musee.org. *Open Tue–Sun
10–12.30, 2–6.*

3 Morgat
Maison des Minéraux
Rte du Cap de la Chèvre
Morgat. Tel: 02 98 27 19 73;
www.maison-des-mineraux.
org. *Open Sun–Fri 10–noon,
2–5.30 (also Sat Jul–Aug).
Closed mornings mid-Sep
to Apr.*

5 Landévennec
Musée de l'Ancienne
Abbaye
Tel: 02 98 27 35 90.
*Open Apr–Jun Sun–Fri
10–6; Jul–Sep daily 10–7 (to
6 Sep); Oct–Nov, Feb–Mar
Sun 10–5.30 (also Mon–Fri
school hols). Closed Dec–Jan.*

6 Brest
Musée-Château National
de la Marine
Brest Château. Tel: 02 98 22
12 39; www.musee-
marine.fr.
*Open Apr–Sep daily
10–6.30; Oct–Dec, Feb–
Mar 1.30–6.30. Closed Jan.*
Conservatoire Botanique
National de Brest
52 Allée du Bot. Tel: 02 98
41 88 95; www.cbnbrest.fr.
*Open Garden: all year, daily
9–6; Pavilion: Jul to mid-Sep
Sun–Thu 2–5.30, Oct–Jun
Wed, Sun 2–4.30;
Greenhouses: Jul to mid-Sep
Sun–Thu 2–5.30.*
Océanopolis
Port de Plaisance. Tel: 02
98 34 40 40; www.
oceanopolis.com. *Open Apr
daily 10–6; May to mid-Sep
daily 9–6/7; mid-Sep–Mar
Tue–Sun 10–5/6. Closed 25
Dec, 2 weeks early Jan.*

8 Ménez-Meur
Ménez-Meur Estate
Hanvec. Tel: 02 98 68 81
71. *Open Mar–Apr, Oct
Wed, Sun, hols 1–5.30;
May–Jun, Sep daily noon–6;*

*Jul–Aug daily 10–7;
Nov–Feb school hols 1–5.*

10 Huelgoat
Arboretum du Pöerop
and Jardin de l'Argoat
Huelgoat. Tel: 02 98 99 95
90; www.arboretum-huel
goat.com. *Open late
Mar–Jun, Sep–Oct Thu–Sun
2–6; Easter, Jul–Aug
Wed–Sun 10–6.*

Back to Nature
Réserve Ornithologique
Cap Sizun. Tel: 02 98 70
13 53. *Open Apr–Jun daily
10–noon, 2–6; Jul–Aug daily
10–6.*

Special to...
Écomusée Moulins-de-
Kerouat
Commana. Tel: 02 98 68 87
76. *Open mid-Mar to Oct
Mon–Fri 10–6, Sun 2–6
(Jul–Aug daily 11–7).*

For History Buffs
Maison des Pilhaouerien
Loqueffret. Tel: 02 98 26 44
50. *Open Apr–Oct. Mon–Sat
2–6 or by reservation.*
Château de Trévarez
St Goazec. Tel: 02 98 26 82
79; www.cdp29.fr. *Open
Apr–Jun, daily 1–6;
Jul–Aug daily 11–6.30; Oct,
Mar Wed, Sat–Sun 2–5.30;
Nov to mid-Jan daily
1.30–6.30. Closed mid-Jan
to Feb.*

TOUR 5

i Place de la Victoire,
Clermont-Ferrand. Tel: 04
73 98 65 00; www.ot-
clermont-ferrand.fr.

i 1 avenue Auguste
Rouzaud, Royat. Tel: 04 73
29 74 70; www.ot-
royat.com.

i 15 place de la
République, La Bourboule.
Tel: 04 73 65 57 71; http://
bourboule.sancy.com.

i Avenue de la
Libération, Le Mont-Dore.
Tel: 04 73 65 20 21;
www.sancy.com.

i Place du Docteur-
Pipet, Besse-en-Chandesse.
Tel: 04 73 79 52 84;
www.sancy.com.

i Les Grands Thermes,
St-Nectaire. Tel: 04 73 88 50
86; www.sancy.com.

i 4 place de l'Hôtel de
Ville, Ambert. Tel: 04 73 82
61 90.

i Château du Pirou,
Thiers. Tel: 04 73 80 65 65;
www.thiers-tourisme.fr.

1 Royat
Maison du Passé
Place Cohendy. Tel: 04 73
29 98 18. *Open mid-Apr to
mid-Oct Mon–Sat 3–6.*

2 Puy de Dôme
Roman temple, exhibition,
information centre
Tel: 04 73 42 22 50. *Open
summer only.*

4 La Bourboule
Musée de Géologie
Botanique
Tel: 04 73 81 11 25 or 04
73 51 35 36. *Open Jul–Sep
Mon–Fri 10–noon, 2–5.*

5 Besse-en-Chandesse
Ski Museum
Tel: 04 73 79 57 30. *Open
Feb, Jul–Aug daily 9–noon,
2–7.*

7 St-Nectaire
Maison du St-Nectaire
Route de Murol. Tel: 04 73
88 57 96. *Open Feb–Mar,
Oct to mid-Nov daily 3–6;
Jul–Aug daily 9–7; Apr–May,
Sep daily 10–noon, 3–7.*
Cornadore grotto
Route de Murol. Tel: 04
73 88 57 97; www.grottes-
du-cornadore.fr. *Open
Feb–11 Nov, 20 Dec–3 Jan
daily 10–noon, 2–6.*

8 Ambert
AGRIVAP museum
Rue de l'Industrie.
Tel: 04 73 82 60 42;
www.agrivap.fr. *Open
Mar–Jun, Sep–Oct Tue–Fri,
Sun 10–noon, 2–6; Jul–Aug
Tue–Sun 10–12.30, 2–6.30.*
Maison de la Fourme
d'Ambert et des
Fromages d'Auvergne
29 rue des Chazeaux.
Tel: 04 73 82 49 23.
*Open Apr–Oct Tue–Sat
10.30–12.30, 3.30–6.30
(also Sun Jul–Aug); Nov–Mar
by appointment only.*

**9 Moulin Richard-
de-Bas**
Ambert. Tel: 04 73 82 03 11;
www.richarddebas.fr.
*Open daily 9.30–12.30, 2–6
(9.30–7 Jul–Aug).*

⓾ Thiers

Musée de la Coutellerie
58 rue de la Coutellerie.
Tel: 04 73 80 58 86; www.
musee-coutellerie-thiers.
com. Open Jul–Aug daily
10–12.30, 1.30–7; Sep–Dec,
Feb–Jun daily 10–noon, 2–6
(closed Mon Oct–May)
Closed Jan.

Special to...
Vulcania
Route de Mazayes, St-
Ours-les-Roches. Tel: 08 20
82 78 28; www.vulcania.
com. Open late Mar to mid-
Nov daily 10–6 (7 Jul–Aug,
and to 11pm Wed). Closed
Mon–Tue Sep–Oct.

For Children
Château de Murol
16 avenue de
Grevenmacher, Aubiere.
Tel: 04 73 26 02 00. Open
Apr–Sep daily 10–6;
Oct–Mar Sat–Sun and
school hols 10–7.
Parc Animalier du Cezalier
Ardes-sur-Couze. Tel: 04 73
71 82 86. Open Apr–Sep
daily 10–7; Oct–Mar Sun
2–dusk.

TOUR 6

ⓘ 12 boulevard de
Fleurus, Limoges. Tel: 05 55
34 46 87; www.tourisme
limoges.com.

ⓘ 28 avenue du Château,
Ségur-le-Château.
Tel: 05 55 73 39 92;
www.offitourisme-
segur.com.

ⓘ Entrée du Haras, place
du Château, Arnac-
Pompadour. Tel: 05 55 98
55 47; www.pompadour.
net.

ⓘ Place de la Libération,
Uzerche. Tel: 05 55 73 15 71;
www.pays-uzerche.com.

ⓘ 2 place Emile Zola,
Tulle. Tel: 05 55 26 59 61;
www.ville-tulle.fr.

ⓘ Place de la République,
Treignac. Tel: 05 55 98 15 04;
www.tourisme-treignac.fr.

ⓘ Rue Vieille, Aubusson.
Tel: 05 55 66 32 12;
www.aubusson.fr.

ⓘ 1 rue Eugène France,
Guéret. Tel: 05 55 52 14 29;
www.ot-gueret.fr.

❷ Arnac-Pompadour

French National Stud Farm
Château Pompadour.
Tel: 05 55 98 51 10. Guided
tours every afternoon.

❹ Tulle

Musée du Cloître
Place Monseigneur
Berteaud. Tel: 05 55 26 22
05. Open May–Oct daily
10–1, 2–6; Nov–Apr Mon,
Wed–Sat 1–6.
Musée de la Résistance et
de la Déportation
2 quai Edmond Perrier.
Tel: 05 55 26 24 36. Open
Mon–Fri 9–noon, 2–6.

❼ Treignac

Museum
Rue du Docteur Fleyssac.
Open Jul–Aug Wed–Mon
2.30–6.30 (Sep–Jun by
appointment, phone Tourist
Office, tel: 05 55 98 15 04).

❾ Aubusson

Musée Départemental de
la Tapisserie
Avenue des Lissiers. Tel: 05
55 83 08 30. Open Wed–
Mon 9.30–noon, 2–6).

❿ Guéret

Musée de la Sénatorerie
22 avenue de la
Sénatorerie. Tel: 05 55 52
07 20. Open May–Oct
Wed–Mon 10–noon, 2–6
(also Tue Jul–Aug), winter pm
only.

For History Buffs
Musée National de la
Porcelaine Adrien
Dubouché
Les Palloux, place Winston
Churchill, Limoges. Tel: 05
55 33 08 50; www.musee-
adriendubouche.fr. Open
Wed–Mon 10–12.30,
2–5.45 (10–5.45 Jul–Aug).
La Tour de Zizim
Bourganeuf. Tel: 05 55 64
12 20 (tourist office). Open
Jul–Aug Wed from 2.30pm.

TOUR 7

ⓘ Le Gabut, La Rochelle.
Tel: 05 46 41 14 68; www.
larochelle-tourisme.com.

ⓘ Quai de Sénac, La
Flotte. Tel: 05 46 09 60 38;
www.ot-laflotte.fr.

ⓘ 2 quai Nicolas Baudin,
St-Martin-de-Ré.
Tel: 05 46 09 20 06;
www.iledere.com.

ⓘ Avenue Sadi Carnot,
Rochefort. Tel: 05 46 99
08 60; www.paysroche
fortais-tourisme.com.

ⓘ 2 rue de Québec,
Hiers-Brouage. Tel: 05 46 85
19 16; www.officede
tourismebrouage.com.

ⓘ Place Henri Barbusse,
Bourcefranc, Île d'Oléron.
Tel: 05 46 85 07 00; www.
ile-oleron-marennes.com.

ⓘ Place Basson Pierre,
Saintes. Tel: 05 46 74 23 82;
www.saintes-tourisme.fr.

ⓘ 7 bis rue du Chat, Place
des Halles, Angoulême.
Tel: 05 45 95 16 84; www.
angouleme-tourisme.com.

ⓘ Place de la Brèche,
Niort. Tel: 05 49 24 18 79;
www.niortmaraispoitevin.
com.

ⓘ Place de la Coutume,
Coulon. Tel: 05 49 35 99 29;
www.niortmaraispoitevin.
com.

ⓘ 8 rue du Grimouard,
Fontenay-le-Comte.
Tel: 02 51 69 44 99; www.
tourisme-sudvendee.com.

❶ Île de Ré

Musée Ernest Cognacq
Av Victor Bouthillier, St-
Martin-de-Ré. Tel: 05 46
09 21 22. Open Mon,
Wed–Fri 10–1, 2–6,
Sat–Sun 2–6.

Phare des Baleines
Le Gillieux, St Clement des
Baleines. Tel: 05 46 29 18 23;
www.lepharedesbaleines.fr.
Open all year daily 9.30 or
10.30–5.30, 6.30 or 7.30
depending on season.

❷ Rochefort

Corderie Royale – Centre
International de la Mer
Tel: 05 46 87 01 90;
www.corderie-royale.com.
Open Apr–Sep daily 9–7 or
8; Oct–Mar daily 10–6.
Maison de Pierre Loti
141 rue Pierre-Loti.
Tel: 05 46 82 91 90.
Open Jul–Sep daily; Oct–Jun
Wed–Mon. Closed Jan.

❼ Niort

Donjon
Rue Duguesclin. Tel: 05 49
28 14 28. Open May to
mid-Sep daily 10–12.30,
2–6; mid-Sep to Apr 2–5.

❽ Coulon

Maison des Marais
Poitevin
5 place Coutume. Tel: 05
49 35 81 04; www.parc-
marais-poitevin.fr. Open
Apr–Oct daily 10–1, 2–6.

❾ Fontenay-le-Comte

Château de Terre-Neuve
Rue de Jarnigarde.
Tel: 02 51 69 17 75. Open
May–Sep daily 9–noon, 2–7.

For History Buffs
Maison de l'Empereur
Rue Napoléon, Aix. Tel: 05
46 84 66 40; www.rmn.fr.
Open all year Wed–Mon
9.30–12.30, 2–5 or 6.

Back to Nature
Lilleau des Niges
Les Portes-en-Ré.
Tel: 05 46 29 50 74;
www.lilleau.niges.reserves-
naturelles.org. Open daily
(except Sat am).
Marais aux Oiseaux
Dolus-d'Oléron.
Tel: 05 46 75 37 54.
Zoodysée
La Forêt de Chizé, Villiers
en Bois. Tel: 05 49 77 17 17.
Open Feb–Mar, Sep–Nov,
Wed–Mon 1–6; Apr daily
10–6; May–Aug daily 10–7.
Closed Dec–Jan.

Special to...
Oyster Bed Tours &
Museum
St-Trojan en Oléron. Tel: 05
46 76 08 16; www.maison-
huitres-oleronaise.fr.
Open all year; phone for
reservation.

TOUR 8

ⓘ 3 cours Olivier de
Clisson, Nantes. Tel: 08 92
46 40 44; www.nantes-
tourisme.com.

ⓘ Place du Minage,
Clisson. Tel: 02 40 54 02 95;
www.mairie-clisson.com.

ⓘ 14 avenue Maudet,
Cholet. Tel: 02 41 49 80 00;
www.ot-cholet.fr.

ⓘ 30 place des Fontaines,
Doué-la-Fontaine. Tel: 02
41 59 20 49; www.ot-
douelafontaine.fr.

ⓘ Place de la Bilange,
Saumur. Tel: 02 41 40 20 60;
www.ot-saumur.fr.

ⓘ Au Château, Baugé.
Tel: 02 41 89 18 07;
www.tourisme-bauge.com.

ⓘ Place Nicolay, Le Lude.
Tel: 02 43 94 62 20.

ⓘ Rue de l'Etoile, Le
Mans. Tel: 02 43 28 17 22;
www.lemanstourisme.com.

ⓘ 7 place Kennedy,
Angers. Tel: 02 41 23 50 00;
www.angers-tourisme.com.

2 Cholet
Musée d'Art et d'Histoire
Avenue de l'Abreuvoir.
Tel: 02 41 49 29 00. *Open
Wed–Sun 10–noon, 2–6;
also open Mon Jul–Aug.*
Musée Paysan
Ferme de la Goubaudière,
Parc de Loisirs de Ribou.
Tel: 02 41 29 09 07. *Open
Apr–Sep Sun 2–6.*
Musée du Textile
La Rivière Sauvageau, rue
du Dr Roux. Tel: 02 41 75
25 40. *Open Wed–Sun
10–noon, 2–6; also Tue
Jul–Aug.*
Musée de la Chaussure
6 rue St-Paul, St André de
la Marche. Tel: 02 41 46 35
65. *Open Mar–Jun, Sep–Oct
Sun–Fri 2.30–6; Jul–Aug
Mon–Fri, Sun 10.30–12.30,
2.30–6; guided tour Sat
4pm, Sun 2.30–6.*
Parc Oriental de
Maulévrier
Maulévrier. Tel: 02 41 55 50
14; www.parc-oriental.
com. *Open Mar–Jun,
Sep–Nov Tue–Sun 2–6 or 7
(also Mon May–Jun, Sep);
Jul–Aug 10.30–7.30.*

3 Doué-la-Fontaine
Bioparc Doué-la-Fontaine
Route de Cholet.
Tel: 02 41 59 18 58;
www.zoodoue.fr. *Open
Feb–Oct 9/10–6.30/7.30*
Musée des Commerces
Anciens
Écuries du Baron Foullon,
route de Soulanger. Tel: 02
41 52 91 58. *Open Feb,
Nov–Dec Fri–Sun 2–6;
Mar–Apr, Oct Tue–Sun 2–6;
May–Jun, Sep Mon 2–7,
Tue–Sun 10–noon, 2–7;
Jul–Aug Mon 2–7, Tue–Sun
10–1, 2–7.*
Arènes
Rue des Arènes. Tel: 02 41
59 20 49 (tourist office).

4 St-Hilaire
Musée du Champignon
Route de Gennes. Tel: 02
41 50 31 55; www.musee-
du-champignon.com. *Open
Feb to mid-Nov daily 10–7.*
Ecole National d'Equitation
Tel: 02 41 53 50 60;
www.cadrenoir.fr. *Guided
tours only Apr to mid-Oct
9.30–4 (closed Sat pm, Sun,
Mon am). No tours during
demonstrations.*

5 Saumur
Château de Saumur
Tel: 02 41 40 24 40. *Open
Apr–Sep Tue–Sun 10–1,
2–5.30.*

6 Baugé
Château/Musée de Baugé
Tel: 02 41 84 00 74;
www.chateau-bauge.com.
*Open May to mid-Sep
10–12.30, 1.30–6.
Otherwise pm only (closed
Nov to mid-Feb).*
La Girouardière Convent
Rue Girouardière. Tel: 02
41 89 12 20. *Open
Wed–Mon 2.30–4.15.*

7 Le Lude
Château du Lude
Place François-de-Nicolay.
Tel: 02 43 94 60 09;
www.lelude.com. *Open
Apr–Sep 2.30–6; gardens
10–12.30, 2–6; closed Wed
Apr to mid-Jun and Sep.*

8 Le Mans Circuit
Musée 24 Heures
Tel: 02 43 72 72 24;
www.sarthe.com. *Open
mid-Apr to Sep daily 10–6;
Oct to mid-Apr Wed–Sun
11–5.*

9 Le Mans
Musée de la Reine
Bérengère
Rue de la Reine Bérengère.
Tel: 02 43 47 38 80. *Open
May–Sep, Tue–Sun
10–12.30, 2–6.30; Oct–Apr,
Tue–Sun 2–6.*
Abbaye Cistercienne de
l'Epau
Rue L'Esterel. Tel: 02 43 84
22 29. *Open daily
9.30–noon, 2–6.*
Musée de Tessé
2 avenue de Paderborn.
Tel: 02 43 47 38 51. *Open
Tue–Sun 10–12.30, 2–6.*

10 Angers
Château d'Angers
2 Promenade du Bout du

Monde. Tel: 02 41 86 48 77.
*Open May–Aug daily
9.30–6.30; Sep–Apr
10–5.30.*

Back to Nature
Chemins de la Rose
Parc de Courcilpleu, route
de Cholet, Doué-la-
Fontaine. Tel: 02 41 59 95
95; www.cheminsdelarose.
fr. *Open mid-May to mid-
Aug daily 9.30–7; mid-Aug
to mid-Sep 10–6.30.*

Special to…
Puy du Fou
30 rue Georges
Clémenceau, Les Epesses.
Tel: 02 51 64 11 11;
www.puydufou.com. *Open
Apr to mid-Sep (see website);
Cinéscénie Jun–early Sep Fri
& Sat 10pm (arrive 1 hour in
advance; booking compul-
sory).*
La Distillerie Cointreau
Carrefour Molière, St-
Barthélémy d'Anjou.
Tel: 02 41 31 50 50. *Guided
tours Tue–Sat 11–6.*

Recommended Walks
Foyer Rural
Jupilles. Tel: 02 43 46 43 92.
*Open Mon–Fri 9–noon,
1.30–6.30.*

For History Buffs
Troglodyte Village
Louresse-Rochemenier.
Tel: 02 41 59 18 15. *Open
Feb–Mar, Nov weekends
and school hols 2–6;
Apr–Oct daily 9.30–7.*

ⓘ 78 rue Bernard-Palissy,
Tours. Tel: 02 47 70 37 37;
www.ligeris.com.

ⓘ 233 quai Général-de-
Gaulle, Amboise. Tel: 02 47
57 09 28; www.amboise-
valdeloire.com.

ⓘ 2 avenue de la
Résistance, Valençay.
Tel: 02 54 00 04 42;
www.pays-de-valencay.fr.

ⓘ Place de la Paix,
Romorantin-Lanthenay.
Tel: 02 54 76 43 89;
www.tourisme-
romorantin.com.

ⓘ Centre Anne de
Beaujeu, Place Jean-Jaurès,
Gien. Tel: 02 38 67 25 28;
www.gien.fr.

ⓘ 2 place de l'Etape,
Orléans. Tel: 02 34 05 05;
www.tourisme-orleans.com.

ⓘ 23 place du Château,
Blois. Tel: 02 54 90 41 41;
www.bloispaysde
chambord.com.

ⓘ 12 rue Rabelais, Vouvray.
Tel: 02 47 52 68 73.

1 Amboise
Château Royal
Tel: 02 47 57 00 98; www.
chateau-amboise.com.
*Open daily from 9, closes 7
Jul–Aug, 6.30 Apr–Jun, earlier
in winter (closed lunchtime
mid-Nov to Feb).*
Chanteloup pagoda
3km (2 miles) south of
Amboise, on Route de
Bléré. Tel: 02 47 57 20 97;
www.pagode-chanteloup.
com. *Open Feb–Mar
Sat–Sun, school hols 2–5;
Apr daily 10–6.30; May–Jun,
Sep 10–7; Jul–Aug 9.30–
7.30; Oct–Nov Mon–Fri
10.30–noon, Sat–Sun 10–5.*

2 Chenonceaux
Château de Chenonceau
Tel: 02 47 23 90 07;
www.chenonceau.com.
*Open daily Apr–early Nov
from 9, closes 5–8, depend-
ing on season; early Nov–
Mar from 9.30, closes 5–7.*

3 Valençay
Château/Motor Museum
Tel: 02 54 00 10 66. *Open
mid-Mar to early Nov
9/9.30–6.30/7.*

**4 Romorantin-
Lanthenay**
Musée Archéologique
Marcel de Marchéville
Le Carroir Doré, 21 rue de
la Pierre. Tel: 02 54 76 22
06. *Phone for appointment.*
Musée de Sologne
Moulin du Chapitre.
Tel: 02 54 95 33 66. *Open
Mon, Wed–Sat 10–noon,
2–6, Sun 2–6.*
L'Espace Matra Automobile
17 rue des Capucins.
Tel: 02 54 94 55 58. *Open
Mon–Fri 9–noon, 2–6,
Sat–Sun 10–noon, 2–6.*

5 Gien
Château and Musée de la
Chasse
Place du Château. Tel: 02
38 67 69 69. *Open Feb–
Mar, Oct–Dec, Wed–Mon

10–noon, 2–5; Apr–Jun, Sep, Wed–Mon 10–6; Aug daily 10–6. Closed Jan.

7 Orléans
Maison de Jeanne d'Arc
3 place du Général-de-Gaulle. Tel: 02 38 52 99 89.
Open Tue–Sun 10–12.30, 1.30–6 (afternoons only Nov–Apr).
Centre Jeanne d'Arc
1 place Gambetta.
Tel: 02 38 65 45 33;
www.jeannedarc.com.fr.
Open Tue–Wed, Fri–Sat 10–noon, 2–6, Thu 2–6.
Musée des Beaux-Arts
Place Ste-Croix. Tel: 02 38 79 21 55. Open Tue–Sun 10–6.
Hôtel Groslot
Place de l'Étape. Tel: 02 38 79 22 30. Open daily, Jul–Sep 9–7; Oct–Jun 10–noon, 2–6 (Sat 4.30–6).
Musée Historique et Archéologique
Place l'Abbé-Desnoyers.
Tel: 02 38 79 21 55.
Open May–Jun, Sep Tue–Sat 1.30–5.45, Sun 2–6; Jul–Aug Tue–Sun 9.30–12.15, 1.30–5.45, Sun 2–6; Oct–Apr Wed 1.30–5.45, Sun 2–6.

8 Chambord
Château de Chambord
Tel: 02 54 50 40 00;
www.chambord.org.
Open daily from 9, closes 5.15–7, depending on season.

9 Blois
Château de Blois
Tel: 02 54 90 33 33;
www.chateaudeblois.fr.
Open daily, Apr–Jun, Sep 9–6.30; Jul–Aug 9–7; Oct–early Nov 9–4; early Nov–Mar 9–12.30, 1.30–5.30.
Les Jacobins Natural History Museum
6 rue des Jacobins.
Tel: 02 54 90 21 00.
Open Tue–Sun 2–6; also Jul–Aug Tue–Fri 10–noon.

10 Vouvray
Château de Jallanges
Vernou-sur-Brenne.
Tel: 02 47 52 06 66;
www.jallanges.com. Open mid-Mar to mid-Oct, 10–noon, 2–6.
Château de Valmer
Chançay. Tel: 02 47 52 93 12. Open May Sat–Sun, hols 10–12.30, 2–7; Jun, Sep

Tue–Sun 10–12.30, 2–6/7; Jul–Aug Tue–Sun 10–7.

Special to...
Le Clos Lucé
Parc Leonardo da Vinci.
Tel: 02 47 57 00 73;
www.vinci-closluce.com.
Open daily 9 or 10–6, 7 or 8 depending on season.
Musée Dunois
Château Dunois, 2 place Dunois, Beaugency.
Tel: 02 38 44 55 23. Open Wed–Mon 10–noon, 2–5.

For Children
Zoo Parc de Beauval
St Aignan-sur-Cher.
Tel: 02 54 75 50 00;
www.zoobeauval.com.
Open daily 9–dusk.
Centre Sciences
6 rue Marcel Proust.
Tel: 02 38 54 61 05;
www.centre-sciences.org.
Open daily 2–6.

For History Buffs
Musée del la Résistance et de la Déportation
Esplanada Charles de Gaulle, Lorris. Tel: 02 38 94 84 19. Open Jul–Aug daily 2–6; Sep–Jun one weekend per month 10–noon, 2–5 (dates vary, call for details).

TOUR 10

ℹ️ 12 cours du 30 Juillet, Bordeaux. Tel: 05 56 00 66 00; www.bordeaux-tourisme.com.

ℹ️ 19 avenue de Lattre de Tassigny, Gujan-Mestras. Tel: 05 56 66 12 65; www.gujanmestras.com.

ℹ️ Esplanade Georges Pompidou, Arcachon. Tel: 05 57 52 97 97; www.arcachon.com.

ℹ️ 55 place G Dufau, Biscarrosse. Tel: 05 58 78 20 96; www.biscarrosse.com.

ℹ️ 38 avenue Maurice Martin, Mimizan. Tel: 05 58 09 11 20; www.mimizan-tourisme.com.

ℹ️ 6 place du Général Leclerc, Mont-de-Marsan. Tel: 05 58 05 87 37; www.montdemarsan.org.

ℹ️ Place Royal, Labastide-d'Armagnac. Tel: 05 58 44 67 56; www.labastide-darmagnac.net.

ℹ️ Place Armagnac, Barbotan-les-Thermes.
Tel: 05 62 69 52 13;
www.mairie-cazaubon.fr.

ℹ️ 7 avenue Mondenard, Nérac. Tel: 05 53 65 27 75.

ℹ️ 11 rue Principale, Sauternes. Tel: 05 56 76 69 13; www.sauternais-graves-langon.com.

1 Gujan-Mestras
Maison de l'Huître
Port de Larros. Tel: 05 56 66 23 71; www.maisonde lhuitre.fr. Open all year 10–12.30, 2.30–6 (closed Sun Sep–May).
Aqualand
145 route des Lacs.
Tel: 05 56 66 39 39;
www.aqualand.fr. Open mid-Jun to early Sep daily 10–6 or 7.

2 Arcachon
Musée Aquarium
2 rue Professeur Jolyet.
Tel: 05 56 83 33 32. Open daily 9.45–12.15, 1.45–6/7.

3 Biscarrosse
Musée de l'Hydraviation
332 avenue Louis Bréguet.
Tel: 05 58 78 00 65;
www.hydravions-biscarrosse.com. Open Wed–Mon 2–6 (daily 10–7 Jul–Aug).
Musée des Traditions et de l'Histoire
216 avenue Louis Bréguet.
Tel: 05 58 78 77 37. Open Jul–Aug daily 9.30–7, closed Sun am; Jun, Sep Tue–Sat 9–noon, 2–6; school hols daily 2–6.

4 Mimizan
Mimizan Museum
8 rue de l'Abbaye. Tel: 05 58 09 00 61. Open all year, telephone for details.

5 Sabres
Écomusée de la Grande Lande
Tel: 05 58 08 31 31;
www.parc-landes-de-gascogne.fr. Open late Mar–early Nov daily, first train 10.10am, last train back 7pm.

6 Mont-de-Marsan
Musée Despiau Wlérick
6 place Marguerite de Navarre. Tel: 05 58 75 00 45.
Open May–Sep daily

10–noon, 2–6; Oct–Apr closed Tue.

7 Labastide-d'Armagnac
Château Garreau
Tel: 05 58 44 84 35. Open Mon–Fri 9–noon, 2–6 (also Sat 2–6, Sun 3–6 Apr–Oct)

9 Nérac
Château de Nérac
Impasse Henri IV. Tel: 05 53 65 21 11. Open Apr–Sep daily 10–6; Oct–Mar Tue–Thu, Sun 2–6

Back to Nature
Parc Ornithologique du Teich
On the A66 Bordeaux to Arcachon road. Tel: 05 56 22 80 93; www.parc-ornithologique-du-teich.com. Open daily 10–6 (to 7 or 8pm in summer).

For Children
Parc Animalier La Coccinelle
135 route Grands Lacs, Gujan-Mestras. Tel: 05 56 66 30 41; www.la-coccinelle.fr. Open mid-Apr to Aug daily 10–6.30/7; Wed, weekends May, Sep; weekends, school holidays noon–6 Oct.
Aventure Parc
Route de Bordeaux, near Biscarrosse. Tel: 05 58 82 53 40. Open Apr–Oct 10–6 or 7. Closed various days except Jul–Aug.

Special to...
l'Atelier des Produits Résineux
Luxey. Tel: 05 58 08 01 39.
Open Jun to mid-Sep daily 10–7.

TOUR 11

ℹ️ 26 place Francheville, Périgueux. Tel: 05 53 53 10 63; www.tourisme-perigueux.fr.

ℹ️ 19 avenue de la Préhistoire, Les Eyzies. Tel: 05 53 06 97 05; www.tourisme-terrede cromagnon.com.

ℹ️ Place Bertran-de-Born, Montignac. Tel: 05 53 51 82 60; www.tourisme-lascaux.fr.

ℹ️ 3 rue Tourny, Sarlat. Tel: 05 53 31 45 45; www.ot-sarlat-perigord.fr.

ⓘ Tourist Information Office
⓫ Number on tour

ⓘ Boulevard Louis-Jean Malvy, Souillac. Tel: 05 65 37 81 56; www.tourisme-souillac.com.

ⓘ L'Hospitalet, Rocamadour. Tel: 05 65 33 22 00; www.rocamadour.com.

ⓘ Place de la Halle, Domme. Tel: 05 53 31 71 00; www.ot-domme.com.

ⓘ 97 rue Neuve d'Argenson, Bergerac. Tel: 05 53 57 03 11; www.bergerac-tourisme.com.

❶ Grotte du Grand Roc
Signposted from Les Eyzies. Tel: 05 53 06 92 70. *Open Apr–Nov Sun–Fri 10–12.30, 2–6 (daily 10–7 Jul–Aug).*

❷ Les Eyzies
Musée National de la Préhistoire
Follow signs for Grotte du Grand-Roc. Tel: 05 53 06 45 45. *Open Jul–Aug daily 9.30–6.30; Sep–Jun Wed–Mon 9.30–noon, 2–5 or 6.*
Abri Pataud
Tel: 05 53 06 92 46. *Open Apr–Oct Sun–Thu 10–noon, 2–6.*
Abri de Cap Blanc
Marquay, Les Eyzies. Tel: 05 53 06 86 00. *Open Sun–Fri 9.30–5.30 (closed 12.30–2 mid-Sep to mid-May).*
Grottes du Roc de Cazelle
Tel: 05 53 59 46 09. *Open all year daily.*
Aquarium du Périgord Noir
Tel: 05 53 07 10 74; www.aquariumperigordnoir.com. *Open Jul–Aug 9–7; shorter hours Apr–Jun, Sep.*

❸ Lascaux II
Off route Montignac–Les-Eyzies. Tel: 05 53 51 95 03. *Guided tours only. High season 8–7; low season 10–5 (closed lunch).*
Régourdou Caves and Museum
Montignac. Tel: 05 53 51 81 23. *Open Feb–Nov daily 11–6 (10–7 Jul–Aug).*

❺ Souillac
Musée de l'Automate
Place de l'Abbaye. Tel: 05 65 37 07 07. *Open Apr–Oct 10–noon, 3–6 (Jul–Aug 10–7); closed Mon Apr–May & Oct; Nov–Mar Wed–Sun 2.30–5.30.*

❻ Gouffre de Padirac
Tel: 05 65 33 64 56; www.gouffre-de-padirac.com. *Open late Mar–early Jul daily 9.30–6.30.*

❽ Domme
Museum
Place de la Halle. Tel: 05 53 31 71 00. *Open Apr–Sep daily 10.30–noon, 2.30–6.*
Caverns
Place de la Halle. Tel: 05 53 31 71 00 (tourist office). *Open Feb to mid-Nov daily 10–noon, 2–6.*

❿ Bergerac
Musée du Tabac
Maison Peyrarède, place du Feu. Tel: 05 53 63 04 13. *Open Tue–Sat 10–noon, 2–5 or 6, Sun 2.30–6.30. Closed Sun Oct–early Apr.*
Musée du Vin et de la Batellerie
5 rue des Conférences. Tel: 05 53 57 80 92. *Open Tue–Sat 10–noon, 2–5.30 or 6.30. Closed Sun Oct–early Apr.*

For History Buffs
La Roque-St-Christophe
Peyzac le Moustier. Tel: 05 53 50 70 45; www.roque-st-christophe.com. *Open daily, Feb–Oct 10–6.30 (8, Jul–Aug); Nov–Jan 2–5.*
Le Thot – Éspace Cro-Magnon
Thonac. Tel: 05 53 05 70 44. *Open Apr–Sep daily 10–6 or 7; Oct–Dec, Feb–Mar 10–12.30, 2–5.30 (closed Jan & Mon in winter).*
Château de Castelnaud
Tel: 05 53 31 30 00; www.castelnaud.com. *Open daily 10–6, 7 or 8.*

For Children
Préhisto-Parc
Tursac. Tel: 05 53 50 73 19; www.prehistoparc.fr. *Open Feb–Nov daily 10–6 (7 Jul–Aug).*
Insectopia
Derriere du Gouffre, Padirac. Tel: 05 65 33 76 76; www.insectopia.fr. *Open Jul–Aug daily 10–6.*

La Féerie du Rail
Rocamadour. Tel: 05 65 33 71 06; www.la-feerie.com. *Open Easter–Oct daily: four to eight shows per day, starting at 11am.*

Back to Nature
Parc Animalier
Route de Cajarc, D14, Gramat. Tel: 05 65 38 81 22; www.gramat-parc-animalier.com. *Open all year daily, Easter–Sep 9.30–7; Oct–Easter 2–6.*
Forêt des Singes
Rocamadour. Tel: 05 65 33 62 72; www.la-foret-des-singes.com. *Open Mar to mid-Nov daily 10–noon, 1–6 (9.30–6.30 Jul–Aug).*
Rocher des Aigles
Rocamadour. Tel: 05 65 33 65 45; www.rocherdesaigles.com. *Open Apr–early Nov 2–6; closed Mon, excluding Jul–Aug.*

TOUR 12

ⓘ Place Royale, Pau. Tel: 05 59 27 27 08; www.pau-pyrenees.com.

ⓘ 3 cours Gambetta, Tarbes. Tel: 05 62 51 30 31; www.tarbes.com.

ⓘ 3 allée Tournefort, Bagnères-de-Bigorre. Tel: 05 62 95 50 71; www.bagneresdebigorre-lamongie.com.

ⓘ 18 allée d'Étigny, Bagnères-de-Luchon. Tel: 05 61 79 21 21; www.luchon.com.

ⓘ Maison du Parc National, Gavarnie. Tel: 05 62 92 49 10; www.gavarnie.com.

ⓘ Place Foch, Cauterets. Tel: 05 62 92 50 50; www.cauterets.com.

ⓘ Place Peyramale, Lourdes. Tel: 05 62 42 77 40; www.lourdes-infotourisme.com.

❶ Tarbes
Musée Massey
Jardin Massey. Tel: 05 62 36 31 49. *Open Wed–Sun 10–noon, 2–6; garden daily, mid-Jun to Sep 7am–8/9pm; Mar–mid Jun and Oct 8–7/8.*

Haras National de Tarbes
Chemin de Mauhourat. Tel: 05 62 56 30 80. *Open Mon–Fri 2–4 for guided tours, on the hour.*

❷ Bagnères-de-Bigorre
Musée Bigourdan du Vieux Moulin
Rue de Hount Blanque. Tel: 05 62 91 07 33. *Open Tue–Fri 10–noon, 2–6.*
Musée Saliès
Place des Thermes. Tel: 05 62 91 07 26. *Open mid-May to Oct Wed–Fri 10–noon, 2–6, Sat–Sun 3–6.*

❹ Bagnères-de-Luchon
Musée du Pays de Luchon
18 allée d'Étigny. Tel: 05 61 79 29 87. *Open daily 9–noon, 2–6.*

❻ Gavarnie
Pyrenees National Park Information Centre
Village centre. Tel: 05 62 92 42 48. *Open all year, Mon–Fri 9–noon, 2–5.*

❼ Cauterets
Pyrenees National Park Information Centre
Tel: 05 62 92 52 56. *Open Mon–Fri 9.30–noon, 3–6.30; closed mid-Oct to mid-Dec & Sun.*
Musée 1900
Boulevard Latapie-Flurin. Tel: 05 62 92 02 02. *Open variable hours; phone to confirm.*

❽ Lourdes
Grotto
www.lourdes-france.org. *Open every morning Masses, at about 10.30am.*
Pavilion Notre-Dame, Musée Bernadette, Musée d'Art Sacré du Gemmail
72 rue de la Grotte. Tel: 05 62 94 13 15; www.gemmail.com. *Open Easter–Oct daily 9–noon, 2–7.*
Musée Pyrénéen
Château, rue du Bourg. Tel: 05 62 42 37 37. *Open daily 9–noon, 1.30–6.30 (9–6.30 mid-Jul to mid-Aug).*

❾ Grottes de Bétharram
Saint Pé de Bigorre. Tel: 05 62 41 80 04; www.grottes-de-betharram.com. *Open mid-Feb to late Mar Mon–*

Fri 2.30–4; late Mar–Oct daily 9–noon, 1.30–5.30

For History Buffs
Maison Natale de Marshal Foch
2 rue de la Victoire, Tarbes. Tel: 05 62 93 19 02. *Open Thu–Mon 10–noon, 2–6.30.*
Musée de Lourdes
Parking de l'Égalité. Tel: 05 62 94 28 00. *Open Apr–Oct daily 9–noon, 1.30–7.*
Musée du Petit Lourdes
68 avenue Peyramale. Tel: 05 62 94 24 36. *Open Apr–Oct daily 9–noon, 1.30–7.*

Back to Nature
Observatoire et Institut de Physique du Globe
Pic du Midi. Tel: 05 62 56 71 11; www.picdumidi.com. *Open Jun–Sep daily 9–7; phone for rest of year.*

For Children
'The Animated Crib'
21 quai St-Jean, Lourdes. Tel: 05 62 94 71 00. *Open Apr–Oct daily 9–noon, 1.30–7.*

TOUR 13

ⓘ 4 la Canebière, Marseille. Tel: 08 26 50 05 00; www.marseille-tourisme.com.

ⓘ Quai des Moulins, Cassis. Tel: 08 92 25 98 92; www.ot-cassis.com.

ⓘ Allées Vivien, Bandol. Tel: 04 94 29 41 35; www.bandol.fr.

ⓘ 334 avenue de la République, Toulon. Tel: 04 94 18 53 00; www.toulontourisme.com.

ⓘ Forum du Casino, 3 avenue Ambroise Thomas, Hyères. Tel: 04 94 01 84 50; www.hyeres-tourisme.com.

ⓘ Quai Jean-Jaurès, St-Tropez. Tel: 04 94 97 45 21; www.ot-saint-tropez.com.

ⓘ 1 boulevard des Aliziers, Grimaud. Tel: 04 94 55 43 83; www.grimaud-provence.com.

ⓘ 8 cours Barthélémy, Aubagne. Tel: 04 42 03 49 98; www.oti-paysdaubagne.com.

❶ Cassis
Musée Municipal Méditerranéen de Cassis
Rue Xavier d'Authier. Tel: 04 42 01 88 66. *Open Wed–Sat, Apr–Sep 10.30–12.30, 3.30–6.30; Oct–Mar 10.30–12.30, 2.30–5.30.*

❸ Bandol
Jardin Exotique Zoo
Commune de Sanary. Tel: 04 94 29 40 38; www.zoosanary.com. *Open daily 9.30–19 (8–noon, 2–6 in winter).*

❹ Toulon
Musée National de la Marine
Place Monsenergue. Tel: 04 94 02 02 01; www.musee-marine.fr. *Open Apr to mid-Sep daily 10–6; mid-Sep to Mar Wed–Mon 10–6.*
Zoo de Toulon
Mont Faron. Tel: 04 94 88 07 89. *Open all year Mon–Sat, Sun 10–5.30; closed when raining.*
Musée Memorial du Débarquement
Sommet du Faron. Tel: 04 94 88 08 09. *Open Tue–Sun 10–noon, 2–5.30 (6.30 May–Sep).*

❺ Hyères
Olbia Archaeological Excavations
D559 Carqueiranne road. Tel: 04 94 57 98 28. *Closed until 2012.*

❼ St-Tropez
Musée de l'Annonciade
Quai de l'Epi. Tel: 04 94 17 84 10. *Open daily 10–noon, 2–6 (closed Tue and Nov).*
Musée de la Citadelle
Citadelle. Tel: 08 92 68 48 28. *Open daily 10–12.30, 1.30–5.30.*

❿ Chartreuse de la Verne
Route de Collobrières. Tel: 04 94 43 45 41. *Open Wed–Mon 11–5 (6 May–Sep).*

⓫ Aubagne
Musée de la Légion Etrangère
Quartier Viénot route Tuilière. Tel: 04 42 18 12 41. *Open Jun–Sep Tue–Wed, Fri–Sun 10–noon, 3–7; Oct–May Wed, Sat–Sun 10–noon, 2–6.*

For Children
OK Corral
Cuges les Pins, on the N8. Tel: 04 42 73 80 05; www.okcorral.fr. *Open Apr–Jun, Sep–Oct Sat–Sun from 10 (also Wed in Jun); Jul–Aug, Easter week, Halloween week daily.*

TOUR 14

ⓘ Palais des Festivals, 1 la Croisette, Cannes. Tel: 04 92 99 84 22; www.cannes.com.

ⓘ 11 place du Général-de-Gaulle, Antibes. Tel: 04 97 23 11 13; www.antibes juanlespins.com.

ⓘ 46 rue St-Sébastien, Biot. Tel: 04 93 65 78 00; www.biot.fr.

ⓘ 22 cours Honoré-Cresp, Grasse. Tel: 04 93 36 66 66; www.grasse.fr.

ⓘ Place Victoria, Gourdon. Tel: 04 93 09 68 25; www.gourdon-france.com.

ⓘ 8 rue Nationale, Castellane. Tel: 04 92 83 61 14; www.castellane.org.

ⓘ Place Marcel Pastorelli, St-André-les-Alpes. Tel: 04 92 89 02 39; www.ot-st-andre-les-alpes.fr.

ⓘ Place de la Mairie, Riez. Tel: 04 92 77 99 09; www.ville-riez.fr/tourisme.

ⓘ Place de l'Église, Moustiers-Ste-Marie. Tel: 04 92 74 67 84; www.moustiers.eu.

ⓘ 2 avenue Carnot, Draguignan. Tel: 04 98 10 51 05; www.dracenie.com.

ⓘ Place St-Sébastien, Mons. Tel: 04 94 76 39 54.

❶ Cap d'Antibes
Musée Napoléonien
Batterie du Graillon, boulevard J F Kennedy. Tel: 04 93 61 45 32. *Open Tue–Sat 10–4.30 (6 mid-Jun to mid-Sep).*

❷ Antibes
Musée Archéologie
Bastion St-André, avenue Maizière. Tel: 04 92 90 54 37. *Open mid-Jun to mid-Sep daily 10–noon, 2–6; mid-Sep to mid-Jun 10–1, 2–5.*

Musée Picasso
Château Grimaldi. Tel: 04 92 90 54 20. *Open Jun–Sep Tue–Sun 10–6 (to 8 Wed, Fri Jul–Aug); Oct–May Tue–Sun 10–noon, 2–6.*

❸ Biot
Musée National Fernand Léger
Chemin du Val de Pome. Tel: 04 92 91 50 30; www.musee-fernandleger.fr. *Open daily 10–5/6 (closed Tue Nov–Apr).*
Écomusée du Verre
5 chemin des Combes. Tel: 04 93 65 03 00; www.verreriebiot.com. *Open Mon–Sat 9.30–7, Sun 10.30–1, 2.30–7.*

❹ Grasse
Musée International de la Parfumerie
2 boulevard Jeu de Ballon. Tel: 04 97 05 58 00; www.museesdegrasse.com. *Open Apr daily 11–6; May–Sep daily 10–7 (to 9 Sat); Oct–to early Nov, late Nov–Mar Wed–Mon 11–6. Closed early–late Nov.*
Musée Jean-Honoré Fragonard
20 boulevard Fragonard. Tel: 04 93 36 44 65. *Open daily 9–6. Closed lunch in winter.*
Musée d'Art et d'Histoire de Provence
2 rue Mirabeau. Tel: 04 93 36 80 20; www.museede-grasse.com. *Open Jun–Sep daily 10–7.*
Musée de la Marine
23 boulevard Fragonard. Tel: 04 93 40 11 11. *Open Mon–Fri 10–12.30, 2–6.*

❺ Gourdon
Château de Gourdon
Musée Historique. Tel: 04 93 09 68 02; www.chateau-gourdon.com. *Closed until 2011.*

⓬ Draguignan
Musée des Arts et Traditions Populaire
15 rue Joseph Roumanille. Tel: 04 94 47 05 72. *Open Tue–Sat 9–noon, 2–6, Sun 2–6.*
Musée de l'Artillerie
Avenue de la Grande Armée. Tel: 04 83 08 13 86. *Open mid-Jan to mid-Dec Sun–Wed 9–noon, 1.30–5.30.*

14 Mons
Museum
Rue Pierre Porre. Tel: 04 94 84 79 50. Open Sat–Sun 2–7 (also Wed pm summer).

For Children
Marineland
Route Nationale 7. Tel: 04 93 33 49 49; www.marine land.fr. Open early Feb–Sep daily 10–6/7 (to 11pm Jul–Aug); Oct–Nov call for hours. Closed Dec–Jan.

Special to...
Etablissement Nevière
Rte de Manosque, Valensole. Tel: 04 92 74 85 28. Open Mon–Fri 8–noon, 1.30–5.30, Sat to 6.

Back to Nature
Réserve Géologique de Haute-Provence
Parc St-Benoît, Digne-les-Bains. Tel: 04 92 36 70 70. Open daily 9–noon, 2–5.30 (later Jul–Aug); closed weekends Nov–Mar.

TOUR 15
---

i 5 Promenade des Anglais, Nice. Tel: 08 92 70 74 07; www. nicetourism.com.

i 59 avenue Denis Seméria, St-Jean-Cap-Ferrat. Tel: 04 93 76 08 90; www.saintjeancapferrat.fr.

i 2 boulevard des Moulins, Monte Carlo. Tel: (377) 92 16 61 16; www.visitmonaco.com.

i Palais de l'Europe, 8 avenue Boyer, Menton. Tel: 04 92 41 76 76; www.menton.fr.

i 19 avenue Jean Médecin, Sospel. Tel: 04 93 04 15 80; www.sospel-tourisme.com.

1 Cap Ferrat
Musée Ephrussi de Rothschild
Tel: 04 93 01 33 09; www.villa-ephrussi.com. Open mid-Feb to Oct daily 10–6 (till 7 Jul–Aug); Nov to mid-Feb Mon–Fri 2–6, Sat–Sun 10–6.

2 Monaco
Palais Princier/Musée des Souvenirs Napoléoniens
Tel: (377) 93 25 18 31;

www.palais.mc. Open Jun–Sep daily 9.30–6.30; Oct to mid-Nov daily 10–5; mid-Dec to May Tue–Sun 10.30–12.30, 2–5. Closed mid-Nov to mid-Dec.
Musée Océanographique and Aquarium
Av St-Martin. Tel: (377) 93 15 36 00; www.oceano.mc. Open daily Apr–Sep 9.30–7 (7.30 Jul–Aug); Oct–Mar 10–6.

3 Menton
Jardin de la Serre de la Madone
74 route de Gorbio. Tel: 04 93 57 73 90; www.serredelamadone. com. Open Tue–Sun 10–5 or 6. Closed Nov.
Musée Cocteau
Bastion du Vieux Port, 2 quai Napoléon-III. Tel: 04 93 57 72 30. Open Wed–Mon 10–noon, 2–6.

5 Sospel
Musée des Fortifications Alpins
Fort St-Roch. Tel: 04 93 04 00 70. Open Jun–Sep Tue–Sun 2–6; Oct–May Sat–Sun and hols 2–6.

For History Buffs
Villa Kérylos
Beaulieu. Tel: 04 93 01 01 44; www.villa-kerylos.com. Open mid-Feb to Oct daily 10–6 (7 Jul–Aug); Nov to mid-Feb Mon–Fri 2–6.

Back to Nature
Jardin Exotique, Grotte de l'Observatoire and Museum of Anthropology
62 boulevard du Jardin Exotique, Monaco. Tel: (377) 93 15 29 80; www.jardin-exotique.mc. Open daily 9–6 or 7 (or sunset in winter).

TOUR 16
---

i 6 rue Auguste, Nîmes Tel: 04 66 58 38 00; www.ot-nimes.fr.

i 24 cours Gambetta, Beaucaire. Tel: 04 66 59 26 57; www.ot-beaucaire.fr.

i 16 boulevard Itam, Tarascon. Tel: 04 90 91 03 52; www.tarascon.org.

i 41 cours Jean-Jaurès, Avignon. Tel: 04 32 74 32 74; www.ot-avignon.fr.

i Place Jean-Jaurès, St-Rémy-de-Provence. Tel: 04 90 92 05 22; www.saint remy-de-provence.com.

i Maison du Roy, Les Baux-de-Provence. Tel: 04 90 54 34 39; www. lesbauxdeprovence.com.

i Boulevard des Lices, Arles. Tel: 04 90 18 41 20; www.tourisme.ville-arles.fr.

i 5 avenue Van Gogh, Stes-Maries-de-la-Mer. Tel: 04 90 97 82 55; www.saintesmaries.com.

i Place Saint-Louis, Aigues-Mortes. Tel: 04 66 53 73 00; www.ot-aigues mortes.fr.

1 Pont du Gard
Route du Pont du Gard, Vers-Pont-du-Gard. Tel: 08 20 90 33 30; www.pont dugard.fr. Open site: daily; Museum, Cinema: Apr–Oct Tue–Sun from 9/9.30, closing 5.30–7 depending on season.

2 Beaucaire
Musée Municipal Auguste Jacquet
Château de Beaucaire. Tel: 04 66 59 90 07. Open Wed–Mon 10–noon, 2–6.

3 Tarascon
L'Espace Tartarin
Cloître des Cordeliers. Tel: 04 90 91 38 71. Open daily 10–noon, 2.30–6.30.
Château Royal
Boulevard du Roi René. Tel: 04 90 91 01 93. Open daily, 9.30–5, 5.30/6.30, depending on season.

4 St-Michel-de-Frigolet
Tel: 04 90 95 70 07; www.frigolet.com. Open all year daily 7–noon, 1.30–6.

5 Avignon
Palais des Papes
Place du Palais. Tel: 04 90 27 50 00; www.palais-des-papes.com. Open daily 9–7 (to 8 or 9 Jul–Aug).

6 St-Rémy-de-Provence
Musée des Alpilles
1 place Favier. Tel: 04 90 92 68 24. Open Tue–Sat, first Sun of month, Mar–Jun, Sep–Oct 10–noon, 2–6;

Jul–Aug 10–12.30, 2–7; Nov–Feb 2–5.
Monastère de St-Paul-de-Mausole
Avenue Van Gogh. Tel: 04 90 92 77 00. Open Apr–Oct daily 9.30–7; Nov–Mar daily 10.15–4.45.
Musée Archéologique
Hôtel de Sade, rue du Parage. Tel: 04 90 92 64 04. Closed for restoration; reopening 2012.
Glanum Roman Site
Avenue Van Gogh. Tel: 04 90 92 23 79. Open Apr–Aug daily 10–6.30; Sep–Mar Tue–Sun 10.30–5.

7 Les Baux-de-Provence
Château and Museum
Tel: 04 90 54 55 56. Open daily spring 9–6.30; summer 9–8.30; autumn 9.30–6; winter 9.30–5.
Cathédrale d'Images
Route de Maillone. Tel: 04 90 54 38 65; www. cathedrale-images.com. Open late Feb–early Jan daily 10–6 (7 Apr–Sep).

8 Arles
Arènes
Rond-Point des Arènes. Tel: 04 90 49 36 74. Open daily, Nov–Feb 10–5; Mar–Oct 9–6 or 6.30.
Théâtre Antique
Rue de la Calade. Tel: 04 90 18 41 20. Open daily, Mar, Apr, Oct 9–noon, 2–5; May–Sep 9–7; Nov–Feb 10–noon, 2–5; closed some days Jul–Aug for concerts.
Fondation Vincent Van Gogh
Palais de Luppé, 24 bis, Rond Point des Arènes. Tel: 04 90 93 08 08. Open Apr–Sep daily 10–6 or 7; Oct–Mar Tue–Sun 11–5.

10 Musée Camarguais
Mas du Pont de Rousty Albaron. Tel: 04 90 97 10 82. Open Apr–Sep daily 9–6; Oct–Mar, Wed–Mon 10–5.

11 Maison du Parc
Tel: 04 90 97 86 32. Closed for construction work..

Parc Ornithologique
North of Saintes-Maries-
de-la-Mer. Tel: 04 90 97
82 62. *Open daily 9–dusk
(from 10am Oct–Mar).*

12 Stes-Maries-de-la-Mer
Musée Baroncelli
Rue Victor Hugo. Tel: 04 90
97 87 60. *Open Apr to mid-
Nov daily 3–6.*

13 Aigues-Mortes
Tour de Constance
Place Anotole-France.
Tel: 04 66 53 61 55. *Open
daily 10–5.30 or 7.*

For History Buffs
Moulin de Daudet
D33, outskirts of Font-
vieille. Tel: 04 90 54 60 78.
*Open Apr–Dec daily 9–6/7;
Feb–Mar daily 10–noon,
2–5. Closed Jan.*

For Children
Tiki III cruises
Pier, Stes-Maries-de-la-Mer.
Tel: 04 90 97 81 68;
www.tiki3.fr. *Cruises operate
late Mar–early Nov daily at
10, 2.30 and 4.15 (also
11.30 and 6 Jul–Aug).*

TOUR 17

i 14 place Stanislas,
Nancy. Tel: 03 83 35 22 41;
www.ot-nancy.fr.

i 5 place de la Fontaine,
Liverdun. Tel: 03 83 24
40 40.

i Place d'Armes, Metz.
Tel: 03 87 55 53 76; http://
tourisme.mairie-metz.fr.

i Pavillion Japiot, avenue
du Général Mangin.
Tel: 03 29 84 55 55;
www.tourisme-verdun.fr.

i Rue du Palais de
Justice, St-Mihiel.
Tel 03 29 89 06 47.

i Parvis de la
Cathédrale, Toul. Tel: 03 83
64 11 69; www.toul.fr.

1 Parc de Haye
Velaine en Haye. Tel: 03 83
23 24 99. *Open daily.*
Motor Museum
Parc de Loisirs, Velaine-en-
Haye. Tel: 03 83 23 28 38;
www.musee-auto-
lorraine.com. *Open all year
Wed, Sat–Sun 2–6; Jul–Aug
daily 2–6.*

3 Metz
La Cour d'Or, Musée
d'Art et d'Histoire
2 rue du Haut-Poirier. Tel:
03 87 20 13 29. *Open 9–5
(10–5 Sat–Sun). Closed Tue.*
Centre Pompidou-Metz
1 parvis des Droits de
l'Homme. Tel: 03 87 15 39
39; www.centrepompidou-
metz.fr. *Open Mon, Wed,
11–6, Thu–Fri 11–8, Sat
10–8, Sun 10–6.*

5 Verdun: Champs de Bataille
Fort de Douaumont
10km (6 miles) north of
Verdun. Tel: 03 29 84 41 91.
*Open Apr–Dec daily 10–5
or 6; Feb–Mar daily 10–1,
2–5*

6 Verdun
Underground Citadel
Avenue du 5ème RAP.
*Open daily, Apr–Sep 9–6 or
or 7; Oct–Mar 10–noon,
2–5. Closed Jan.*
Musée de la Princerie
16 rue de la Belle Vierge.
Tel: 03 29 86 10 66.
*Open Apr–Oct daily
9.30–noon, 2–6.*

7 St-Mihiel
Benedictines' Library
Rue du Palais de Justice.
Tel: 03 29 89 06 47. *Open
Apr–Jun, Sep–Oct weekends
2–6; Jul–Aug Wed–Mon 2–6.*

For History Buffs
Maison de Robert
Schuman
Rue Robert Schuman, Scy-
Chazelles. Tel: 03 87 60 19
90. *Open Apr–Oct, Thu–Tue
10–noon, 2–6.*

Special to...
Maison Lorraine du
Polyculture
94 Grande Rue, Lucey.
Tel: 03 83 63 85 21. *Guided
tours by reservation.*

TOUR 18

i Place Bellecour, Lyon.
Tel: 04 72 77 69 69;
www.lyon-france.com.

i 3 place Hôtel de Ville,
Villars-les-Dombes. Tel: 04
74 98 06 29; www.villars-
les-dombes.com.

i Place du Champ de
Foire, Châtillon-sur-
Chalaronne. Tel: 04 74 55
02 27.

i Place de l'Hôtel de
Ville, Amplepuis.
Tel: 04 74 89 30 24;
www.amplepuis.fr.

i Place Maréchal de
Lattre de Tassigny, Roanne.
Tel: 04 77 71 51 77;
www.leroannais.com.

i 9 place Jean-Baptiste
Galland, Chazelles-sur-
Lyon. Tel 04 77 54 98 86;
www.cc-forez-en-
lyonnais.fr.

1 Musée Henri Malartre
645 rue du Musée,
Rochetaillée-sur-Saone.
Tel: 04 78 22 18 80;
www.musee-malartre.
com. *Open Tue–Sun, holiday
Mon 9–6 (10–7 Jul–Aug).*

3 Parc des Oiseaux
Off N83 near Villars-les-
Dombes. Tel: 04 74 98 05
54; www.parc-des-
oiseaux.com. *Open
Mar–Nov daily 9.30 or
10–5.50 or 7.*

5 Châtillon-sur-Chalaronne
Apothecairerie
Place St Vincent de Paul.
Tel 04 74 55 15 70. *Open
Apr–Sep Tue–Sun 10–noon,
2–6 (7 in Jul–Aug); Oct to
mid-Nov weekends only.*

7 Amplepuis
Musée Barthélémy
Thimonnier
Place de l'Hôtel de Ville.
Tel: 04 74 89 08 90.
Open daily 2.30–6.30.

8 Roanne
Musée du Tissage
Place Vaucanson, Bussières.
Tel: 04 77 27 33 95. *Open
Apr–Oct Sat–Sun 3–6 (daily
Jul–Aug); closed Nov–Mar.*
Musée Déchelette
22 rue Anatole France.
Tel: 04 77 23 68 77. *Open
Wed–Mon 10–noon, 2–6
(10–6 Sat, 2–6, Sun).*

9 Chazelles-sur-Lyon
Atelier-Musée du Chapeau
16 Route de St-Galmier.
Tel: 04 77 94 23 29; www.
museeduchapeau.com.
*Open Wed–Mon (also Tue
Jul–Aug) 2–6.*

For Children
Parc de la Tête d'Or
Tel: 04 78 89 02 03. *Park*

*open Apr–Sep daily
6am–11pm (9pm winter);
zoo daily 9–5 (6.30 in
summer).*

**For Children/For
History Buffs**
Musée Ampère/Maison
d'Ampère
Poleymieux. Tel: 04 78 91
90 77. *Open Sat 2–6, Sun
10–noon, 2–6 or by
reservation.*

For History Buffs
Maison Monsieur Vincent
12 places des Halles,
Châtillon-sur-Chalaronne.
Tel: 04 74 55 26 64.
*Telephone for an appoint-
ment.*

For Children
Musée d'Allard
13 Boulevard de la
Préfecture, Montbrison.
Tel: 04 77 96 39 15. *Open
Wed–Mon 2–6.*

Back to Nature
Parc de Courzieu
Montmain la Côte, Cour-
zieu. Tel: 04 74 70 96 10;
www.parc-de-courzieu.fr.
*Open mid-Mar to Aug daily
10–7; Sep to mid-Nov
noon–6.*

TOUR 19

i 14 rue de la
République, Grenoble.
Tel: 04 76 42 41 41;
www.grenoble-isere.com.

i 5 bis place du Palais de
Justice, Chambéry. Tel: 04 79
33 42 47; www.
chambery-tourisme.com.

i Place Maurice Mollard,
Aix-les-Bains.
Tel: 04 79 88 68 00;
www.aixlesbains.com.

i 1 rue Jean-Jaurès,
Annecy. Tel: 04 50 45 00
33; www.lac-annecy.com.

i Place de l'Eglise, La
Clusaz. Tel: 04 50 32 65 00.

i Grande Rue, Beaufort.
Tel: 04 79 38 37 57.

i Place de la Gare,
Bourg-St-Maurice. Tel: 04
79 07 12 57;
www.lesarcs.com.

i Val-d'Isere. Tel: 04 79
06 06 60;
www.valdisere.com.

[i] Place de la Cathédrale,
St-Jean-de-Maurienne. Tel:
04 79 83 51 51; www.saint
jeandemaurienne.com.

**1 La Grande
Chartreuse**
Musée de la Grande
Chartreuse
La Correrie. Tel: 04 76 88
60 45; www.musee-
grande-chartreuse.fr. Open
daily, May–Sep 10–6.30;
Apr, Oct–Nov Mon–Fri
1.30–6, Sat–Sun 10–6.

2 Chambéry
Château
Rue Basse du Château.
Tel: 04 79 33 42 47. Guided
tours only, all year.
Musée des Beaux-Arts
Place du Palais de Justice.
Tel: 04 79 33 75 03. Closed
until late 2011.
Musée Savoisien
Square Lannoy-de-Bissy.
Tel: 04 79 33 44 48. Open
Wed–Mon 10–noon, 2–6.
Galerie Eurêka
Place François Mitterand.
Tel: 04 79 60 04 25. Open
Tue, Fri 2–7, Wed, Sat 2–6
(Tue–Sat 2–6 during school
holidays).

3 Aix-les-Bains
Temple of Diana and
Museums
Place Mollard. Tel: 04 79 88
68 00. Open for guided
tours only, Thu 2.30.
Musée Faure
10 boulevard des Côtes.
Tel: 04 79 61 06 57. Open
Wed–Mon 10–noon,
1.30–6 (closed Mon
Nov–Feb).

4 Annecy
Castle Museum
Place du Château. Tel: 04
50 33 87 30. Open daily
10.30–6 (closed lunchtime &
Tue Oct–May).
Palais de l'Île and Museum
3 passage de l'Île. Tel: 04 50
65 08 14. Open daily
10.30–6 (closed Tue and
lunchtime Oct–May).

5 Beaufort
Cheese Co-operative
Avenue du Capitaine Bulle.
Tel: 04 79 38 33 62;
www.cooperative-de-
beaufort.com.
Demonstrations daily:
Apr–Sep 9–12, 7–10;
Oct–Mar 9–12. Shop:

May–Sep daily 8–noon, 2–6
(7 Jul–Aug); closed Sun
Oct–Apr.

7 Bourg-St-Maurice
Musée des Minéraux
32 avenue du Maréchal
Leclerc. Tel: 04 79 07 12 74.
Open Jul–Aug Tue–Sat
10–noon, 3–7, Sun–Mon
3–7.

10 Modane
Fort St-Gobain
Tel: 04 79 05 21 25. Open
Apr–Nov Fri–Mon 10–noon,
2–7 (daily Jul–Aug);
Dec–Mar by reservation.

**11 St-Jean-de-
Maurienne**
Musée de Costumes
Ancien Evêché. Tel: 04 79
83 51 51 (tourist office).
Open school summer
holidays Mon–Sat 10–noon,
2–6.
Opinel Knife Museum
Avenue Henri Falcoz. Tel:
04 79 64 04 78; www.
opinel-musee.com. Open
Mon–Sat 9–noon, 2–7.

For Children
Luge d'Été
Télépherique de la
Patinoire, La Clusaz. Tel: 04
50 32 65 00 (tourist
office). Open mid-Jun to
early Sep daily; telephone for
hours.
Funicular railway
Bourg-St-Maurice. Tel: 04
79 07 12 57 (tourist
office). Open late Jun-late
Aug daily 8.30–7.30 (every
half hour).

For History Buffs
Museum of the French
Revolution
Vizille Château. Tel: 04 76
68 07 35; www.musee-
revolution-francaise.fr.
Open Wed–Mon 10–12.30,
1.30–5 or 6.

TOUR 20

[i] 17 place de la
Cathédrale, Strasbourg.
Tel: 03 88 52 28 28; www.
ot-strasbourg.com.

[i] 86 rue Wilson, Ste-
Marie-aux-Mines. Tel: 03 89
58 80 50.

[i] 7 rue de la 1ère
Armée, Thann. Tel: 03 89
37 96 20; www.ot-thann.fr.

[i] 9 avenue du Maréchal-
Foch, Mulhouse. Tel: 03 89
35 48 48; www.tourisme-
mulhouse.com.

[i] Hôtel de Ville,
Guebwiller. Tel: 03 89 76
10 63; www.tourisme-
guebwiller.fr.

[i] 4 rue Unterlinden,
Colmar. Tel: 03 89 20
68 92; www.ot-colmar.fr.

[i] 38 rue du Général
de Gaulle, Kaysersberg.
Tel: 03 89 71 30 11;
www.kaysersberg.com.

[i] 10 boulevard Leclerc,
Sélestat. Tel: 03 88 58
87 20; www.selestat-
tourisme.com.

**2 Ste-Marie-aux-
Mines**
St Barthélemy Mine Tour
Rue de la Sermonnette.
Tel: 03 89 58 72 28. Open
Jul–Aug daily 10–noon, 2–6,
or by appointment Apr–Jun
& Sep.
Maison de Pays and
Musée Minéralogique
Place Prensureux.
Tel: 03 89 58 56 67. Open
Jun–Sep daily 10–7.

3 Thann
Musée des Amis de Thann
Halle aux Blés, 24 rue
St-Thiébaut. Tel: 03 89 37
05 68; www.genealogie
thann.org. Open Jul–Aug
Tue–Sun 2–6; Jun, Sep
Fri–Sun 2–6.

4 Mulhouse
Musée des Beaux-Arts
4 place Guillaume-Tell.
Tel: 03 89 33 78 11. Open
Wed–Mon 10–noon, 2–6.
Cité du Train
2 rue Alfred-de-Glehn.
Tel: 03 89 42 83 33; www.
citedutrain.com. Open Feb–
Dec daily 10–5 (6 Apr–Oct).
Musée National de
l'Automobile
192 avenue de Colmar.
Tel: 03 89 33 23 23. Open
daily 10–6 (5 Nov–Mar).

**5 Écomusée de Haute
Alsace**
8km (5 miles) southeast of
Guebwiller via D430.
Tel: 03 89 74 44 74;
www.ecomusee-alsace.fr.
Open late Mar–early Nov,
Dec daily 10–6 or 7 (closed
Mon–Tue in May)

6 Guebwiller
Musée Theodore Deck
1 rue du 4-Février. Tel: 03
89 74 22 89; www.ville-
guebwiller.fr. Open Mon,
Wed–Fri 2–6, Sat–Sun
10–noon, 2–6.

7 Colmar
Musée d'Unterlinden
1 rue d'Unterlinden. Tel: 03
89 20 15 50; www.musee-
unterlinden.com. Open
May–Oct daily 9–6; Nov–
Apr Wed–Mon 9–noon, 2–5.
Musée Bartholdi
30 rue des Marchands.
Tel: 03 89 41 90 60; www.
musee-bartholdi.com.
Open Mar–Dec Wed–Mon
10–noon, 2–6.

8 Kaysersberg
Musée du Docteur
Schweitzer
126 rue du Général de
Gaulle. Tel: 03 89 47 36 55.
Open Apr to mid-Nov daily
9–noon, 2–6.

9 Riquewihr
Musée Dolder
Rue Général de Gaulle.
Tel: 03 89 73 23 23. Open
Apr–Oct weekends 10.30–1,
2–6 (daily Jul–Aug).
Tour des Voleurs
Rue des Juifs. Tel: 03 89 49
08 40. Open mid-Apr to
Oct daily 10.30–1, 2–6.
Musée de la
Communication en Alsace
and Mail Coach Museum
Cour du Château.
Tel: 03 89 47 93 80;
www.shpta.com. Open
early Apr–Oct, late Nov to
mid-Dec daily 10–5.30.

10 Sélestat
Bibliothèque Humaniste
1 rue de la Bibliothèque.
Tel: 03 88 58 07 20. Open
Mon, Wed–Fri 9–noon, 2–6,
Sat 9–noon (also Sat–Sun
2–6 Jul–Aug).

For Children
Luge d'Été
La Vue des Alpes, Villar
sur Thur, Le Grand Ballon.
Tel: 03 89 76 14 40. Open
weekends May–Jun; daily
Jul–Aug 2–6.
Montagne des Singes
Kintzheim. Tel: 03 88 92 11
09; www.montagnedes
singes.com. Open Mar–Nov
daily 10–noon, 1–5 or 6
(10–6 Jul–Aug).

Volerie des Aigles
Kintzheim. Tel: 03 88 92 84
33; www.voleriedesaigles.
com. *Open Apr to mid-Nov;
see website or phone.*

Special to...
**Parc des Cigognes et des
Loutres**
Hunawihr. Tel: 03 89 73 72
62; www.cigogne-loutre.
com. *Open Apr–Oct daily
10–noon, 2–5 (6/7 in high
season). Open lunchtime Jul–
Aug; Mar, Nov Wed, Sat–Sun.*

For History Buffs
**Château de Haut-
Koenigsbourg**
Tel: 03 88 82 50 60;
www.haut-koenigsbourg.
net. *Open daily all year*
Musée de l'Abri
Hatten. Tel: 03 88 80 14 90.
*Open mid-Jun to mid-Sep
daily 10–noon, 2–6, Sat–Sun
10–6; Mar to mid-Jun, mid-
Sep to Nov, Thu–Sun
10–noon, 2–6 (weekends
lunchtime).*

TOUR 21

ⓘ 12 boulevard
Clemenceau, Calais.
Tel: 03 21 96 62 40; www.
calais-cotedopale.com.

ⓘ Forum Jean Noël,
Boulogne. Tel: 03 21 10
88 10; www.tourisme-
boulognesurmer.com.

ⓘ Palais de l'Europe,
place de l'Hermitage, Le
Touquet. Tel: 03 21 06 72
00; www.letouquet.com.

ⓘ 21 rue Carnot, Mont-
reuil. Tel: 03 21 06 04 27.

ⓘ 41 rue des Potiers,
Desvres. Tel: 03 21 92 09 09.

❸ Boulogne
Château-Musée
Rue de Bernet. Tel: 03 21
10 02 20. *Open Mon, Wed–
Sat 10–12.30, 2–5.30, Sun
10–12.30, 2.30–6.*

❺ Domaine du
Marquenterre
**Parc Ornithologique du
Marquenterre**
25 bis chemin des
Garennes, St-Quentin-en-
Tourmont. Tel: 03 22 25
68 99; www.parcdu
marquenterre.com. *Open
daily 10–5, 6 or 7.30.*

❻ Le Crotoy
Bay of the Somme Railway
Tel: 03 22 26 96 96; www.
chemin-fer-baie-somme.
asso.fr. *Open Apr–early Nov,
several departures daily on
weekends and during Jul,
Aug; phone for other details.*

❾ Desvres
Maison de la Faïence
Rue Jean Macé. Tel: 03 21
83 23 23; www.desvres
museum.org. *Open Jul–Aug
daily (ex Mon am) 9.30–
12.30, 2–6.30; Oct–Mar
Tue–Sun 2–5.30); Apr–Jun,
Sep Tue–Sun 9.30–12.30,
2–6.30.*

For History Buffs
**Colonne de la Grande
Armée**
Avenue de la Colonne,
Wimille. Tel: 03 21 80
43 69. *Open all year
(exterior only; monument
closed for restoration).*

For Children
Nausicaà
Boulevard Ste-Beuve,
Boulogne-sur-Mer.
Tel: 03 21 30 98 98;
www.nausicaa.fr. *Open
Feb–Dec daily 9.30–6.30
(7.30, Jul–Aug); Jan 2–6.30.*
Aqualud
Front de Mer, Le
Touquet–Paris Plage. Tel: 08
25 74 77 07; www.aqualud.
com. *Open mid-Feb to Jun
Wed–Sun 10.15–5.45 (also
Mon–Tue school hols);
Jul–Aug daily 10–7 (to
11pm some Sats); Sep to
mid-Nov Sat–Sun
10.15–5.45.*
Bagatelle Fun Park
D940, Merlimont, south of
Le Touquet. Tel: 03 44 62
31 31; www.parcbaga
telle.com. *Open Apr–Sep
most days from 10.30. Rides
close 5.30–6, depending on
number of visitors.*

TOUR 22

ⓘ 6 bis rue Dusevel,
Amiens. Tel: 03 22 71 60 50;
www.amiens.tourisme.com.

ⓘ 115 place du Général
de Gaulle, Picquigny.
Tel: 03 22 51 46 85.

ⓘ Place des Héros, Arras.
Tel: 03 21 51 26 95;
www.ot-arras.fr.

ⓘ 70 place d'Armes,
Douai. Tel: 03 27 88
26 79; www.ville-douai.fr.

ⓘ Place du Parvis Gautier
de Mortagne, Laon.
Tel: 03 23 20 28 62; www.
tourisme-paysdelaon.com.

ⓘ Place de l'Hôtel-de-
Ville, Pierrefonds. Tel: 03 44
42 81 44; www.pierre
fonds-tourisme.net.

ⓘ Place de l'Hôtel-de-Ville,
Compiègne. Tel: 03 44 40
01 00; www.compiegne-
tourisme.fr.

ⓘ 2 bis rue René de
Girardin, Ermenonville.
Tel: 03 44 54 01 58; www.
otsi-ermenonville.com.

ⓘ 1 rue Beauregard,
Beauvais. Tel: 03 44 15 30 30;
www.beauvaistourisme.fr.

❶ Samara
Route de St-Sauveur,
La Chaussée Tirancourt.
Tel: 03 22 51 82 83;
www.samara.fr. *Open
Mon–Fri 9.30–5.30,
Sat–Sun 10–6.30.*

❷ Grottes de Naours
Rue des Carrières.
Tel: 03 22 93 71 78; www.
grottesdenaours.com.
*Open Feb to mid-Nov daily
10–noon, 2–5 (9.30–6.30
Apr–Aug).*

❸ Battlefields of the
Somme
**Historial de la Grande
Guerre**
Château de Péronne.
Tel: 03 22 83 14 18; www.
historial.org. *Open mid-Jan
to mid-Dec daily 10–6.*

❹ Arras
Musée des Beaux-Arts
22 rue Paul-Doumer.
Tel: 03 21 71 26 43. *Open
daily (ex Tue) 9.30–noon,
2–5.30.*

❻ Douai
**Belltower and Hôtel de
Ville**
Rue de la Mairie. Tel: 03 27
88 26 79. *Guided tours daily
from 11am (10 Jul–Aug).*

❼ Centre Historique
Minier Lewarde
Fosse Delloye. Tel: 03 27 95
82 82. *Open Mar–Oct daily
9–5.30; Nov–Feb Mon–Sat
1–5, Sun 10–5.*

❽ Laon
**Musée d'Art et
d'Archéologie**
32 rue Georges-Ermant.
Tel: 03 23 22 87 00. *Open
Tue–Sun Jun–Sep 11–6;
Oct–May 2–6.*

❾ Blérancourt
**Museum of Franco-
American Co-operation**
Château de Blérancourt.
Off D939. Tel: 03 23 39 60
16; www.museefranco
americain.fr. *Due to reopen
end 2011. Gardens open all
year daily 8–7.*

❿ Pierrefonds
Château
Rue Viollet-le-Duc. Tel: 03
44 42 72 72. *Open May–
Sep daily 9.30–6; Oct–Apr
Tue–Sun 10–1, 2–5.30.*

⓫ Compiègne
Palace and Museums
Place du Général-de-
Gaulle. Tel: 03 44 38 47 02.
Open daily (ex Tue) 10–6.
Musée Antoine Vivenel
2 rue d'Austerlitz. Tel: 03
44 20 26 04. *Open Tue–Sat
9–noon, 2–5 or 6, Sun 2–6.*
Musée de la Figurine
28 place de l'Hôtel de Ville.
Tel: 03 44 40 72 55.
*Open Tue–Sat 9–noon, 2–5
or 6, Sun 2–6.*

⓬ Ermenonville
Abbaye Royal de Chaalis
Fontaine-Chaalis. Tel: 03 44
54 04 02; www.chaalis.fr.
*Open daily 11–6 (5.30 and
closed lunch mid-Nov to Feb).*

⓭ Beauvais
**Galérie Nationale de la
Tapisserie**
22 rue St-Pierre. Tel: 03 44
15 39 10. *Open Feb–Dec
daily 10.30–5.30.*
**Musée Départemental de
l'Oise**
1 rue du Musée. Tel: 03 44
10 40 50. *Open Feb–Dec
daily 10–noon.*

For Children
Parc Astérix
10km (6m) south of Senlis.
Tel: 08 26 30 10 40;
www.parcasterix.fr. *Check
website for opening times.*
La Mer de Sable
Ermenonville. Tel: 08 25 25
20 60; www.merdesable.fr.
*Open early Apr–Aug 10–6
(closed Mon–Tue Apr–Jun),
Sep weekends*

TOUR 23

ⓘ 2 rue Guillaume de Machault, Reims. Tel: 08 92 70 13 51.

ⓘ 3 quai des Arts, Châlons-en-Champagne. Tel: 03 26 65 17 89.

ⓘ 5 place Général Leclerc, Ste-Menehould. Tel: 03 26 60 85 83.

ⓘ 35 rue du Ménil, Sedan. Tel: 03 24 27 73 73; www.sedan-bouillon.com.

ⓘ 4 place Ducale, Charleville-Mézières. Tel: 03 24 55 69 90; www. charleville-mezieres..org.

ⓘ 3 quai d'Orfeuil, Rethel. Tel: 03 24 38 54 56.

❷ Châlons-en-Champagne
Musée du Cloître Notre-Dame-en-Vaux
Rue Nicolas Durand. Tel: 03 26 69 99 61. *Open Wed–Mon 10–noon, 2–5/6.*

❺ Varennes-en-Argonne
Musée d'Argonne
9 rue Louis XVI. Tel: 03 29 80 71 14. *Open Apr–Jun, Sep Sat, Sun 3–6; Jul–Aug Mon–Sat 3–6, Sun 10.30–noon, 3–6.*

❻ Parc de Vision de Belval
Belval Bois-des-Dames. Tel: 03 24 30 01 86. *Open May–Aug Wed–Mon 12.30–6 (from 10.30 Sun).*

❼ Sedan
Château-Fort and Military Museum
Tel: 03 24 29 98 80. *Open daily 10–5.*

❽ Charleville-Mézières
Musée Rimbaud
Quai Arthur Rimbaud. Tel: 03 24 32 44 65. *Open Tue–Sun 10–noon, 2–6.*

❾ Musée de l'Ardenne
31 place Ducale. Tel: 03 24 32 44 60. *Open Tue–Sun 10–noon, 2–6.*

For Children
Karting Centre
Lonny. Tel: 03 24 54 99 82; www.karting-lonny.fr. *Open Jul–Aug daily 2–7.*

TOUR 24

ⓘ 4 place du Port Villiers, Chalon-sur-Saône. Tel: 03 85 48 37 97; www.chalon-sur-saone.net.

ⓘ 6 boulevard Perpreuil, Beaune. Tel: 03 80 26 21 30.

ⓘ 2 place Gaveau, Semur-en-Auxois. Tel: 03 80 97 05 96; www.ville-semur-en-auxois.fr.

ⓘ 6 rue Bocquillot, Avallon. Tel: 03 86 34 14 19.

ⓘ Rue St-Etienne, Vézelay. Tel: 03 86 33 23 69; www.vezelaytourisme.com.

ⓘ 2 place St-Christophe, Château-Chinon. Tel: 03 86 85 06 58; www.ot-chateauchinon.com.

ⓘ 13 rue Général Demetz, Autun. Tel: 03 85 86 80 38; www.autun-tourisme.com.

❶ Beaune
Hôtel-Dieu
Rue de l'Hôtel-Dieu. Tel: 03 80 24 45 00; www.hospices-de-beaune.com. *Open daily 9–5.30 or 6.30 (closes 11.30–2 mid-Nov to Mar).*
Musée du Vin de Bourgogne
Rue d'Enfer. Tel: 03 80 22 08 19. *Open daily 9.30–5/6 (closed Tue Dec–Mar).*

❷ Flavigny-sur-Ozerain
Crypt Tours
Abbaye de Flavigny. Tel: 03 80 96 20 88; www.anisde flavigny.com. *Open Mon–Fri 9–noon, 2–6, Sat–Sun 10–12.30, 1.30–7.*

❹ Avallon
Musée de l'Avallonnais
Rue du College. Tel: 03 86 34 03 19. *Open Jul–Sep Wed–Mon 2–6.*
Musée du Costume
6 rue Belgrand. Tel: 03 86 34 19 95. *Open mid-Apr to Oct; guided tours 10.30–12.30, 1.30–5.30.*

❻ St-Brisson
Maison du Parc du Morvan
Tel: 03 86 78 79 57; www.parcdumorvan.org. *Open Apr to mid-Nov Mon–Fri 9.30–12.30,*

2–5.30, Sat 10–12.30, 2–5, Sun 10–1, 3–5.30.
Musée de la Résistance
Maison du Parc du Morvan. Tel: 03 86 78 72 99. *Open Apr–Oct Wed–Mon 10–1, 2–5 or 6.*

❼ Château-Chinon
Musée du Costume
4 rue du Château. Tel: 03 86 85 18 55. *Open Jul–Aug daily 10–1, 2–7; rest of year Wed–Mon. Closed Jan.*
Musée du Septennat
6 rue du Château. Tel: 03 86 85 19 23. *Open Jul–Aug daily 10–1, 2–7; rest of year Wed–Mon 10–noon or 1, 2–6. Closed Jan.*

❽ Autun
Musée Rolin
5 rue des Bancs. Tel: 03 85 52 09 76. *Open Apr–Sep, Wed–Mon 9.30–noon, 1.30–6; Oct–Mar Wed–Mon 10–noon, 2/2.30–5.*

For History Buffs
Époisses Château
Tel: 03 80 96 40 56; www. chateaudepoisses.com. *Open Jul–Aug Wed–Mon 10–noon, 2–6; park & garden open all year daily 9–7.*

TOUR 25

ⓘ Place de la Cathédrale, Chartres. Tel: 02 37 18 26 26; www.chartres-tourisme.com.

ⓘ 8 place de la Libération, Rambouillet. Tel: 01 34 83 21 21.

ⓘ 47 rue Langlois, Milly-la-Forêt. Tel: 01 64 98 83 17; www.millylaforet.com.

ⓘ 41 Grande Rue, Barbizon. Tel: 01 60 66 41 87.

ⓘ 4 rue Royale, Fontainebleau. Tel: 01 60 74 99 99; www.fontainebleau-tourisme.com.

ⓘ 4 bis place de Samois, Moret-sur-Loing. Tel: 01 60 70 41 66.

ⓘ Mail-Ouest, Maison 'Les Remparts', Pithiviers. Tel: 02 38 30 50 02.

❶ Rambouillet
Château
Tel: 01 34 83 00 25. *Open Wed–Mon 10–11, 2–5.*

Bergerie Nationale and Museum
Parc du Château. Tel: 01 61 08 68 70; www.bergerie-nationale.educagri.fr. *Open Wed–Mon 10–11.40, 2–4.30 or 5.*
Espace Rambouillet Wildlife Reserve
Yvelines, southeast of Rambouillet on the D27. Tel: 01 34 83 05 00; www.espacerambouillet.onf.fr/. *Open daily 10–5 or 6.30. Closed Dec & Jan.*

❸ Barbizon
Auberge Ganne
92 Grande Rue. Tel: 01 60 66 22 27. *Open Wed–Mon 10–12.30, 2–5.30.*

❹ Fontainebleau
Palace
Tel: 01 60 71 50 70; www.musee-chateau-fontainebleau.fr. *Open Wed–Mon 9.30–5 or 6; gardens 9–5, 6 or 7.*
Musée d'Art et d'Histoire Militaire
88 rue St Honoré. Tel: 01 60 74 64 89. *Open Tue–Sat 2–5.30.*

❺ Moret-sur-Loing
Le Conservatoire du Vélo
Site Prugnat. Tel: 01 64 70 62 52. *Open May to mid-Sep, Wed–Fri 2–6, Sat–Sun 10–12, 2–6.30.*

❼ Pithiviers
Musée d'Art et d'Histoire
17 rue de la Couronne. Tel: 02 38 30 50 02 (tourist information office). *Closed temporarily for renovation, phone for details.*
Musée des Transports
Rue Carnot. Tel: 02 38 30 50 02 (tourist information office). *Phone for details.*

Special to...
Conservatoire National des Plantes à Parfum, Médicinales, Aromatiques et Industrielles (CNPMAI)
Route de Nemours. Tel: 01 64 98 83 77; www.cnpmai.net. *Open Apr–Oct Tue–Sun 10–5; Mar, Nov Sat–Sun 10–5.*

For History Buffs
Château de Rouville
Malesherbes. Tel: 02 38 34 78 25. *Park and chapel only. Apr–Sep Fri–Sun 10–noon, 2–6.*

INDEX

Index & Acknowledgements

The Automobile Association
wishes to thank the following libraries and photographers for their assistance in the preparation of this book.
HEMIS/ALAMY 65, 77, 80.
The remaining photographs are held in the Association's own library (AA WORLD TRAVEL LIBRARY) with contributions from:
P ATTERBURY 140, 142; A BAKER 83, 86, 87, 88/9, 91, 93, 95, 96, 98, 104; P BENNETT 76; S DAY 22, 23, 24/5, 84; J EDMANSON 20, 58, 59, 61; P KENWARD 32, 41, 42, 43, 44, 49, 62, 63, 66, 67, 68, 71, 73, 78; R MOORE 5, 9, 11, 14, 17, 19, 33, 37, 51, 52/3, 54, 55, 57, 82, 106/7, 115, 117, 118, 120; R MOSS 15; D NOBLE 155, 156; T OLIVER 34, 35, 38, 45, 101, 108, 109, 111, 114, 128, 130, 131, 137, 138, 139, 143, 154; D ROBERTSON 110, 113, 133, 135, 141; C SAWYER 6, 7, 8, 10, 12, 13, 16, 18, 99; N SETCHFIELD 79; M SHORT 134, 150, 151, 152, 153; B SMITH 21, 30, 36, 39, 46, 47, 60, 64, 69, 70, 74, 75, 81, 85, 94, 100, 103, 112, 116, 119, 122, 123, 124/5, 127, 129, 144, 146/7, 148, 149, 157; R STRANGE 2, 26, 27, 28, 29, 50, 90, 92, 97, 105, 126; R VICTOR 31.

Contributors
Verifiers: Penny Phenix and Terry Arsenault   **Copy editors:** Audrey Horne, Dilys Jones
Indexer: Marie Lorimer

Atlas

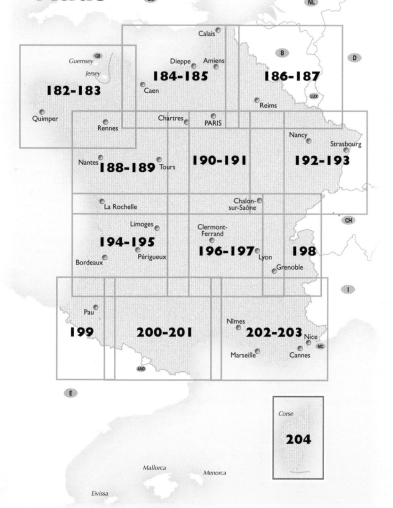

GB

NL

Guernsey GB

Jersey

182-183

Calais

Dieppe Amiens

184-185

Caen

B

D

186-187

LUX

Reims

Quimper

Chartres

PARIS

Rennes

Nancy

Strasbourg

Nantes **188-189** Tours

190-191

192-193

La Rochelle

Chalon-sur-Saône

CH

Limoges

Clermont-Ferrand

194-195

Périgueux

196-197 Lyon

198

Bordeaux

Grenoble

I

Pau

Nîmes

199

200-201

202-203 Nice

MC

Marseille

Cannes

AND

E

Mallorca

Menorca

Corse

204

Eivissa

Toll-free motorway	Local road	National park, natural reserve
Toll motorway	Secondary road	⊕ International airport
Interchange; service area	▼ 63 ▼ Distance in kilometres	⚔ Castle, fortress
≡ 2007 ≡ Motorway under construction (opening year)	Scenic route	☀ Panoramic view
╪═╪ Motorway in tunnel	╪--╪ Railway and tunnel	**PARIS** Town or place of great tourist interest
National road	*Bastia* Ferry route and destination	**Blois** Interesting town or place
Regional road	International boundary	Raphaël Other tourist town or place

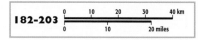

182-203   0 10 20 30 40 km
          0   10   20 miles

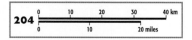

204   0 10 20 30 40 km
      0   10   20 miles

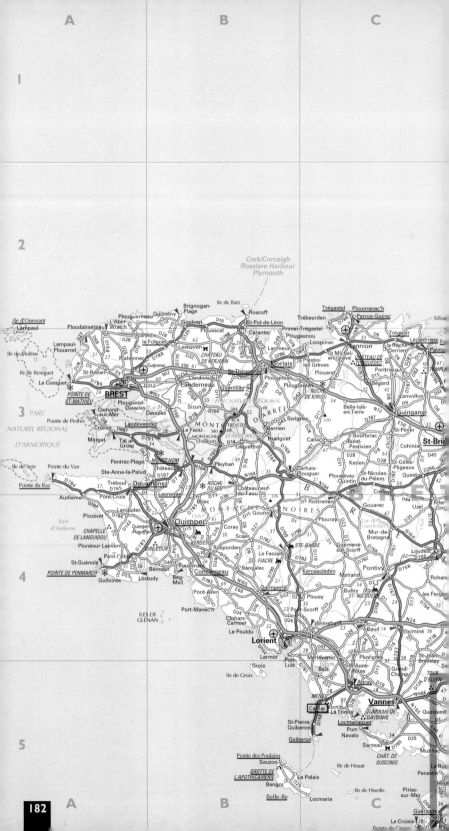

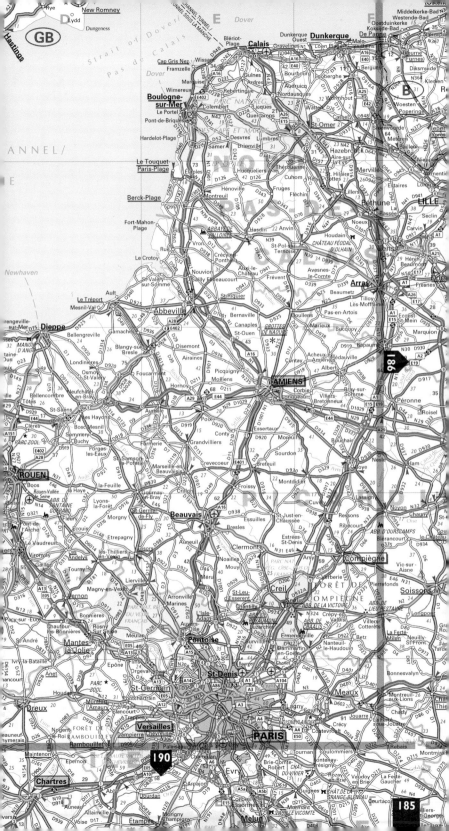

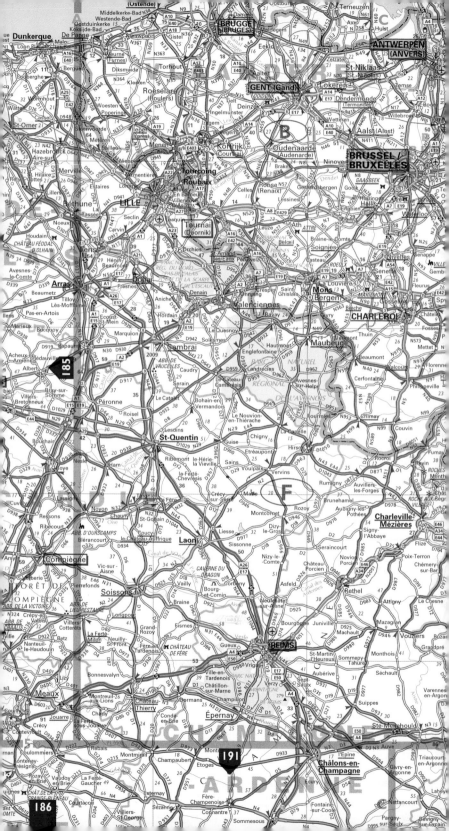

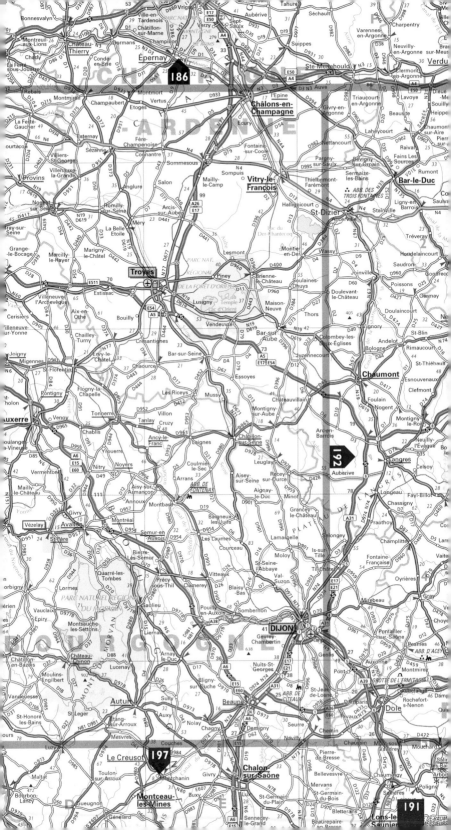

SAARLAND
Merzig
Saarlouis
Völklingen
Forbach
SAARBRÜCKEN
Neunkirchen
St Wendel
Homburg
Zweibrücken
Kaiserslautern
Pirmasens
Neustadt an der Weinstrasse
Frankenthal
LUDWIGSHAFEN
MANNHEIM
Speyer
Landau
Bruchsal
KARLSRUHE
Ettlingen
Pforzheim
Rastatt
Baden Baden
Sarreguemines
St-Avold
Sarrebourg
Saverne
Haguenau
Wissembourg
Bitche
STRASBOURG
Kehl
Offenburg
Freudenstadt
Lahr
Sélestat
Colmar
St-Dié
Emmendingen
FREIBURG IM BREISGAU
Villingen Schwenningen
Donaueschingen
Tuttlingen
Rottweil
MULHOUSE
Lörrach
BASEL
Waldshut
Schaffhausen
Singen
Winterthur
ZÜRICH
Baden
Aarau
Olten
Solothurn
Biel/ Bienne
BERN
Luzern
Zug
Schwyz
CH
D
PARC NATUREL REGIONAL DES VOSGES DU NORD
PFÄLZERWALD

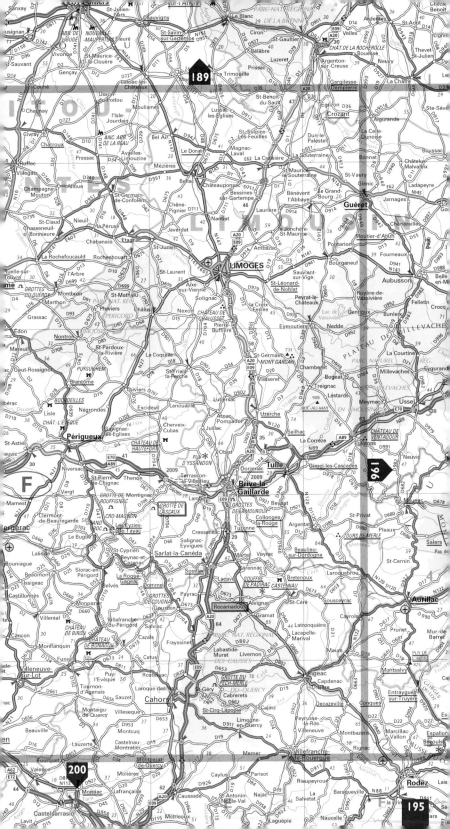

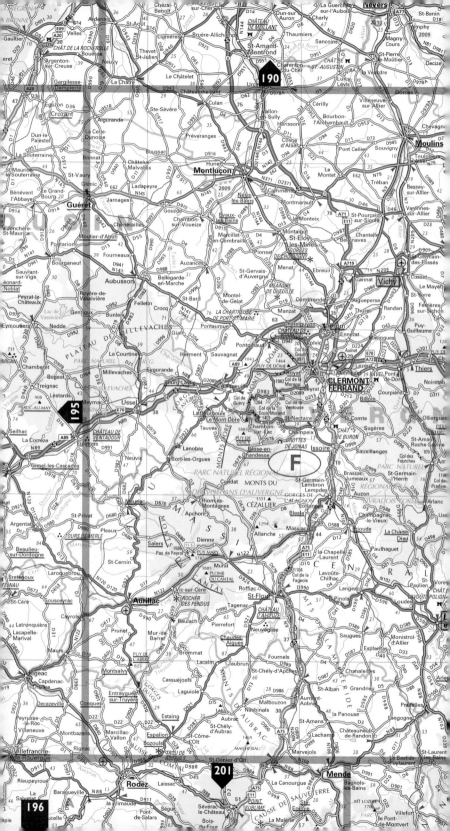

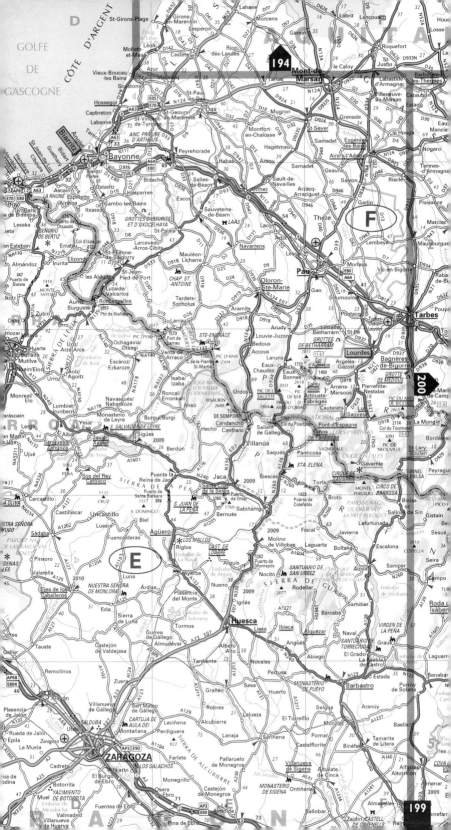

ATLAS INDEX

Atlas Index

206